College and Career Ready in the 21st Century

MAKING HIGH SCHOOL MATTER

D1504418

College and Career Ready in the 21st Century

MAKING HIGH SCHOOL MATTER

James R. Stone III
Morgan V. Lewis

Teachers College, Columbia University
New York and London

Published by Teachers College Press, 1234 Amsterdam Avenue, New York, NY 10027

Library of Congress Cataloging-in-Publication Data

Stone, James R., 1948–
College and career ready in the 21st century : making high school matter / James R. Stone III, Morgan V. Lewis.
  pages cm
 Includes bibliographical references and index.
 ISBN 978-0-8077-5323-1 (pbk.)
  1. Vocational education—United States. 2. Technical education—United States. 3. High schools—United States. I. Lewis, Morgan V., 1935– II. Title.
 LC1045.S745 2012
 370.1130973—dc23

                                                                    2011045683

ISBN 978-0-8077-5323-1 (paper)

ISBN 978-0-8077-5324-8 (hardcover)

Printed on acid-free paper

Manufactured in the United States of America

19 18 17 16 15 14 13   8 7 6 5 4 3 2

Contents

Preface

Education in the United States, especially high school education, has become increasingly narrow in focus. In the name of improving education for all students, high schools have become the new middle school. That is, there is no intrinsic value in a high school education except to prepare all youth for the next level of education, presumably college.

While no doubt well intended, we argue that the net result of such a focus is a system that ill-serves perhaps as many as 60% of the students who start 9th grade. This is the estimated percentage of those who will never complete a college credential.

Efforts to increase academic rigor and attainment are not new. In the 1950s the Soviets launched Sputnik and a generation of youth was directed toward becoming, literally, rocket scientists. In 1963 that effort was modified by an expanded federal investment in vocational education, Public Law 88-210. By the late 1970s, Japanese and German manufacturers were successfully competing against American manufacturers and the impulse again was to focus on education. This, and other influences, led to the *A Nation at Risk* report that began what has become nearly 30 years of education reform churn with schools and teachers under constant criticism. Within a decade, however, thoughtful reformers recognized the folly of a single curriculum for all students and thus came youth apprenticeships, the school-to-work movement and other efforts to provide multiple pathways for young people to succeed.

Then came No Child Left Behind. This reform effort, like those that came before, was predicated in part on assumptions about how the presumed decline in American education would bring down our economic competitiveness. Yet today's major economic competitors, China and India, hardly have education systems America would seek to emulate. So there must be something other than education that explains a nation's economic competitiveness. As further evidence of the disconnect between education and economic robustness, one only needs to look at where some of the most advanced manufacturing plants in the United States have been located in recent years: Boeing and BMW in South Carolina; Toyota in Kentucky; Mercedes in Alabama; General Electric in Mississippi. The educated workforce argument would argue for locating such sophisticated, highly technical enterprises in New Jersey, Massachusetts, Minnesota, or Iowa. Clearly, more than education is at play in economic competitiveness.

There are other, more important reasons to examine why and how we should structure multiple opportunities for young people in high school today. The most compelling is that despite all the efforts over the past several decades, only a minority of 9th graders will complete a 2- or 4-year college degree. There are many reasons for this. Certainly, rapidly rising costs of higher education represent a barrier. The capacity of higher education, especially that of community college systems, limits options for many. And, as we will discuss, many high school graduates are simply not capable of mastering the academics demanded of traditional 4-year colleges, but possess other talents valued in the labor market.

In today's lexicon the phrase "college and career ready" has gained traction. We suggest that perhaps we should simply discuss "career ready" recognizing that some career pathways require 4 years of college or more and others a 2-year post-high-school technical degree, but there still remain many that require only a high school level of education. The high school diploma, we argue, should be coupled with some signal that the graduate is prepared to be employed, a credential that documents the skills that have been acquired.

As Barton (2006) has observed, high school is the last education opportunity paid for wholly by the public. Its purpose has to be to do the best it can to provide all who leave it the foundation necessary to enter, or further prepare for, adult life. For this reason, we propose an approach, a strategy, to once again make high school matter.

Finally, we would like to express our appreciation to our colleagues at the National Research Center for Career and Technical Education who conducted much of the research reported in this book with funding provided by the Office of Vocational and Adult Education, U.S. Department of Education. We also wish to thank the hundreds of educators and thousands of students who cooperated in this research. Needless to say, the views expressed are our own and may not be shared by our colleagues or the Office of Vocational and Adult Education.

CHAPTER 1

Rhetoric and Meaningful High School Reform

Education's contribution to the American economy has been a fundamental assumption of those who advocate for skill training as a part of public education since the beginning of the 20th century (Commission on National Aid to Vocational Education, 1914/1974). It was not until the 1960s, however, when the federal government expanded its role in financing vocational education and what was then called "manpower training," that this contribution began to receive continuing examination. Becker's 1964 book *Human Capital* summarized the available knowledge and provided a rationale for efforts to improve both individual and societal well-being through education and training. Educators welcomed this explicit endorsement of what they had long contended, but few foresaw that if they were credited for their contributions to growth they could also be blamed when the economy slipped.

In the late 1970s and early 1980s the American economy experienced an unusual and damaging combination of high inflation with little or no economic growth—a combination that was labeled "stagflation." The global economic dominance that America had enjoyed after World War II as other industrialized nations rebuilt their economies was fading. During this period, also, the number of new entrants into the labor force began to decline as the last of the Baby Boomers completed their education and sought employment. Employers had fewer applicants from which to choose and often were disappointed with the skills of those they hired.

In 1980, in the midst of stagflation, Ronald Reagan was elected president. Among the issues on which he had campaigned was a promise to eliminate the federal Department of Education, which had been created under the Carter administration. His Secretary of Education, Terrel Bell, had been appointed with the understanding that he would close the department (Borek, 2008). To provide support for such a decision, Secretary Bell established a commission to examine the quality of education. In 1983 the National Commission on Excellence in Education issued its report, *A Nation at Risk*. That report did not lead to the elimination of the Department of Education, but it did launch a movement to improve education that continues to this day.

THE RHETORIC

The basic argument of *A Nation at Risk* was that the quality of American education had declined and this decline was directly linked to the poor economic conditions the nation was experiencing. If the decline was not reversed, the future was dire:

> Our Nation is at risk. Our once unchallenged preeminence in commerce, industry, science, and technological innovation is being overtaken by competitors throughout the world. . . . the educational foundations of our society are presently being eroded by a rising tide of mediocrity that threatens our very future as a Nation and a people. (National Commission on Excellence in Education, 1983, p. 5)

The commission provided no analyses of the link between education and the economy to support its assertions. Nevertheless, the report focused public attention on a number of indicators, such as the poor performance of American students in international comparisons of test performance, to launch a host of reform initiatives. Virtually every state increased the number of academic credits required for high school graduation and specified the subjects in which these credits were to be earned (Zinth & Dounay, 2007). These increases were accompanied by a variety of efforts to improve the preparation of teachers, to adopt rigorous standards, and to require more accountability. One result of the convergence of these initiatives was the passage in 2001 of the No Child Left Behind legislation, which requires highly qualified teachers for core academic subjects and adequate yearly progress and establishes sanctions to be applied when these requirements are not met.

Have the many reforms of the past 2 decades achieved their goals? The rhetoric of those advocating for more rigorous academics implies they have not:

> It is clear that the science and engineering problem begins early in the K–12 pipeline. We are losing our future scientists and engineers around the junior high school years. Less than 15% of U.S. students have the prerequisites even to pursue scientific/technical degrees in college. U.S. high school students underperform most of the world on international math and science tests. And most have little interest in pursuing scientific fields. (Council on Competitiveness, 2005, p. 49)

The National Summit on Competitiveness (2005) has one fundamental and urgent message:

> If trends in U.S. research and education continue, our nation will squander its economic leadership, and the result will be a lower standard of living for the American people. . . . By 2015 [the country needs to] double the number of bachelor's degrees awarded annually to U.S. students in science, math, and engineering, and increase the number of those students who become K–12 science and math teachers. (pp. 2, 5)

The National Center on Education and the Economy (2007) echoes this message:

> If we continue on our current course, and the number of nations outpacing us in the education race continues to grow at its current rate, the American standard of living will steadily fall relative to those nations, rich and poor, that are doing a better job. (p. xix)

MORE IS NOT BETTER—IT MAY BE WORSE

These assertions are the same as those in *A Nation at Risk*, despite the changes that occurred after that report was released. In 1982, high school graduates earned an average 12.9 academic credits; by 2005, this average had increased to 17.4 (Snyder, Dillow, & Hoffman, 2009). The average student in 2005 had, in effect, experienced 1 full year more academic courses than his or her 1982 counterpart. During these 2 decades, however, scores of 17-year-old students on the reading test in the National Assessment of Educational Progress (NAEP) changed very little, moving within a five-point range between 285 and 290 with the lowest average score occurring in 2004 (Rampey, Dion, & Donahue, 2009). In the same period the average number of credits earned in both science and mathematics increased more than a full credit (2.2 to 3.3 in science and 2.6 to 3.7 in math; Snyder, Dillow, & Hoffman, 2009) and the NAEP score in mathematics rose from a low in 1982 of 298 to 305 in 1990 (Plant & Provansnik, 2007). This was a statistically significant increase, but there has been no significant improvement in the past 18 years. The content of the NAEP science tests changed in the mid-1990s but there was a significant decline in scores between the early 1970s and the mid-1990s. With the newer tests, only 21% of students tested as proficient in 2009 (NAEP, 2011).

For almost 30 years our nation has asked its students to take more courses in the core academic disciplines. Standards have been adopted with the goal of making these courses more rigorous. These reforms have not produced improved performance on tests that measure what these courses are designed to teach. There is no question that in a global economy with high rates of technological change, a sound basic education is essential for all workers. Unfortunately, the current approach of more academics and more rigor, especially in science and mathematics, is not producing the outcomes that are desired.

STEM and College and Career Ready

The emphasis on science and mathematics has created the STEM acronym: Science, Technology, Engineering, and Math. Performance in science and mathematics courses has traditionally served a sorting function, identifying those students who are encouraged to prepare for entry into science and engineering occupations. The prevailing assumption, reflected in the quotations presented above and in the continuing rhetoric today, is that if more students take more of these courses, the nation will produce more engineers and scientists. As a result of having more of these workers, the nation will produce the technological innovations that will enable American workers to compete with their low-wage counterparts in other nations.

For many, STEM is primarily, if not exclusively, about science and mathematics education, not career and technical education (STEM Education Coalition, 2011). Others think of STEM as a set of skills nested in specific occupations such as accountants, software engineers, electrical and mechanical engineers, scientists of all varieties, operations research analysts, and database administrators, among many others. STEM programs for such occupations generally lead to careers in these areas. Most, if not all, narrowly defined STEM occupations require a baccalaureate or more for entry. Such occupations account for only 5–7% of current or expected employment in the United States (Carnevale, Smith, & Strohl, 2010). That said, such is the importance of STEM that STEM-related occupations have disproportionately contributed to job creation and wealth creation in the past century and no doubt will do the same in years to come.

But how many scientists and engineers do we really need? Lowell and Salzman (2007) have tracked the flow of students through the science and engineer education pipeline. Their analysis found that the education system produces qualified graduates far in excess of demand. The most recent data show that 16% of first-time bachelor's degree recipients majored in STEM (Cataldi et al., 2011). Each year there are more than three times as many 4-year-college graduates competing for science and engineering occupations as there are openings. From 1985 to 2000, an average of about 435,000 U.S. citizens and permanent residents graduated with bachelor's, master's, and doctoral degrees in science and engineering. Over the same period, there were about 150,000 jobs added annually to the science and engineering workforce.

An update of this analysis (Lowell, Salzman, Bernstein, & Henderson, 2009) found the same or even increasing rates of retention in the STEM pipeline from high school to college, college to first job, and college to mid-career job, but less retention among the highest performing students. The data analyzed provided no reasons for this decline among the best science and engineering graduates, but the authors state: "This analysis does strongly suggest that students are not leaving STEM pathways because of lack of preparation or ability. . . . The problem may not be that there are too few STEM qualified college graduates, but rather that STEM firms are unable to attract them. Highly qualified students may be choosing a non-STEM job because it pays better, offers a more stable professional career, and/or [is] perceived as less exposed to competition from low-wage economies" (p. iii).

Another frequent claim is that China and India produce far more engineers than the United States and this gives them an advantage in the global economy. The basis of this claim lies in how each country defines an engineer. A study conducted at Duke University (Wadhwa, Gereffi, Rissing, & Ong, 2007) found that in China many skilled tradesmen, such as mechanics, and graduates of 2- and 3-year programs are counted as engineers. National data were difficult to obtain in India, and the sources that were available included a wide variety of occupations in computer science. A survey of 58 corporations engaged in offshoring engineering jobs, reported in the Duke study, found the top reason for hiring in other countries was lower salary costs. This survey yielded little evidence that implied there is a shortage of engineers in the United States.

A study by the McKinsey Global Institute (Farrell, Laboissière, Rosenfeld, Stürze, & Umezawa, 2005) also supports the Duke findings. The McKinsey study involved interviews with human resource managers of 83 multinational companies. These managers reported that 8 out of 10 engineering graduates in the United States could successfully work in their companies while fewer than 3 out of 10 in India and 1 out of 10 in China could do so.

Although all CTE programs address some aspects of science, mathematics, and most certainly technology, not all are focused on engineering or engineering-related jobs. Many CTE programs do, however, address STEM-related careers, the second focus of the STEMEd Caucus. These include careers in automotive technology, medical technology, nursing, process control, machining financial management, and many other kinds of occupations. In a very real sense, all occupationally oriented career and technical education is STEM-related. Some of these occupations require a bachelor's degree or more, but many can be found in the subbaccalaureate labor market and vary in the amount and kinds of mathematics and science they require (ISEEK Careers, 2011).

Dropout Rates

One possible, unintended consequence of the increased emphasis on moving all youth to college, the focus on STEM, and the consequent narrowing of the high school curriculum may be to exacerbate the stubbornly persistent high dropout rate. Presently the United States ranks 23rd among leading industrialized nations in the proportion of youth who complete secondary education (Organisation for Economic Cooperation and Development [OECD], 2008).

High school dropouts are difficult to identify and measure. State and local methods of reporting dropouts vary widely, and it is in the self-interest of educational agencies to define and count dropping out in ways that minimize the number. In some measures, individuals who obtain a General Educational Development (GED) certificate are counted and in others they are not. There is one indicator, however, that can be applied uniformly across states: the ratio of the number of graduates reported by state educational agencies to the number of 17-year-olds in the population. Barton (2005) reported this figure for the past 130 years, from school years 1869–1870 through 1999–2000. The ratio reached a peak at 77% in 1969 declined to 70% in 1995 and stayed at approximately that level for the remainder of the period examined. This indicator is lower than most other measures of dropouts, but it has the advantage that it is not influenced by reporting policies of local school districts or the self-report and nonresponse biases inherent in population surveys and longitudinal studies of defined cohorts of students. An analysis of different sources and methods by Heckman and LaFontaine (2007) found somewhat higher graduation rates than Barton, but the same decline starting in the early 1970s.

The best estimates imply that between 20% and 30% of students do not graduate from high school. Many of these dropouts earn GEDs, but their economic and social outcomes are significantly lower than those of high school graduates who do not go on to college, and do not differ significantly from those of similar dropouts without such certificates (Heckman & LaFontaine, 2006). The real challenge facing high school education is not to increase the rigor of what is taught but to provide a more appropriate curriculum for those who find the typical academic class boring and frustrating. In the following chapters, we present evidence that these students are unlikely to benefit from more rigorous academics taught in the traditional manner.

It is unfortunate but true, as any high school teacher will attest, that for many students the typical academic class is an ordeal, not an opportunity.

There are teachers who can reach such students, but they are the exception. Even with the best preservice preparation and continuing professional development, no significant number of mathematics teachers will become like the late Jaime Escalante and be capable of teaching calculus to inner-city students. And even he taught only those students who were willing to do the extra studying that was needed. The very fact that the film *Stand and Deliver*, based on Escalante's experiences, was made underscores how unusual his success was (Mathews, 1988).

As students are required to take more academic courses, and as these courses are made more demanding, which outcome becomes more likely for those students who have difficulty in these courses? Will they study harder to meet these higher standards or will they leave school? The final exit from high school is the result of a process of disengagement from school that begins much earlier, often in the elementary grades (Beatty, Neisser, Trent, & Heubert, 2001). Requiring a more rigorous curriculum, absent other changes in instruction and support, will not reverse this process. If increased rigor does anything, it is likely to accelerate disengagement. There is an alternative— teaching academics in the context of how they are used in occupations—that has a higher probability of producing the improvements that are desired. In the next section, we outline the components of such an alternative.

A CAREER-FOCUSED APPROACH TO MAKING HIGH SCHOOL MATTER

Let us be clear in what we recommend. We are not trying to change the high school curriculum for all students. The career education effort in the 1970s (Herr, 1977) and school-to-work in the 1990s (Hughes, Bailey, & Mechur, 2001) attempted to bring about total curriculum reform with little lasting effect. There are new efforts in this regard that will be discussed in Chapter 2. The dominant curriculum produces the results desired for that proportion of the student population who performs well in academic classes. These students, too, find their classes to be boring, but they have accepted the rules of the game (Fried, 2005; Tripp, 1993). They study enough to get good grades and are prepared for college and the access to management, scientific, and professional occupations that obtaining a college degree makes possible. We focus in this book on those students for whom the academic classroom is a poor match with their interests and learning styles. These are the students who are most likely to "major" in CTE or could benefit from a robust CTE. Over the years, this group of students has been called the "forgotten half" or the "neglected majority." By whatever name, they represent a substantial proportion of high school students today.

With the current emphasis on college for all, one not involved in secondary education might think that CTE has faded from the high school. That is hardly the case. Three types of CTE courses are offered in virtually all high schools: family and consumer sciences, general labor market preparation, and occupationally specific preparation.[1] Family and consumer sciences have their origins in home economics education, one of the three occupational areas authorized to receive funding in the first federal vocational education legislation, the Smith-Hughes Act of 1917. Today the content of family and consumer sciences includes human development; personal and family finance; housing and interior design; food science, nutrition, and wellness; textiles and apparel; and consumer issues (American Association of Family and Consumer Sciences, 2011). General labor market preparation includes career exploration, introduction to technology, and basic computer applications, such as keyboarding/word processing. Occupational courses teach skills within career clusters and increase in specificity as students advance.

Statistics on enrollment by subject area are obtained from transcript studies and the most recent available are for students who graduated in 2005. In that year virtually all graduates (97%) took at least one CTE course. The average graduate earned a half credit (0.51) in family and consumer sciences, a second half credit (0.46) in general labor market preparation, and three credits (3.0) in occupational courses. Over nine out of ten graduates (92%) took at least one occupational course, and slightly more than one of every five graduates (21%) earned three or more credits in a sequence of related courses within a defined occupational area. Analysts who examine the effectiveness of CTE have adopted the term *concentrators* for students who earn three or more credits in one occupational area.

Some of the students who take several related CTE courses have clear occupational goals and use their courses to prepare for future careers. Many more, however, are still in the exploratory stage of career development. For these students, occupational classes and work-based learning provide a test of how well their interests and abilities align with the occupations they are considering. Some take CTE courses just to escape academic classes. Whatever their reasons, it is our contention that CTE classes have the potential to enhance student engagement in their education, and this engagement can be used to improve the skills needed for success in the new economy.

All occupations that require technical skills that must be acquired through training provide opportunities for incorporating instruction designed to increase students' literacy, mathematical, and scientific skills and understanding.

This is our basic proposition. We concede that the typical CTE course does not always capitalize on these opportunities. Nevertheless, the potential is there, and in our judgment this potential is more promising than asking students to take more traditional academic courses. In this book we present the evidence upon which we base this judgment and suggest the kinds of initiatives that should be pursued if the potential is to be realized. Before making this argument, however, we question the prevailing claim that the skills needed to be college and career ready are the same. The primary source of this claim is an analysis by the test company ACT (2006) in which it linked the performance of students on its college readiness examination to the performance of workers on its WorkKeys examination. In Chapter 2 we analyze the academic standards and courses that are said to define college and career readiness. We argue that defining career readiness primarily in academic terms ignores the employability and technical skills that employers seek and that CTE courses develop. Chapters 3, 4, and 5 extend our argument by describing how CTE can enhance *engagement* in education, improve academic and technical *achievement* through contextualized instruction, and ease the *transition* to further education and employment. Chapter 6 presents the evidence on the effects of CTE participation on earning and examines the charge that CTE is a means of perpetuating existing inequalities in society. Chapter 7 offers a scenario on how engagement, achievement, and transition could be affected if a district made a long-term effort to improve the rigor and relevance of its CTE programs.

Engagement

Engagement in one's education is difficult to measure, but there is one indicator about which few would quarrel: graduation from high school. Educators have long acted on the belief that CTE can retain students who are bored and frustrated in academic classes by guiding them into these courses. One consequence of this practice was the "dumping ground" label that came to be associated with vocational education. This label was one of the factors that caused the members of the American Vocational Association to change the name of their organization to the Association for Career and Technical Education.

Regardless of the negative connotations, studies have found that increased enrollment in CTE courses is associated with lower dropout rates. For many students, learning skills whose utility is self-evident provides a sense of purpose to their studies. And there is emerging evidence that young people who have such a sense are more likely to become productive adults who express satisfaction with their lives (Damon, 2008). The studies we discuss in Chapter 3 used quite different methodologies, intensive cases studies, and statistical analysis of data from national surveys of young people. Both approaches have indicated that as participation in CTE courses increases, graduation rates increase. There are exceptions to this generalization that we discuss in the context of the studies.

Achievement

In Chapter 4 we address how CTE instruction can increase achievement, especially in academics. From its origins in the manual training movement of the late 19th century, the field now called CTE has claimed that it can contribute to the learning of academic skills. Calvin Woodward (1883/1974), the most prominent proponent of this claim, put it this way:

> I advocate manual training for all children as an element in general education. I care little what tools are used, so long as proper habits (morals) are formed, and provided the windows of the mind are kept open toward the world of things and forces, physical as well as spiritual.
>
> We do not wish or propose to neglect or underrate literary and scientific culture; we strive to include all elements in just proportion. When the manual elements which are essential to a liberal education are universally accepted and adopted into American schools, the word "manual" may very properly be dropped. (pp. 60–61)

"Developing a better teaching process" was one of the arguments used by the Commission on National Aid to Vocational Education (1914/1974) to make the case for federal funding. After the Smith-Hughes Act was passed in 1917, and federal support became a reality, however, the field evolved essentially separate from academic instruction. Instead of the infusion and vitalization of general education that Woodward, Dewey (1913/1974), and others had hoped for, the field concentrated on teaching the technical skills needed for entry into occupations that require less than a bachelor's degree.

Though poorly realized, the hope for a better teaching process persisted. When *A Nation at Risk* shook the education world, vocational educators responded with *The Unfinished Agenda* (National Commission on Secondary Vocational Education, 1984). The agenda that this report addressed was the potential of vocational education to improve learning for all students:

> In this report we argue for a more balanced approach to attaining excellence in secondary schools. . . . Vocational education must be a significant part of a quality high school education. Many young people enter high school already turned off to the learning process. More of the same is not the answer. Motivat-

ing students not only to do better, but also, in many cases, to remain in school is a critical task of education. Vocational education is frequently the catalyst that reawakens their commitment to school and sparks a renewed interest in the academic skills. (p. 2)

The same year in which *The Unfinished Agenda* was published, federal vocational education legislation was reauthorized with the Carl D. Perkins Vocational and Technical Education Act of 1984.[2] The reauthorizations of this act in 1990 and 1998 incorporated an emphasis on academics that culminated in the 2006 Perkins Act. This act requires that career technical education be evaluated by student performance on several indicators, the first of which is attainment of challenging academic content and achievement standards. In Chapter 4 we present studies that have begun to demonstrate how CTE can meet this mandate.

Transition

Even though we think it unrealistic to expect all students to pursue postsecondary education, we recognize that many occupations require preparation beyond high school. CTE is changing so that students who wish to continue their education are prepared to do so. The association that represents CTE educators has published a position paper in which the first recommendation is "Establish postsecondary preparation and expectations for all" and the second is "Develop education systems that integrate all levels" (Association for Career and Technical Education, 2007, p. 1). The 2006 Perkins legislation requires all districts that received funds authorized by that act to offer at least one program of study that aligns secondary education with postsecondary education and leads to an industry-recognized credential or certificate at the postsecondary level or an associate or baccalaureate degree. We discuss the changes taking place in CTE to facilitate transition to postsecondary education in Chapter 5.

Another transition that CTE has traditionally attempted to facilitate is the one directly into employment. Despite the emphasis on college for all, a substantial proportion of young people who enter the 9th grade do not continue their education after high school. Out of an average 100 entering high school students, 70 will graduate on time and 44 will directly continue their education (Greene & Winters, 2006; National Center for Higher Education Management Systems, 2009). If any of those 26 who do not enter postsecondary education take several CTE courses and obtain employment in the occupations they studied, they will earn more than their counterparts without such preparation (Silverberg, Warner, Fong, & Goodwin, 2004). In Chapter 6, we summarize the evidence on the economic returns to high school training and the opportunities that will be available in "middle-skill" occupations that offer attractive wages and stable employment.

The New 3 Rs

In Chapter 7 we relate engagement, achievement, and transition to what many are referring to as the "new 3 Rs" of education: rigor, relevance, and relationships. *Rigor* translates into expecting more of students, challenging them to work hard to understand complex concepts and, most important in the era of No Child Left Behind, requiring them to demonstrate their understanding on standardized tests. *Relevance* means making the concepts that are studied meaningful by relating them to interests and concerns of students. *Relationships* require teachers, counselors, and administrators who know their students as individuals and provide them with the personal and educational support they need to achieve their potential.

The pedagogy and content of CTE courses, like the pedagogy and content of any class, can be lax or rigorous. But more than traditional academic classes, CTE courses have an inherent potential to add relevance to academic learning and to enhance the relationships that contribute to an effective learning environment. Quality CTE courses taught by skilled instructors are characterized by four attributes that distinguish the CTE learning experience from others in a typical high school:

- *Relevance of the instruction:* Students do not have to ask, "Why do I have to learn this?" The answer is inherent in the content.
- *Less full-class lecture and discussion:* In CTE classes much instruction is individualized, with students engaged in hands-on activities and teachers serving primarily as coaches and guides. Such one-to-one interaction encourages the development of teacher-student relationships.
- *More time with students:* Students who concentrate in CTE typically spend half the school day in occupational classes over 2 or more years. This time, coupled with individualized instruction, allows for both the teachers and the students to get to know each other, forming small learning communities that nurture both engagement and achievement.
- *Opportunities for success:* Many students find in CTE courses a match for their learning styles and interests and perform better that they do in academic classes.

Some may question whether CTE courses can claim rigor as one of their attributes. In terms of occupational skills, the tests of rigor are the tasks themselves. Electrical circuits must be properly wired or fuses are blown. Foundations must be solid or structures sag and break. Ingredients must be accurately measured and combined or dough does not rise. In the past these were the only types of skills that CTE was required to teach. In an era of educational reform and pressured by the demands of a rapidly changing labor market, more is required. Secondary-level CTE programs that receive federal funds must, by law, demonstrate that they teach academic skills while simultaneously preparing youth and adult learners for pathways to high-skill, high-paid, or high-demand occupations. In the chapters that follow, we examine how CTE can continue to honor its historic mission of teaching occupational skills while also preparing young people to be lifelong learners who will be capable of acquiring the new skills that a continually changing economy will require.

SUMMARY

For almost 3 decades education has been criticized for not providing students with the skills needed to maintain the competitiveness of the American economy in global markets. This criticism has resulted in more demanding graduation requirements, rigorous standards for what high school graduates should know, and high-stakes testing. Trends in student performance on the NAEP over this period indicate that these efforts have not produced the improvements desired. High school dropout rates have remained high and pressure for increased rigor may cause them to rise even higher. In this chapter we propose a different approach, one that draws upon student involvement in occupations they have chosen to study to enhance the learning of academic skills. High-quality CTE courses offered as part of career pathways that lead to a variety of occupations can increase student engagement, improve their academic achievement, and ease their transition to further education or employment. In this book we present the evidence supporting these claims and outline the changes that will be needed if this potential is to be realized.

CHAPTER 2

College and Career Ready for the 21st Century

The prevailing emphasis on more academics has resulted in the widely ac-cepted goal of college and career ready for all. Most of the reports and policy papers addressing this topic equate career ready with college ready. The American Diploma Project (Achieve, 2004, 2010) has defined college and career ready with sets of benchmarks for English and mathematics that all students should reach to receive a diploma. The website of Achieve, Inc. (http://www.achieve.org) reports that 35 states have committed to clos-ing the gap between what colleges and employers expect from high school graduates and what these graduates actually can do. Common Core State Standards for English language arts and mathematics have been endorsed by the National Governors Association Center for Best Practices and the Council of Chief State School Officers (2011); by the summer of 2011, ac-cording to the Common Core website (http://www.corestandards.org), 42 states, the District of Columbia, and the U.S. Virgin Islands had formally adopted these standards. The National Center on Education and the Econ-omy (2007) has stated that the goal of high school should be to prepare all students to do college-level work without the need for remediation; to ensure such preparation "Boards of Examination" would be established in each state to develop syllabi for core subjects and examinations to assess competence in these subjects.

Thus the means recommended to prepare college-ready graduates are high standards and expectations, rigorous courses aligned with standards, and tests to ensure that students meet those standards. Presumably, career readiness comes with the same requirements. The evidence contradicts the rhetoric, however. Paul Barton (2006) at ETS, Peter Cappelli (2008) at the Wharton School, and other labor market experts argue that being prepared for college is not the same as being prepared for successful transition into the workforce.

FIGURE 2.1. The Skills Needed to Be College and Career Ready

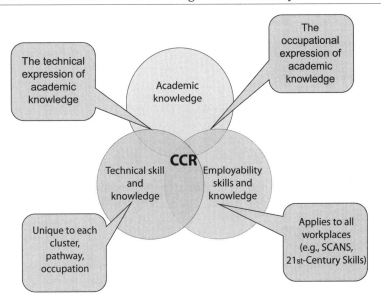

DEFINING COLLEGE AND CAREER READY

Perhaps we ought to consider an alternative framework that more clearly defines what *college and career ready* means. To be career ready, a graduate must have mastery of three kinds of skills, not just one. First and most obvious, *academic knowledge* is important—especially the occupational expression of academic knowledge; for example, graduates should know how to use mathematics or science to solve real workplace problems. Second, *employability skills*—often called "soft skills"—apply to all workplaces and include such personal qualities as responsibility, self-management, and integrity. Third, *technical skills* are unique to specific occupational areas, although for many students, instruction in a specific occupational context offers opportunities to develop all three types of skills.

Figure 2.1 presents our concept of college and career ready, which includes employability and technical skills. Education is, of course, primarily academics, and a sound base of academic skills is essential to all functioning in a complex, rapidly changing world. To be career ready, however, an individual must also have employability skills and the technical skills and knowledge required for specific occupations. The overlap of the circles indicates that the three types of skills build upon each other, and the nonoverlapping sectors signify the unique contribution of each set. It is the overlap or the intersection of these three domains of knowledge that point to the potential for CTE to add value to the high school experience of many youth. Academic skills are expressed in the acquisition of technical as well as occupational or employability skills.

Employability Skills

As one examines what employers want from their employees, it is clear that many opportunities are available to non-college-degreed youth if they possess the proper skills and training that could be provided by secondary CTE programs and postsecondary CTE programs both for the degree and certificate programs. Barton (2005) and Mathematica Policy Research, (2002) conclude that employers place a higher premium on hiring individuals who show good work habits, confidence, and leadership skills—often described as "soft skills." These are skill sets that are often lacking in many youth, yet are the kinds of skills that are the focus of quality high school CTE programs.

Employability skills are often referred to by the SCANS acronym (used in Figure 2.1), which stands for Secretary's Commission on Achieving Necessary Skills (1991). The secretary referred to is Secretary of Labor Lynn Martin, who appointed a commission that identified generic competencies needed in all jobs and what the commission labeled "foundation" skills that underlie these competencies. The foundation skills include basic academic skills, thinking skills (e.g., creative thinking, problem solving) and personal qualities (e.g., responsibility, self-management, integrity/honesty). It is these personal qualities that are most often thought of as employability skills.

The 21st-century skills noted in Figure 2.1 are to a large degree an updating and elaboration of SCANS (Partnership for 21st Century Skills, 2009). As with SCANS, the base is academic skills. Woven through the teaching of all core subjects are five "21st-century interdisciplinary themes":

- Global awareness
- Financial, economic, business, and entrepreneurial literacy
- Civic literacy
- Health literacy
- Environmental literacy

Building on this base are three sets of additional skills: (1) learning and innovation; (2) life and career; and (3) information, media, and technology. As of the summer of 2011, some 15 states had entered into formal agreement with the Partnership for 21st Century Skills to infuse the 21st-century framework into their standards, assessment, and professional development.

In November 2010 the Association for Career Technical Education and the National Association of State Directors of Career Technical Education Consortium joined with the Partnership to publish *Up to the Challenge*. This report makes the case that CTE programs that incorporate the 21st-century framework provide the preparation for successful careers and should be made widely available to students.

In 1990 the reauthorization of federal legislation for vocational education required measures of the attainment of academic skills as one of the indicators by which programs were to be evaluated. This was a major shift for a field whose primary focus had been the teaching of occupational skills. This same legislation also required that "the goal of each program shall be to give a student experience in, and understanding of, all aspects of the industry [AAI] in which the student is preparing to enter" (P.L. 101-392, Sec. 113(b)(9)). Each subsequent reauthorization has continued this requirement. The AAI noted in Figure 2.1 indicates that such understanding is a part of the occupational expression of academic knowledge. Unfortunately, the legislation provided no guidance as to what the AAI was to include. Vocational educators tried a variety of approaches to respond to this requirement (Andrew, 1996), and the method that came to be most widely adopted was to broaden the initial courses within defined occupational areas. The AAI requirement was established during a period when vocational educators were seeking ways to expand their programs to provide preparation for both entry-level employment and postsecondary education. Global competition and rapid rates of technological change had raised the level of skills needed for success in the labor market, and many occupations required more preparation than could be provided at the secondary level.

CTE's Contribution

To master these kinds of skills and successfully transition into adulthood, youth must be engaged in learning and achieve in demonstrable ways. A necessary first condition to successful transition to adulthood is a successful high school experience. We are all too aware of the persistently high number of youth who fail to complete high school—and the attendant consequences of this failure in both personal and economic terms. Research from Johns Hopkins University and the National Research Center for Career and Technical Education (NRCCTE) has shown that participation in career and technical education (CTE) can increase the likelihood of completing high school, especially for students who enter high school with lower measured academic ability (Plank, DeLuca, & Estacion, 2005; Castellano et al., 2007). Plank and his colleagues found that a ratio of one CTE class for every two core academic classes increased the chances students would graduate.

CTE participation has other benefits. The workplace of the 21st century, experts argue, requires that all workers be able to communicate with coworkers and customers, collaborate in evolving work teams, think critically and solve problems, and demonstrate creativity and innovation. If one of the goals of education is to prepare young people with these employability skills, where in the high school curriculum can they be developed? Two pedagogic opportunities are readily available in all quality CTE programs: CTE student organizations (CTSOs) and work-based learning (WBL).

CTSOs like SkillsUSA, DECA, FBLA, HOSA, and others provide participants with opportunities to develop the kinds of nonacademic employability skills called for in the SCANS and 21st-Century Skills reports. Research from the NRCCTE has shown that key elements of CTSOs are linked to increased academic engagement, employment and college aspirations, and career self-efficacy (Alfeld et al., 2007). This research is discussed in Chapter 4.

Our counterparts in Europe have long understood the value of WBL. The Organization for Economic Cooperation and Development (OECD, 2010) conducted an extensive analysis of vocational education and training (VET, the European equivalent of CTE) in its member countries. The cross-country synthesis of these studies showed that WBL-intensive approaches are especially effective in meeting the developmental needs of youth and in preparing them for advanced studies in polytechnics and applied science university programs. High-quality CTE programs in the United States have shown similar results.

It has been widely reported that, on average, U.S. school children perform less well academically than their peers in most other advanced nations. As discussed in Chapter 1, internal measures, most notably the National Assessment of Educational Progress (NAEP), show little progress and actual declines in reading skills and science knowledge of U.S. high school students during the past 2 decades; math skills have remained essentially static. These dismal results come despite an increase from an average of roughly 13 academic credits earned by high school graduates in the early 1980s to nearly 20 today. These data suggest that piling on more course requirements is not getting us where we want to be. An alternative to simply adding more academics to the curriculum is to leverage the potential of curriculum integration to enhance the underlying academic content in occupational coursework. In Chapter 4 we discuss national studies that have shown curriculum integration to significantly improve the math, science, and literacy skills of CTE students.

A more dynamic vision of college and career readiness focuses on the many students who are often bored and frustrated in the increasingly narrow curriculum being offered in U.S. high schools. CTE that emphasizes academics and engages students in intensive WBL experiences can keep students in school, teach them academic skills they will actually use in the workplace, and contribute to their successful acquisition of postsecondary credentials.

To those who would label such a vision "tracking," we suggest that the most pernicious track we offer young people today is the dropout track. A high-quality, technically and academically rigorous career pathway that employs the proven pedagogic strategies of an integrated curriculum, CTSOs, and intensive WBL are what our students, our schools, and our economy need. We present a fuller discussion on CTE and issues of tracking in Chapter 6.

SIGNALING THE LABOR MARKET

One explanation for the nation's "college for all" emphasis is that a college degree has become a proxy for employability or work readiness (Stone & Alfeld, 2006). Believing that the high school diploma no longer signifies meaningful achievement and lacking a national system of industry credentials, employers rely on college degrees. Recent national data indicate that there have been increases in college enrollment and completion since the early 1970s, the ramifications of which are still unclear. Rosenbaum (2001) found that only 42% of U.S. high school graduates complete and graduate from college within 10 years of leaving high school. Other studies put the success rate much lower, with less than 20% of all students completing a 4-year degree within 6 years (National Center for Public Policy and Higher Education, 2004). Regardless, such degrees are coming at increased costs to students and their families. The Public Interest Research Group (Swarthout, 2006) found that more than two thirds of college graduates leave with debt and between 23% and 55% of new graduates leave with debts described as unmanageable.

Labor market trends indicate that many opportunities are available to non-college-degreed youth if they possess the kinds of skills and training provided by secondary CTE programs and postsecondary CTE degree and certificate programs. Stone and Alfeld (2006) identified the basic skills for success in the modern workplace as reliability, positive attitude, willingness to work hard, 9th-grade or higher mathematics abilities, 9th-grade or higher reading abilities, the ability to solve semistructured problems at levels much higher than today's high school graduates, the ability to work in groups, the ability to make effective oral and written presentations, and the ability to use personal computers to carry out simple tasks. Other reports (Barton, 2005; Mathematica Policy Research, Inc., 2002) concluded that employers place a higher premium on hiring individuals who show good work habits, confidence, and leadership skills—the so-called soft skills. Many of these skills can be developed through classroom- and work-based CTE experiences.

In an NRCCTE study Bartlett (2004) conducted what to our knowledge is the only systematic test of the signaling value of industry-recognized certificates. The certificates used in his study were A+ in information technology issued by CompTIA (Computing Technology Industry Association) and ASE issued by the Institute for Automotive Service Excellence. To test the influence such certification had on hiring decisions, Bartlett prepared 12 fictitious resumes with various combinations of education (high school diploma only, certification, associate degree, and associate degree and certification) and work experience (none, less than 2 years, and 2–4 years). A randomly selected sample of managers responsible for hiring for entry-level positions in Atlanta, Minneapolis, and Portland were asked to rank the 12 resumes in terms of suitability for hiring. As would be expected, the resumes with 2–4 years of related work experience were most likely to be ranked first. Two thirds (67.4%) of the auto managers ranked first the resume with this level of experience, an associate degree, and ASE certification. Surprisingly, this same combination, but with A+ certification, was ranked first by less than one quarter (23.4%) of the information technology managers. Slightly more than one third (34.6%) of these managers ranked the associate degree and 2–4 years of experience highest, and slightly more than one quarter (26.2%) selected A+ certification plus 2–4 years. Further analyses of the signaling power of the two educational qualifications found a uniform preference for the associate degree regardless of work experience in the information technology sample. Interviews with the managers found that many in information technology believed the associate degree indicated a broader, more complete understanding of the field, and some expressed doubts about the rigor of the A+ test. Even though Bartlett studied only two industry-recognized credentials, it is clear that their signaling value varies across employers and is influenced by the factors, including testing, underlying certification.

Because the labor market in the United States is not well organized with respect to qualification, the challenge is to identify signals beyond formal education that the labor market will recognize. These signals would be based on certifying skill attainment. Stone (2009) identified definitional, measurement, and timing issues related to assessing technical skills. Several states are addressing these issues from different perspectives. Some are using industry-driven approaches. CISCO certification in IT and Certified Nursing Assistant in health care have been adopted by many states. A number of states are creating their own employability certifications. The extent to which industry recognizes these as a signal is unclear.

ACADEMIC SKILLS NEEDED TO BE COLLEGE AND CAREER READY

As discussed earlier, academic skills have an expression in the workplace. The issue is what skills are necessary for the workplace that are also necessary for successful college transition and success. We turn to an examination of mathematics as it represents a key sorting mechanism for higher education, especially for STEM occupations.

Math Myopia

Findings about the workplace needs for mathematics, such as those discussed in Chapter 1, have had little impact on the push for more academics. Reports such as *The Toolbox Revisited* (Adelman, 2006) and *Ready or Not: Creating a High School Diploma that Counts* (Achieve, 2004) have succeeded in equating studying mathematics at the algebra II level and above with increased postsecondary success. Achieve (2008) examined a small selection of technical occupations (e.g., aircraft maintenance technician) and highlighted what it identified as higher level math that is embedded in the standards that have been set for the American Diploma Project. But how much mathematics do most jobs really require? A survey of 2,300 workers found that virtually all, 94%, used basic arithmetic, but only 22% reported using anything more advanced (Handel, 2007). When the respondents to this survey are limited to upper level white-collar workers, only 30% reported using algebra. Carnevale and Desrochers (2003) reported an analysis of the mathematics needed for different job levels using the paradigm developed for the National Adult Literacy Survey. Workers in higher paying jobs have taken more advanced mathematics. Nevertheless, they note:

> Clearly, algebra II is the threshold mathematics course taken by people who eventually get good jobs in the top half of the earnings distribution. And the more mathematics beyond algebra II, the better the odds of eventually landing a job in the top 25 percent of the earnings distribution. Yet even a casual analysis of the distribution of occupations demonstrates that relatively few of us—fewer than 5 percent—make extensive use of geometry, algebra II, trigonometry, or calculus on the job. (p. 26)

Carnavale and Desrochers (2003) also discuss the mismatch between the mathematics that students learn in school and what they will eventually need on the job:

> Mathematical skills are the best general proxy for demonstrating the increasing economic returns to reasoning ability in the new economy. It is much less clear, however, that the content and methods of the current mathematics curriculum

are aligned with the uses of mathematics in the world of work. Most Americans seem to have taken too little, too much, or the wrong kind of mathematics. Too many people do not have enough basic mathematical literacy to make a decent living even while many more people take courses in high school such as geometry, algebra, and calculus than ever will actually use the mathematical procedures taught in these courses. (p. 25)

Studying mathematics does not impart the skills that are rewarded in the new economy so much as it identifies those who have these skills. The reference to "too little, too much, or the wrong kind of mathematics" addresses the central thesis of this book: Asking students to study more traditional academic courses will not produce workers with the skills employers want and need. There is no question that students who earn high school credits in trigonometry, precalculus, and calculus are more likely to obtain postsecondary degrees. To assume, however, that requiring more such courses will lead to more college graduates confuses cause and effect. It is not these courses, by themselves, that improve the likelihood of obtaining degrees. Students who succeed in advanced mathematics have a combination of skills, knowledge, and motivation that enables them to do well in school. Simply requiring students to take more higher level courses will have little impact on the characteristics that produce this success. The more likely result of higher requirements is more dropouts.

Working Math

In Figure 2.1, Math-in-CTE and CI are noted as examples of the technical expression of academic knowledge. "Math-in-CTE" refers to an experiment conducted by the National Research Center for Career and Technical Education that tested the effects of enhanced mathematics instruction in five occupational areas (Stone, Alfeld, & Pearson, 2008). The design and outcomes of this study are presented in Chapter 4. The "CI" in the figure refers to contextualized instruction, which grounds the teaching of skill and knowledge within specific applications. Teaching in occupational context is the core of what we propose in order to improve the learning of those students who struggle in academic courses. Students who have difficulty in core subjects are typically assigned to drill and practice courses and tutoring that involve more of the same type of instruction that has served them poorly throughout their education.

As noted in Chapter 1, ACT (2006) is the primary source for the claim that college ready and career ready require the same types of skills. Their analysis focused on Zone 3 occupations as defined in the O*Net data generated by the U.S. Department of Labor. Zone 3 occupations pay a family-sustaining wage but do not require a 4-year-college degree. By examining the math and reading requirements for these jobs and comparing them to ACT scores necessary to be college ready, they concluded:

> Our new finding has important implications for U.S. high school education. It suggests that all high school students should be educated according to a common academic expectation that prepares them for both postsecondary education and the workforce. This means that all students should be ready and have the opportunity to take a rigorous core preparatory program in high school, one that is designed to promote readiness for both college and workforce training programs. (p. 1).

Assuming the validity of their analysis,[1] an examination of the tables in the ACT report is revealing. The algebra skills necessary to obtain a 20–23 on the ACT math exam, identified in the Summary, include the following:

- Solve routine two-step or three-step arithmetic problems involving concepts such as rate and proportion, tax added, percentage off, and computing with a given average
- Exhibit knowledge of elementary number concepts including rounding, the ordering of decimals, pattern identification, absolute value, primes, and greatest common factor
- Evaluate algebraic expressions by substituting integers for unknown quantities
- Add and subtract simple algebraic expressions
- Solve routine first-degree equations
- Perform straightforward word-to-symbol translations
- Multiply two binomials
- Evaluate quadratic functions, expressed in function notation, at integer values

The equivalent list of WorkKeys (Level 5) skills includes the following:

- Solve problems that include a considerable amount of extraneous information
- Calculate using several steps of logic
- Perform single-step conversions within or between systems of measurement
- Look up and use a single formula
- Calculate using mixed units (e.g., 3.5 hours and 4 hours 30 minutes)

- Find the best deal using one- and two-step calculations and then compare results
- Calculate percentages, percentage discounts, or percentage markups
- Divide negative numbers
- Decide what information, calculations, or unit conversions to use to solve the problem
- Use exponents, including exponents in fractions and formulas (ACT, 2006)

Mapping these skills against math course content in two states (California and Oklahoma) shows that algebra I is the highest level of math required to address these skills. The separate list of statistical thinking also fits within algebra I or pre-algebra coursework. The short list of geometry concepts similarly were found in a single high school geometry course.

One can conclude from this analysis that the math requirements for college and career ready can be met with at most, 2 years of high school math. This is consistent with the National Center on Education and the Economy's Board Examination System that a number of states have signed onto (Pat Trotter, personal communication, July 7, 2011). This, of course, runs counter to the many states that now require algebra II or more for high school graduation.

In addition to the kinds of math skills detailed above, the emerging workplace, and indeed society as a whole, requires that our schools help students think like scientists. More than memorizing periodic tables or plant classifications, the 21st-century workplace and society more generally require citizens with the ability to confront problems as a scientist does: formulate a hypothesis, gather relevant data, analyze the data, and draw conclusions. This requires instruction that makes explicit the connections among scientific concepts and principles by applying the concepts to real problems. More specifically, the Center for Curriculum Materials in Science (CCMS) approach emphasizes curricular coherence based on these characteristics: (a) interconnectedness of core knowledge, (b) connections between ideas of science and phenomena in the real world, (c) connections between new ideas and prior knowledge, and (d) connections between scientific ideas and the enterprise that produced them (Kali, Linn, & Roseman, 2008). The authors further promoted *contextualized* science learning through the use of real-world problems and inquiry-based projects. CCMS modeling, based on empirical research, closely parallels the approach of the evidence-based contextualized approach employed by the Math-in-CTE model discussed in Chapter 4.

Other Voices

Although most calls for high school reform stress "college for all," there have been some who have questioned this emphasis. One of the most prominent or, in the eyes of many, infamous, is Charles Murray, coauthor with Richard Herrnstein of *The Bell Curve* (1994). This book argued that the positions achieved in American society (and their accompanying status and economic rewards) are primarily determined by individual ability, which is best reflected by IQ. This argument is controversial in itself, but Murray and Herrnstein compounded their notoriety by linking differences in IQ among races to genetic factors. Needless to say, these propositions provoked much criticism, but Murray has not been swayed (Herrnstein died shortly before *The Bell Curve* was published). Murray has continued to argue that differences in intellectual ability, as measured by IQ tests, explain much of the inequality present in American society. In his 2008 book *Real Education*, he charges that our entire education system is living a lie:

> The lie is that every child can be anything he or she wants to be. No one really believes it, but we approach education's problems as if we did. We are phobic about saying out loud that children differ in their ability to learn the things that schools teach. Not only do we hate to say it, we get angry with people who do. We insist that the emperor *is* wearing clothes, beautiful clothes, and that those who say otherwise are bad people. (p. 11)

In our experiences as teachers at the secondary and university levels and in our years of research on education, we have never encountered an educator who claimed that every child could be anything he or she wanted to be. We have known hundreds of teachers who tried to help their students become all they were capable of becoming. Teachers, probably more so than any other occupation, are aware of individual differences, and they respond to these differences in how they teach and what they expect from students. We are in agreement, however, with these statements from *Real Education*:

> Despite the current obscurity of vocational education, most school systems around the country still maintain substantial programs and facilities. The label for them is no longer vocational education, but CTE (career and technical education). . . . Moreover, the empirical evidence in favor of CTE is not in dispute. CTE works. Giving high-school students the option of taking technical courses increases the likelihood they will graduate from high school. High-school students who pursue the vocational track do better in the job market, in terms of both employment rates and wages, than those who stay in the academic track but don't belong there. (pp. 149–150)

Murray further argues that few students enroll in CTE because of the "misbegotten, pernicious, wrong-headed idea that not going to college means you're a failure" (p. 150). With this statement we could not agree more, and it is this "wrong-headed idea" that we would most like to see changed. In Chapter 6 we discuss the broader issue that underlies much of Murray's work—class structure in capitalistic economies—and the roles of education, in general, and CTE, specifically, in perpetuating this structure.

The emphasis on college as the only route to a satisfying career has been questioned by another prominent social scientist, James Rosenbaum, but he has received little of the attention received by Murray. Rosenbaum presented his position in the 2001 book *Beyond College for All,* and more recently in an article for *American Educator,* the flagship publication of the American Federation of Teachers (Rosenbaum, Stephan, & Rosenbaum, 2010). In the 2010 paper, Rosenbaum and his coauthors identify what they consider the three elements of college for all that have the most potential for harm: the idealization of the BA degree, the promise of easy college access, and the cultivation of stigma-free remediation.

The idealization of the BA degree arises primarily from the well-documented difference in the lifetime earnings of workers with a bachelor's degree and those with only a high school diploma. This gross comparison ignores the wide variation in earnings of both groups and, echoing Murray, the variability accounted for by differences in academic ability. In *Beyond College for All* (2001) Rosenbaum reported analyses of longitudinal studies that found that among all students who earned bachelor's degrees, those in the lowest quartile on high school achievement had earnings below those with average achievement. The gross high school–BA comparison also ignores the differences across majors. Degrees that require advanced science and mathematics, such as engineering and accounting, yield a far larger economic payoff than a liberal arts or education degree (Carnevale, Strohl, & Melton 2011). For those who seek postsecondary education, our society is very forgiving with regard to prior academic performance. Unlike most industrialized nations that limit postsecondary access to those who have performed well at the secondary level, we provide a range of options from nonselective 4-year colleges to open-entry community colleges. For poorly prepared students, Rosenbaum et al. (2010) see such access as a false promise. All who apply gain admission, but if they do not pass placement tests, they have to take developmental (i.e., remedial) courses, a level that many never progress beyond. A national longitudinal study of young people who had graduated in 1992 found that by the year 2000, only 20% of those who had a C average or lower in high school had earned any type of postsecondary credential (Rosenbaum, 2001). A more recent follow-up in Florida, which has probably the best system for tracking post-high-school experiences of any state, found virtually the same result: 19% of those who left school in 1999 with a C average or lower earned a postsecondary credential of any type in the 6-year period after high school (Jacobson & Mokher, 2009). The Florida study also found that postsecondary persistence and certificate attainment were higher for C-average or lower students who enrolled in occupational programs rather than courses that prepared them to transfer to 4-year colleges.

Rosenbaum et al. (2010) identify "stigma-free remediation" as the third potentially harmful aspect of college for all. This involves the use of the adjective *developmental* for the postsecondary courses that poorly prepared high school graduates must take and the lack of information students have about such courses. The "developmental" label has replaced "remedial," and it was adopted to avoid discouraging students. "Developmental" is less pejorative, but it still results in students spending time and money on courses that yield no college credit. Research conducted by Rosenbaum in the Chicago area found that many high school students were unaware of the need to pass the placement tests used by community colleges (Rosenbaum, Deil-Amen, & Person, 2006). This research also found little discussion of developmental courses and how they may delay program completion in college catalogs, websites, or even in the advice given by college staff.

College for all emerged to encourage students to set high goals, but it has discouraged educators from giving students realistic information about the demands of postsecondary education. It has also led to a devaluing of occupations that do not require a bachelor's degree. Rosenbaum would like schools to be more honest with their students and provide them with information about a range of opportunities for rewarding careers.

To underscore Rosenbaum's appeal for more honesty, we present Table 2.1 and Figure 2.2. We prepared Table 2.1 by drawing on three sources; Figure 2.2 was developed by the U.S. Census Bureau (2011b). The statistics presented in the two are not fully consistent, but both indicate that college for all is unrealistic for a large percentage of young people.

Table 2.1 presents our estimates of the number of 9th-grade students who earn some type of postsecondary credential. We prepared this table by drawing on three sources. The first is Greene and Winters (2006), who used data from the Common Core Data collected by the National Center for Education Statistics to estimate national dropout rates. The second is the National Center for Higher Education Management Systems (2011) and draws upon data on the number of students who enter college each year that are assembled by that Center. The third is Skomsvold, Radford, and Berkner (2011), who analyzed data from a follow-up survey of a nationally representative sample of students who began postsecondary education for

TABLE 2.1. The College and Career Pipeline

9th-Grade Cohort	Benchmarks	Initial Workforce Credentials[4]
100 enter 9th grade	70% complete high school on time[1]	30 enter as high school dropouts
70 complete high school	63% immediately start college[2]	26 enter as high school graduates
44 start college	50% dropout[3]	22 enter with some college, but no credential
	9% earn a certificate within 6 years[3]	4 enter with a postsecondary certificate
	9% earn an associate degree within 6 years[3]	4 enter with an associate degree
	31% earn a bachelor's degree within 6 years[3]	14 enter with a college degree

Sources. [1]Greene & Winters (2006); [2]National Center for Higher Education Management Systems (2011); [3]Skomsvold, Radford, & Berkner (2011); [4]An unknown number of individuals in each of these cells will go on to obtain more education or credentials later in life.

Note. Estimates of how many adults 25 years of age and older hold a bachelor's degree vary. *The Current Population Survey* (U.S. Census Bureau, 2011a) reports that 29.5% hold a bachelor's degree or higher. But this is a survey that is subject to respondent bias. Other estimates, such as those from Symonds, Schwartz, & Ferguson (2011), show that 59% of 27-year-olds have "some college." The *Chronicle of Higher Education* (2011) estimates 27.5% of adults have a 2- or 4-year college degree (see note 4 above).

the first time during the 2003–04 school year. The data used were collected in 2009, 6 years or more after the students had left high school.

The data we drew upon for Table 2.1 indicate that 30% of a typical cohort does not graduate from high school. The Census Bureau chart (Figure 2.2) indicates half as many dropouts. Part of this discrepancy may be self-report bias, because most census statistics are based on surveys of individuals. In addition, the Census Bureau counts those who report they obtained a GED as high school graduates. The report we cite used data collected from schools on the number of 9th-grade students enrolled and the number of diplomas awarded 4 years later.

The difference in the percentage of those earning a bachelor's degree is more difficult to explain. The Census Bureau figure for those with a bachelor's or higher degree is 30%, which includes those who spent time in graduate school but did not receive a degree. The longitudinal survey of those entering postsecondary education, which we cite, found only 14% received a bachelor's within 6 years after they originally enrolled. Some of those who did not obtain a degree when they were followed up may do so at a later date, but it is unlikely that enough will do so to come close to the Census Bureau figure. Regardless of the differences between the table and chart, it

FIGURE 2.2. Educational Attainment of Adults 25 Years of Age or Older in the United States as of the 2010 Census

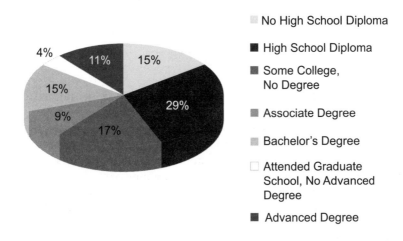

- No High School Diploma
- High School Diploma
- Some College, No Degree
- Associate Degree
- Bachelor's Degree
- Attended Graduate School, No Advanced Degree
- Advanced Degree

Source. U.S. Census Bureau (2011a)

is clear from both that at least half of all students entering the 9th grade are unlikely to obtain a college degree.

We found support for CTE in an unlikely source: *The Death and Life of the Great American School System.* In this 2010 book Diane Ravitch recants the support she had given over the previous 2 decades to those critics of American education who would like to see an open market for educational services. These critics believe that if we set high standards, hold teachers accountable, and give parents the opportunity to choose the schools their children attend, the better schools will attract students and the weaker schools will lose them. As this movement gained strength, Ravitch saw it was doing just what many of its proponents hoped: "undermining public education" (p. 13). She describes changes made in the New York City and San Diego school districts that focused on management, choice, incentives, and sanctions that failed to yield the improvements expected. She concludes that curriculum and instruction are the keys to improving students' knowledge and skills. With all its flaws, Ravitch believes public education is essential "because it is so intimately connected to our concepts of citizenship and democracy and the promise of American life" (p. 14).

Ravitch does not address the college-for-all mantra directly, but in her concluding chapter she presents the components that a curriculum for public education should include. And here, to our surprise, we found support for the type of CTE that we too would like to see: a curriculum that prepares young people for employment but one that also includes the arts and sciences, "so that they too may gain a sense of life's possibilities" (p. 232). With properly prepared and supported teachers, the CTE classroom can contribute to learning in the arts and sciences.

MULTIPLE PATHWAYS, MULTIPLE WAYS OF WINNING

The representatives of CTE who have been the most visible opponents of college for all are Kenneth Gray and Edwin Herr. Both of these authors were teachers, guidance counselors, and administrators in high schools before moving to the university level. Their understanding of students' abilities and interests has roots in their extensive personal interactions as well as in their research. In 1995 Gray and Herr coauthored *Other Ways to Win*, a book that received such a good reception that they published a second edition in 2000 and a third in 2006. The message of all three editions has been consistent: Too many students in the middle two quartiles of academic ability are pushed into a college preparatory curriculum that is a poor match for their interests and skills. The majority of students who follow this path start but do not complete a baccalaureate, and even among those who obtain degrees, many have to accept employment below their level of preparation. College for all discourages students from considering a host of occupations for which workers are in high demand and that offer earnings comparable to those of college graduates. In addition, the cost of training for such occupations is far less than 4 years of college. Gray and Herr believe that schools have a responsibility to serve all their students—those who are at risk of dropping out and those who will enter the workforce directly after high school, as well as those preparing for college.

In thinking about multiple ways of winning, schools have begun to organize curriculum in different ways to address this issue. We briefly describe several approaches in the following discussion. These are not mutually exclusive approaches although each is driven by different logics.

USDE Career Clusters/Pathways

One approach that emerged to align academic and technical content and secondary and postsecondary instruction was "career clusters" within which there are "career pathways." Career clusters organize occupations by the goods and services they provide to society. The Office of Vocational and Adult Education, the unit of the U.S. Department of Education that administers the federal role in CTE, has adopted the following 16 clusters for funding and reporting activities receiving federal funds:

- Agriculture, Food, and Natural Resources
- Architecture and Construction
- Arts, Audio/Video Technology, and Communications
- Business, Management, and Administration
- Education and Training
- Finance
- Government and Public Administration
- Health Sciences
- Hospitality and Tourism
- Human Services
- Information Technology
- Law, Public Safety, Corrections, and Security
- Manufacturing
- Marketing, Sales, and Service
- Science, Technology, Engineering, and Mathematics
- Transportation, Distribution, and Logistics

Within each of the clusters, there are career pathways that specify the skills and knowledge to be acquired to enter occupations at various levels within the cluster. These levels range from occupations that can be entered directly following high school to those that require postgraduate study. A career pathway becomes increasingly focused as a student progress through it. The National Career Clusters Framework, which is supported by the National Association of State Directors of Career Technical Education Consortium, has developed detailed statements of the skills and knowledge required for each of the pathways in the 16 clusters. These skills and knowledge are organized into four levels and show pathways from high school through college:

- Foundational academic expectations: learning standards in core academic subjects established by the separate states for secondary students
- Essential: apply to all clusters and pathways and students should be able to demonstrate them in the context of the pathways they are studying
- Cluster (foundation): apply to all pathways within a cluster
- Pathway: apply to all careers within a pathway

The first two levels apply to all clusters. The Common Core State Standards for language arts and mathematics should produce highly uniform expectations for these two content areas. Each cluster has unique knowledge and skills that all students should be able to demonstrate. It is within these foundation skills that the information relevant to AAI ("all aspects of the industry") is presented. As students' understanding of clusters increases, they should select pathways consistent with their aspirations and abilities. Career Pathways provide the framework for what Perkins IV defines as a "programs of study" that lead to defined occupations, most of which require education and training beyond high school. We discuss this concept in greater detail in Chapter 5. Pathways/programs of study help students and their parents identify the academic and technical courses that students should take to be prepared to pursue their careers of choice. [2]

Linked Learning

California has one of the most visible efforts to initiate multiple pathways: Linked Learning. This initiative is being led by ConnectEd, the California Center for College and Career, with funding from the James Irvine Foundation. Linked Learning pathways have all the components specified for programs of study by Perkins IV, as well as requiring WBL ("work-based learning") and support services. They are built around industry themes, combining rigorous academic and technical content in coordinated, nonduplicative sequences from high school to postsecondary education. The academic component includes 2 years of a foreign language as well as advanced mathematics. Linked Learning pathways are designed to enable young people to obtain postsecondary credentials that lead to successful careers and satisfying civic and family lives (Saunders & Chrisman, 2011).

When the ConnectEd website (http://www.connectedcalifornia.org/) was accessed in the summer of 2011, nine school districts in California were listed as having received grants of one million dollars or more to implement Linked Learning pathways as a primary reform strategy within their high schools. Two other districts have received planning grants. This funding supports extensive planning, technical assistance, and professional development to develop a shared commitment among district and school leaders, faculty, and community partners, as well as the actual curriculum and instructional skills needed for the pathways.

Tough Choices, Tough Times

The National Center on Education and the Economy (2007) has proposed a much different approach to improving student performance. The core of their proposal is the establishment of Boards of Examination in each state that would establish syllabi for core academic subjects and develop examinations to assess learning of the skills and knowledge specified in the syllabi. The standard for passing these examinations would be scores that would enable students to enter the community colleges in their states without the need for remedial courses. Students would take these examinations at the end of their 10th year of schooling. Those who pass would go on to community colleges or could take 2 additional years of high-level academics such as Advanced Placement courses or an International Baccalaureate program. Those who do not pass would take additional academics designed to bring them to the level needed to pass the state qualifying examination.

We have already questioned whether more of the same, that is, remedial academic courses, are likely to improve the performance of students for whom such instruction has proved inadequate in the past. High-stakes tests linked to specific standards and syllabi may provide direction and motivation to most students, but more traditional academic courses are unlikely to bring about significant improvement in those students who need a different approach. We discuss this issue at greater length in Chapter 3.

Schools with Occupational Themes

In 2004 the Committee on Increasing High School Students' Engagement and Motivation to Learn, a committee of the National Research Council (NRC) and the Institute of Medicine (IOM), published a report that synthesized the available research on the psychological, organizational, and pedagogic variables associated with the motivation to learn in structured educational settings. The findings and conclusions of this committee represent the consensus of leading scholars who included a chapter that presents the evidence on the effectiveness of structuring schools around occupational themes. The committee identified six practices common to such schools that have the potential to enhance motivation and engagement:

1. Programs motivating students allow for close adult-student relationships.
2. Engagement increases in environments where students have some autonomy in selecting tasks and methods and in which they can construct meaning, engage in sense making on their own, and play an active role in learning, rather than the passive role typical of teacher-centered classrooms.
3. Motivation and engagement are enhanced in well-structured educational environments with clear, meaningful purposes.

4. Motivation is enhanced in settings with a challenging curriculum, high expectations, and a strong emphasis on achievement.
5. Motivation and engagement are enhanced when students have multiple paths to competence.
6. Helping students develop education and career pathways can enhance their understanding of school and their motivation to participate fully. (NRC & IOM, 2004, pp. 172–176)

The research findings underlying each of these practices are presented in the report. The committee raised the following caveat: "Although this summary represents an idealized version of schools with occupational themes, it does reflect the goals of most programs" (p. 172). The committee examined the evidence from schools that were attempting comprehensive reforms, such as career academies, but these practices also reflect the kind of CTE that we would like to see in all secondary schools. Good CTE programs, whatever their settings (comprehensive high schools, career centers, or career academies), follow these practices to prepare students for broad occupational clusters rather than specific occupations. They teach academics in occupational context and give students the skills they need both to enter the labor market and to continue their education after high school. Unfortunately, such programs are at present more the exception than the norm. If CTE is to realize its potential, more programs will have to incorporate these practices, especially a challenging curriculum, high expectations, and a strong emphasis on achievement.

HOW OTHER NATIONS PREPARE THEIR YOUTH

As we were nearing the end of work on this book, the Organisation for Economic Cooperation and Development (OECD) and the Harvard Graduate School of Education published reports supporting our views: *Learning for Jobs* (OECD, 2010) and *Pathways to Prosperity* (Symonds et al., 2011). These organizations could hardly be considered advocates for CTE, but both recommend occupational training at the secondary level that meets the needs of employers for specific skills and ensures that students have the academic foundation and career/employability skills needed in all occupations. These are the relevant recommendations from the OECD report, which uses the acronym VET for vocational education and training:

- Through VET systems, provide young people with the generic, transferable skills to support occupational mobility, and lifelong learning and with the occupationally specific training to meet employers' immediate needs.

- Immediate job skills need to be complemented with wider, career development competencies.
- Ensure all students in vocational programs have adequate numeracy and literacy skills to support lifelong learning and career development. Identify and tackle weaknesses in this area.
- VET programs need to prepare students for further study and jobs. (OECD, 2010, pp. 20–21)

The idea that job preparation and academic preparation are not mutually exclusive outcomes is an important observation discussed in this report. The OECD report repeats the familiar argument that developed countries need highly skilled workers if they are to compete with the low wages in developing countries and advances five reasons why occupational training at the secondary level helps meet this need. First, employers have little incentive to provide training in general skills. Training in firm-specific skills benefits employers, but training in general skills benefits workers who can use these skills to seek employment at high wages. Second, training makes young people more "job ready" and thus reduces the risk and expense of hiring them. Third, those who are well prepared at the secondary level are more likely to engage in continued learning to update and learn new skills throughout their careers. Fourth, in the absence of specific measures to raise skills levels, countries can fall into a "low-skill equilibrium" in which there are no incentives to upgrade skills. High skill levels can have just the reverse effect and encourage investment and economic growth. Fifth, secondary occupational training has a labor market payoff. The first four reasons arise primarily from economic theory, and we do not discuss them further. There is, however, an extensive research base underlying the fifth reason and we review this evidence in Chapter 6.

The Harvard report, *Pathways to Prosperity,* focuses on the bleak prospects for young people who do not have skills needed in the workforce. Increasingly, a high school diploma no longer provides entry into jobs paying enough to support a family nor, in the words of the Harvard report, "a passport to the American Dream" (p. 2). The labor market rewards skills that are acquired through prolonged study either in the classroom or in structured on-the-job training. Symonds et al. present data similar to those we reviewed in Chapter 1 on the lack of progress on NAEP reading and math scores, dropouts, and postsecondary completion rates.[3] They also cite some of the research presented in the OECD report: In comparison with the United States, countries where half or more of all upper secondary students participate in VET score higher on standardized tests, have higher completion rates for secondary education, and experience a smoother transition to employment. The United States is an outlier among its industrialized competitors in offering its youth access to high-quality CTE. The result is in the evidence provided by the OECD and Harvard reports.

To improve the opportunities available to young people, *Pathways to Prosperity* recommends multiple pathways to careers, some of which would involve modern CTE programs that emphasize academic as well as technical skills:

> These programs also advance a broader pedagogical hypothesis: that from late adolescence onward, most young people learn best in structured programs that combine work and learning, and where learning is contextual and applied. Ironically, this pedagogical approach has been widely applied in the training of our highest status professionals in the U.S., where clinical practice (a form of apprenticeship) is an essential component in the preparation of doctors, architects, and (increasingly) teachers.
>
> When it comes to teenagers, however, we Americans seem to think they will learn best by sitting all day in classrooms. If they have not mastered basic literacy and numeracy skills by the time they enter high school, the answer in many schools is to give them double blocks of English and math. (Symonds et al., 2011, p. 38)

In additional to multiple pathways, the Harvard report recommends greatly expanded involvement of employers in upper secondary education and a new social compact with youth. Such a compact would describe how educators, employers, and government will provide pathways to youth and what will be expected from youth in return. We too would welcome such changes in the way we prepare young people for life, but our objective in this book is more modest: We would like to see all CTE educators enhance instruction in the academic content that is inherent in their curricula. In the following chapters we provide the rationale for such an approach and give some examples of the results it can produce if applied correctly. Before moving to these topics, we discuss career guidance and its key role in assisting students to set occupational goals and to plan programs of study consistent with these goals.

CAREER GUIDANCE: THE MISSING LINK

Occupational training at the secondary level is opposed by many educators because it requires young people to identify career objectives before they are developmentally ready to do so. [4] Work in many ways signifies who we are—defining our personalities, our habits, and our lifestyles. Finding the right career can lead to a lifetime of satisfaction, but not finding the right career can lead to poor self-esteem, lowered self-efficacy, a lack of life satisfaction, and even depression (Csikszentmihalyi & LeFevre, 1989; Haworth & Hill, 1992; Wang, Lesage, Schmitz, & Drapeau, 2008; Warr, 2007).

Frank Parsons, the founding father of career counseling, recognized the importance of finding the "right" work. In *Choosing a Vocation*, published in 1909, Parsons wrote:

> An occupation out of harmony with the worker's aptitudes and capacities means inefficiency, unenthusiastic and perhaps distasteful labor, and low pay; while an occupation in harmony with the nature of the man means enthusiasm, love of work, and high economic values—superior product, efficient service, and good pay. (p. 3)

Research has verified Parsons's observations: People who find satisfaction in their work exhibit higher levels of commitment, competency, and productivity and report higher levels of life adjustment (Auty, Goodman, & Foss, 1987; Henderson, 2000; Mueller, 2003; Stott, 1970).

Developing a career is a process, not a single decision. Unfortunately, not enough attention is paid to assisting young people to engage in thoughtful, thorough career development. One of the issues facing schools is that students are confronted with substantial career and life decisions at an early age with limited opportunities for career exploration. Students are expected to choose and follow a program of study that will prepare them to exit high school with the skills necessary to continue their education or to enter the workforce. Career and technical education students must choose specific occupational areas even though most do not continue the same career emphasis upon completing high school (Bishop, 1989; Levesque et al., 2008).[5] Too often, students are offered few opportunities to engage in career exploration and given little useful information on postsecondary options (Dykeman, Wood, Ingram, Pehrsson et al., 2003). The result is that career development is often a by-product of the educational curriculum, with a "figure it out as you go along" mentality prevalent among educators and students regarding career exploration.

In this section, we present an overview of career development using the framework of Super's (1957) life-span, life-space theory with special emphasis on the growth and exploration stages of development. We also review research relevant to the need for improved career development services for K–12 students.

The Life-Span, Life-Space Perspective of Career Development

Career theories are the framework that counselors, psychologists, and educators use to understand the career development process and provide career guidance. Career theory has a long and complex history and includes many perspectives on how to understand the career development process. Theories include trait-and-factor, stage, and social learning, to name just a few (Osipow & Fitzgerald, 1996). In addition, the development of career theory has not proceeded down a linear path. Like any complex field of study, career theories have grown out of one another, merged, and branched off in other directions, thus weaving an intricate path with the goal of understanding the hows and whys of the career process. The core of most career theories, however, is the same: an effort to explain the "evolving sequence of a person's work experiences over time" (Arthur, Hall, & Lawrence, 1989, p. 8).

From among the several competing theories of career development, we present Super's (1957) life-span, life-space theory because it is a general theory with a perspective that addresses career development at different stages. Although other theories could have been presented, Super's theory seemed appropriate due to its capacity to address student needs at different stages and because it recognizes the need for intentional efforts toward career development. After its original publication, the theory has evolved in response to research and social changes, resulting in its most recent formulation in Super, Savickas, and Super (1996).

The career development process is unique to every person. Gender, ethnicity, ability, personality, socioeconomic status, family, geography, and opportunity all play a part in the development of one's career path, to varying degrees. Super's life-span, life-space theory takes into account many of these aspects. According to Herr (1997), Super's theory incorporates the notion of multiple-role environments that include work, family, educational, and community roles, each with varying demands and levels of significance that occur at different developmental stages in life.

In addition to the traditional trait-and-factor approach of career development theory (the process of matching an individual to a career according to his or her personality, ability, and interests), Super's theory incorporated life stages, self-concept, and social context as three areas of influence in the career development process. (Patton & McMahon, 2006).

Super's theory was established on a life-span perspective and recognized that career development does not end in young adulthood but continues throughout life. Furthermore, the work of Super and his colleagues "changed the focus of career choice from that of a static point-in-time event to that of a dynamic process where career development was viewed as an evolving process of life" (Patton & McMahon, 2006, p. 53). Super recognized the complexity of the career development process and worked to develop a comprehensive theory to transcend other theories that did not address the complexity of human development and environmental influences.

Super, however, recognized that his own theory lacked comprehension and integration, identifying it as "a loosely unified set of theories dealing with specific aspects of career development taken from developmental, differential, social and phenomenological psychology and held together by self-concept or personal-construct theory" (Super, 1984, p. 194).

Super's theory posits that people progress through five stages during the career development process: growth, exploration, establishment, maintenance, and disengagement. It should be noted that Super's theory is not a rigid stage theory in which an individual's age dictates his or her progression from stage to stage, a process referred to as *maxicycling*. In fact, Super contended that movement through the five stages could be a flexible process through which people could recycle through certain stages. Super referred to this process as *minicycling*. We provide a brief description of each of the stages with our central focus on the growth and exploration stages. We then explore relevant research pertaining to career development and applications to CTE.

The growth stage is the process through which individuals, typically children and adolescents, are introduced to a variety of occupations, and it is the time in which they begin to develop their self-concept (Super, 1957). Self-concept, in the context of career, is "the constellation of self attributes considered by the individual to be vocationally relevant" (Super, 1963, p. 20). According to Giannantonio and Hurley-Hanson (2006), self-concept includes "one's abilities, personality traits, values, self-esteem, and self-efficacy" (p. 320). It is during this growth stage that individuals are exposed to occupations through family, school, community, and the media, among other sources. Through their experiences in home, school, and community, young people develop a sense of autonomy and industry, begin to develop work-related skills and habits, and identify relevant role models, all while developing a better understanding of their own interests along with a burgeoning awareness of their own abilities (Patton & McMahon, 2006; Super et al., 1996).

During the exploratory stage, individuals engage in experiences that aid in developing their vocational identity by explicitly investigating careers and taking part in education, training, and other work-related experiences. Through these experiences, they learn more about themselves, their interests, and their abilities, which furthers the development of their self-concepts. Individuals apply what they learn through the exploratory process by matching their interests and abilities to occupations and applying their self-concept to both work and life roles (Super, 1957). Moreover, exploration is believed to be intrinsically motivated by natural curiosity (Blustein, 1988, 1997).

The establishment stage is a period of employment in which the individual is focused on establishing a stable work environment and working toward career advancement. The major goal during this stage is for the individual to stabilize his or her role within a career context. Some individuals may work toward promotion and advancement in their careers, thus increasing their job-related responsibilities (Patton & McMahon, 2006).

Maintenance is the fourth stage in which "individuals are concerned with maintaining their self-concept and their present job status" (Giannantonio & Hurley-Hanson, 2006, p. 323). Nevertheless, some may decide to make career changes during the maintenance phase (e.g., moving to other organizations or positions or changing occupations). According to Super's theory, this results in the individual recycling through the exploration and establishment stages—referred to as a *minicycle*. The central focus for the individual, however, is toward preserving or maintaining his or her position within an established career (Patton & McMahon, 2006).

The final stage, disengagement, is the process of disengaging from the world of work, which usually comes in the form of retirement. During this stage, the individual engages in the process of planning for retirement, begins to reduce his or her workload, and finally leaves the work setting.

The stages described here are only a part of Super's theory. As stated earlier, Super's theory is elaborate and includes other significant constructs. For example, Super developed a Life-Career Rainbow that provides a graphic representation of the life-span, life-space theory, including the stages of career development and life-roles (Super, 1984). Super also developed the Archway Model, a graphic representation of the personal and social constructs that affect career development. Career development begins early in life and continues throughout one's life, During this process, one's self-concept is formed and cemented through one's experiences. In the following sections, we address this process during the growth and exploration stages, including a discussion of relevant research. Finally, we examine the role that CTE may play in the career development process.

The Growth Stage

As stated earlier, career development is a process that happens over an individual's lifetime. Most educators and counselors, however, focus their career development efforts on adolescence and young adulthood. Placing the focus solely on these later stages ignores the growth stage, which is the foundation for the subsequent stage of exploration. The growth stage is characterized as the starting point of self-concept development and the beginning stage of vocational identity development.

According to the life-span, life-space theory, the growth stage begins in childhood and extends into middle adolescence (4 to 13 years of age; Stead & Schultheiss, 2003). This stage is characterized by exploration through learning, play, and fantasy (Patton & McMahon, 2006; Wood &

Kaszubowski, 2008). Engagement in these activities sets the stage for self-concept development by helping children gain better knowledge about their strengths and weaknesses and likes and dislikes.

Super (1963) identified three constructs related to self-concept of vocational development: formation, translation, and implementation. Schultheiss and Stead (2004) provided an explanation for the development of self-concept, beginning with the formation process, which occurs in childhood and persists throughout development. Formation requires identification with key figures in the child's life and includes role playing and reality testing. Translation is the process of transforming the self-concept into occupational terms that "occurs through identification, experience, and awareness of one's own attributes" (p. 115). Finally, implementation emerges during adolescence and young adulthood and consists of individuals implementing or applying their self-concepts within the context of their chosen calling (e.g., training for their first jobs).

Super (1990) outlined nine dimensions associated with the career development of children in the growth stage of development, which have been further defined by Stead and Schultheiss (2003) and Wood and Kaszubowski (2008): (a) curiosity—the desire to learn more about the world; (b) exploration—engaging in activities that lead to information about self and others in an effort to meet curiosity needs; (c) information—seeking and applying career information; (d) interests—awareness of likes and dislikes; (e) locus of control—maintaining a sense of control over the environment; (f) key figures—the recognition of role models or those who influence one's life and decisions; (g) time perspective—an understanding of time in planning for events; (h) self-concept—one's identity, encompassing one's roles and behaviors in the context of relationships; and (i) planfulness—an understanding of the importance of planning and preparation. These dimensions are part of the everyday learning and growth experiences of children and have been corroborated by research to some extent. Schultheiss, Palma, and Manzi (2002) investigated the application of Super's dimensions in 4th- and 5th-grade students and found eight of the nine dimensions to be present in childhood career development with some slight modifications to Super's theory (as cited in Schultheiss & Stead, 2004). In addition, Super's dimensions relate well with Erikson's (1963) theory of psychosocial development in that these dimensions are characteristic of the three stages of early, middle, and late childhood development in which children exercise their autonomy, express their natural inclination toward taking initiative, and engage in industrious activities.

Theories need research to help legitimize their application. Unfortunately, little research has examined Super's theory as applied to children. In general, career development research is not concentrated on the career development of children; instead, research has historically focused on adolescence and adulthood (Auger, Blackhurst, & Wahl, 2005; Stead & Schultheiss, 2003; Wood & Kaszubowski, 2008). However, research does support the theory that children think about careers and identify with vocational constructs. For example, research conducted on children as young as 5 has found that they display realistic and stable career goals across time (Trice & King, 1991). Moreover, they tend to be influenced by their parents, in that their vocational aspirations correlate with their parents' occupations (Trice & Knapp, 1992). Children also demonstrate an awareness of careers as they relate to gender, often engaging in gender-typing of careers at young ages and, over time, broadening their definitions of gender and career. In addition, children display a coherent structure in their occupational choices (Trice, Hughes, Odom, & Woods, 1995).

The findings from these studies corroborate several of the dimensions related to the growth stage. For instance, exploration, information, and curiosity are involved in the contemplation of careers. The concept of key figures is applicable to children's identification with their parents' occupations. The dimensions of information and curiosity also play a role in children's understanding of gender and career and the eventual loosening of gender and career stereotypes.

Several studies have examined the longitudinal aspects of career as they relate to childhood. Trice (1991a) demonstrated that, in general, children maintain the same career goals over the course of a school year. Trice (1991b) examined the first realistic career aspirations of middle-aged adults and found that 59% of them had identified their first career aspiration before the age of 13. Furthermore, it was found that 41% of the sample's childhood career aspirations matched their adult occupations, and 46% of the sample's adolescent career aspirations matched their adult occupations. Finally, Trice and McClellan (1993), using data from a 1926 study on gifted individuals, found strong concordance between childhood career aspirations and early adult attainment. More research is needed to examine Super's theory as it applies to the growth stage and Super's later stages of career establishment and maintenance.

Although limited in scope, research is available that demonstrates the need for career exposure and interventions earlier in childhood development. Rojewski and Kim (2003) examined the occupational aspirations, vocational preparation, and work experiences of work-bound and college-bound individuals through longitudinal data gathered while the participants were in the 8th and 10th grades. They compared their findings with the sample's postschool transition activities (e.g., college or employment) and found that the work-bound individuals had exhibited poorer academic performance, had a higher sense of external locus of control, and had lower academic and occupational aspirations than their college-bound counterparts. The authors assert that these characteristics are "firmly established by grade 8" (p. 103). Furthermore, the gap between the college-bound group and the work-bound group widened through the 10th grade. The importance of these data, as explained by the researchers, is that students are "pretty well 'locked in' to a particular orientation toward occupations and adult life early in their lives" (p. 104). Targeted career development interventions during the growth stage could widen the range of occupations compatible with children's emerging vocational self-concepts.

No one would advocate for occupational preparation in elementary schools. However, preliminary research has demonstrated that career-infused curriculum in Grades K–8 improves student career maturity (Cassidy, 2007). Efforts such as this may set the stage for preparing students to make informed decisions with regard to choosing their program of study upon entering high school, thus enhancing the growth stage of career development. Overall, the limited research on childhood career development demonstrates the need for increased application of career interventions during childhood and more research into the career development process of children.

The Exploration Stage

Super believed that children developed certain traits during the growth stage, readying them for the exploration stage of career development. These traits consist of the nine dimensions previously outlined in the growth stage (Super, 1990). According to Savickas and Super (1993), these constructs develop in childhood, strengthen in adolescence, and function as determinants of adolescent career maturity. Furthermore, it is during adolescence that the exploration stage begins (lasting into young adulthood, 14 to 24 years of age) and the advancement of career maturity and further development of the self-concept occurs. The exploratory process was first included in an explicit career development theory by Ginzberg, Ginsburg, Axelrad, and Herma (1951) and integrated in Super's life-span, life-space theory.

The exploration stage is characterized by the tasks of adolescence and young adulthood. Individuals within this age range are typically seeking opportunities to explore careers through education and work experiences. Individuals in this stage begin to narrow their career desires and options and seek training or education in their fields of interest, aiding in the development of a vocational identity (Patton & McMahon, 2006) or vocational self-concept. *Vocational self-concept* has been defined as "the constellation of self attributes considered by the individual to be vocationally relevant, whether or not they have been translated into a vocational preference" (Super, 1963, p. 20). Jordaan (1963) further explained that "vocational exploration is the process of clarifying the self-concept and translating it into occupational terms, of acquiring the understanding of occupations necessary for this translation, and of trying out this vocational self-concept in vocationally relevant activities" (p. 54).

The exploration stage consists of substages or tasks, including crystallization, specification, and implementation. According to Jordaan (1963), the exploratory stage is a period of realistic choices in which the individual seeks knowledge about himself or herself and the world, experiments, and searches for new experiences and perspectives in an effort to "increase his understanding of reality" (p. 50). Through the exploration process, the individual *crystallizes* his or her career interests by narrowing choices, then *specifies* a vocational choice, which may come in the form of work, training, or education, and then *implements* a vocational choice and makes it a reality via training or education.

The exploration stage is critical to students developing a sense of vocational identity and an overall sense of self, and identity development is a crucial stage in overall adolescent development. Erikson (1963) considered identity development as the primary task of adolescence. Identity development and vocational decision making are closely linked, in that individuals who possess well-developed career interests also display an overall stronger sense of self (e.g., Blustein, Devenis, & Kidney, 1989; Vondracek, Schulenberg, Skorikov, Gillespie, & Wahlheim, 1995; Weyhing, Bartlett, & Howard, 1984). Additionally, Erikson (1959) considered one's occupational identity as key to overall identity development: "In general it is primarily the inability to settle on an occupational identity which disturbs young people" (p. 92). The work of Super and Erikson demonstrates the bidirectional influence of career exploration and vocational identity. In essence, one strengthens the other, creating the groundwork for movement into the establishment stage of development.

Research efforts have established a link between identity formation, self-concept, and career development and decision making. Gushue, Scanlan, Pantzer, and Clarke (2006) examined the career development of African-American students and found that higher levels of career decision-making self-efficacy were related to a more differentiated vocational self-concept and more engagement in career exploration. In a similar study with Latino students, Gushue, Clarke, Pantzer, and Scanlan (2006) found that students with higher levels of career decision-making self-efficacy possessed a more differentiated identity and were more engaged in the career exploration process. Shoffner and Newsome (2001) conducted a study with gifted adolescent females in an effort to examine career exploration, commitment, and life-role salience. They found that vocational exploration and commitment contributed strongly to the identity development of this population.

These studies demonstrate the influence of exploration on vocational identity development: Engagement in exploratory activities enhances the career development process.

Age and gender also influence exploration and career decision making, with older students engaging in more exploration than younger students. Specifically, Wallace-Broscious, Serafica, and Osipow (1994) found that 12th-grade students engaged in more career planning and exploration than 9th-grade students. Additionally, they found that 12th-grade students reported higher levels of career decidedness, females engaged in more planning and exploration than males, and females had higher levels of career decidedness than males. Furthermore, the researchers found that students' identity status played a role in predicting their levels of career certainty, indecision, exploration, and planning. This study was based on Super's and Erikson's theoretical constructs of exploration and identity development and supported these constructs as fundamental to the career development process.

External efforts appear to foster career development and aid in the development of vocational identity. Lapan, Aoyagi, and Kayson (2007) found that career development efforts can have long-term effects in aiding students in transitioning from adolescence to young adulthood. Enhanced career development efforts in high school resulted in the participants making greater progress toward career awareness, exploration, and planning. The participants reported greater success in transitioning into life roles, had a better sense of direction in their work, and expressed a greater sense of life satisfaction.

Exploration in K–12 Settings and CTE

Evidence supports the importance of growth and exploration in helping individuals develop their vocational identities and engage in thoughtful career decision making. What efforts do schools take to help students engage in career exploration? Is there a difference in the career exploration outcomes of students who are enrolled in traditional educational programs versus those who are enrolled in CTE programs?

Career development efforts in high school settings have been portrayed as hit and miss, in that students do not typically receive comprehensive guidance services and do not engage in career planning activities to help them achieve their career goals (Hollenbeck & DebBurman, 2000; Hughes & Karp, 2004). This lack of focus on career development in K–12 programming was delineated by Bloch (1996) in a multistate survey of high school principals and counselors that revealed a lack of commitment to the career development of students, in particular for those considered at risk for dropping out. Helwig (2004) examined the career development issues experienced by a group of students over a 10-year period in which data were gathered six times throughout their K–12 educational experiences. The students in this sample reported mediocre satisfaction with their school's role in helping them engage in career development activities, such as making a connection between school subject and occupational direction, feeling supported by their school in searching for a career direction, and feeling supported by their school with career preparation.

Other large-sample studies echo the finding that students are not receiving the career development experiences and information they need to develop their vocational identities and help them progress through the growth and exploratory stages of career development. Wimberly and Noeth (2005) reported on a large-scale study conducted by ACT in which 2,942 students in the 8th, 9th, and 10th grades completed the Educational Planning Survey. The survey examined issues related to high school programs, class selection, and the helpfulness of school, family, and friends in educational planning and decision making. Over 77% of the students reported that they planned to attend college; however, only two thirds of these students described their high school program as a college preparatory program—indicating a discrepancy between career guidance and program choice. In regard to exploration, 78% of the sample indicated that they had begun the exploration process by considering types of education, training, and work options upon graduation from high school, while 22% of the sample had not explored postgraduation education and/or training program or work options. Furthermore, although most of the sample had set educational or career goals, they were not engaged in planning activities. When comparing these data with the constructs of Super's theory, the majority of the sample had crystallized their vocational goals but had not engaged in the specification and implementation steps needed to make their goals a reality.

Wimberly and Noeth (2005) illuminated the potential problem with this lack of comprehensive exploration: When these students eventually approach postsecondary planning, they likely will find that they have missed such key steps as taking appropriate courses, participating in precollege programs, and obtaining postsecondary planning information from teachers and counselors. By failing to plan early, they may be closing the door on viable postsecondary education, training, and employment options for their future. The authors concluded that middle and high school students are not taking a college preparatory curriculum that would help them prepare for postsecondary education.

The cited research on traditional educational experiences indicates that there is a general lack of focus on career development practices in traditional high school settings. In addition, few comprehensive studies examine the effectiveness of career development interventions. Dykeman, Wood, Ingram, Gitelman et al. (2003) described career development studies as "singular and isolated, often without consideration or measure of students' level of career development" (p. 18). On a positive note, the limited research that is available on CTE programs that attempt to link high school with postsecondary experiences (e.g., career pathways, school-to-work, Tech Prep, career magnets) shows more promise in engaging students in career development activities—if not directly, then at least peripherally, indicating that career development may be a by-product of engagement in CTE programs. This research is reviewed in Chapter 5.

Programs of study, as specified by Perkins IV, require students to make decisions that, at a minimum, impact the last 2 years of high school and the first 2 years of postsecondary education. The theory and research we have reviewed suggest that virtually all high school students making these decisions are still in the exploratory stage of career development. Perkins IV emphasizes the need for career guidance, academic counseling, and professional development for educators in an effort to arm them with the knowledge and skills needed to assist students in the career exploration process. Although Perkins IV recognizes the role of career development in aiding students in making career-related decisions, the legislation does not emphasize the importance of helping students engage in the identity development and career exploration needed to make informed decisions. Instead, the legislation focuses on the development of rigorous programs. These programs, in turn, seek to educate students on the knowledge and skills needed to engage in meaningful careers. However, the question remains, is this enough to allow students to proceed successfully through the exploration stage and into the establishment stage of development in which they can sustain long-term careers?

Few studies have explicitly examined the effect of participating in CTE courses on career development. There were, however, a few efforts to examine career development in the context of school-to-work (STW) programs. For example, in 1999 the *Career Development Quarterly* produced a special issue on the role of career development theory in STW transition. Lent and Worthington (1999) acknowledged that although career development experts contributed to STW policy, research, and practice, those who are actually knowledgeable about career development process and theories (e.g., vocational and school counselors) had little impact on STW policy and implementation. In addition, Blustein, citing Worthington and Juntunen (1997), explained that the STW literature is rich in many ways, but "tends to downplay the experience of the individual" (Blustein, 1999, p. 349), which is contradictory to career development. Hansen (1999) explained that, "In the zeal to prepare students for the workforce, the human dimension—student development—has been forgotten" (p. 357). This statement emphasizes the need for a stronger emphasis on the growth and exploration stages of career development, which would include fostering the natural inclination of children and adolescents to learn more about themselves in the context of vocation.

In the following chapters we review studies that have examined the effect of participation in CTE programs on engagement, achievement, transition, and labor market outcomes. On the whole, these studies indicate that CTE contributes to the career development process. It appears to make this contribution even if students do not continue their educations or obtain employment in the occupational areas they study. For most high school students, the decision to study certain occupations is as much exploration as it is preparation for employment. The relevance of their courses may produce increased educational involvement even if experiences in these courses eventually lead to decisions to seek different occupational goals.

Improving Guidance and Counseling

In 1909 Frank Parsons wrote:

> We guide our boys and girls to some extent through school, then drop them into this complex world to sink or swim as the case may be. Yet there is no part of life where the need for guidance is more emphatic than in the transition from school to work—the choice of a vocation, adequate preparation for it, and the attainment of efficiency and success. (p. 4)

Some students and educators may wonder, after reading this passage, if much has changed in the 100-plus years since Parsons wrote these words. Although efforts have been made to engage students in the educational process and prepare them for the world of work, there is much still to do. Career development should become an intentional process in the education of students. In addition, career development needs to occur earlier, during the growth stage of development, while children are engaging in the processes of learning, play, and fantasy. These experiences, according to Super and other theorists, provide children with the tools to develop and clarify their career aspirations and thereby prepare them for the exploration phase of development that occurs during adolescence and young adulthood.

In 2007 the National Governors Association Center for Best Practices identified a number of features or practices thought to enhance high school reform and economic competitiveness. Among the practices cited was career education in Grades K–12. Most students in school today have little access to good career guidance. Given the constraints on most school budgets, it is unlikely that new staff can be added to address this vital component of the high school experience. One solution to this problem may lie in combining school and community resources. By distributing the career guidance function across and among caring adults in a variety of settings, we may be able to enhance the career development opportunities available to young people. One example of this kind of model was initially proposed by the Institute for Student Achievement (ISA) project at the National Center for Restructuring Education, Schools and Teaching at Teachers College, Columbia University. Contrary to traditional models of counseling, this approach brings together academic teachers, administrators, and counselors to work with students. Core components of distributed counseling include:

- *Team collaboration and integration of counseling strategies.* The team members collaboratively develop goals and strategies for supporting students, meet to discuss the progress of individual students, and integrate counseling and academic subjects.
- *A dedicated counselor integrated into the team.* The ISA counselor provides direct counseling to individual students and groups of students. As a full participant in the team, the counselor helps team members develop the skills and knowledge to help them collaborate in advising students.
- *Teachers as advisers.* The teacher's role is expanded to include serving as adviser, monitoring and supporting his or her students' development socially and emotionally as well as academically.
- *Student-support mechanisms.* Teams put in place a variety of structures and strategies to support students' academic, social, and emotional development. Two common strategies that are used to help teams support students' progress are team case conferencing and advisory programs.
- *Consistent communication with parents.* Teachers have sustained and purposeful interaction with parents, regularly communicating with them about their child's performance.
- *College preparation.* A 4-year college-preparatory sequence of activities is developed by the team. Through these activities, students and families are informed of and actively engaged in the process of preparing for college. (Allen, Nichols, Tocci, Hochman, & Gross, 2006)

If we combine this approach with the programmatic approach described in a Wisconsin study (Rubin, 2011) that identified approaches respondents (e.g., students, parents, counselors, administrators) felt would improve students' transition from high school to work, we would include:

- Community-based career information
- Systematic and regularized career awareness activities that begin in middle school
- Structured job shadowing
- Career plans that build on the practical knowledge gained through job shadowing
- Guidance services fully integrated with the school curriculum

Further, if we embed concepts emerging from the federal legislation requiring "programs of study," we could begin to imagine a more holistic, comprehensive college and career guidance system that would increase college and career readiness for all students.

Based on our preliminary review of the literature, features of a distributed guidance model would include, but not be limited to:

- Identification of one or more career-focused guidance teams that will include school counselors, teachers, administrators, and community members
- A professional development plan for all team members
- Identification of student support services to be provided
- Identification of community resources for career-related experiences
- A college and career readiness guidance plan

If career guidance and counseling is to be effective, it must become a total school/community responsibility. A small number of counselors, each one dealing with hundreds of students, cannot do what needs to be done. These counselors must become leaders and resources for a much broader approach that involves all those who influence the occupational knowledge and aspirations of young people.

SUMMARY

In this chapter, we question the prevailing assumption that college ready is the same as career ready. Career ready involves academic, technical, and employability skills. The current myopic focus on academics alone, particularly in the form of advanced mathematics, ignores the realities of the labor market. The college degree has become a signal that young people have the skills and traits that employers seek, and there is no question that those with degrees earn more than those without. Such comparisons, however, ignore the wide variability in earnings of college graduates, the potential of middle-skilled occupations, and the limited success that students who complete high school with a C average or lower have in postsecondary education.

Career clusters and career pathways have been developed to provide meaningful career development and technical training at the secondary level that allows students to progress as far with a broad occupational area as their ability and aspirations will take them. The Linked Learning initiative in California is assisting selected school districts to use such pathways to bring about major change in how their high schools operate. Two major reports from Harvard University and the Organisation for Economic Co-operation and Development have made the case for increasing access to technical training and WBL at the secondary level.

We conclude the chapter by citing the need for an increased emphasis on career guidance. Virtually all high school students are in the exploratory stage of their career development. They need to test their evolving vocational identities against the realities of occupations. Technical training and WBL provide opportunities for such testing. The concept of guidance must be expanded from the limited contacts that students have with counselors to a responsibility shared by all adults with significant work-related contact with youth.

CHAPTER 3

Student Engagement: The Necessary Condition

It is a given in education that student engagement is essential to learning. While its importance is universally accepted, engagement is a difficult concept to define and measure. Any observer will notice the differences between a classroom where the students are engaged and one where they are not, but identifying the factors that create these differences has proved challenging. Engagement emerges from a complex interaction of community, school, parents, teachers, students, and content, each of which varies on many dimensions. A synthesis of the available research concluded that engagement is a "meta" concept with behavioral, attitudinal, and cognitive components (Fredricks, Blumenfeld, & Paris, 2004).

There is one indicator of engagement, however, about which there is little disagreement: high school graduation. Withdrawal prior to graduation is the final act of disengagement. If students do not remain in school, all efforts to improve their ability to function in a rapidly changing, information-driven economy are futile. As expectations for better academic performance increase—accompanied by tests to measure if the expectations have been met—the pressure on struggling students increases. The debate as to whether this pressure causes such students to improve their performance or simply withdraw from school is unresolved.

In this chapter, we present the views of spokespersons for each side of this debate, as well as the implications for CTE. There is little question that when test results have major consequences, they become prone to influences that can distort them from their intended purpose. It appears equally clear, despite claims to the contrary, that these consequences can have a motivational effect on students. The challenge, therefore, is to harness the motivation component while controlling the distorting influences. This is a challenge to which we think CTE has a special, if not unique, capacity to respond.

Some of the research that we present shows that taking an appropriate combination of CTE and academic courses increases the probability that students will graduate from high school. This finding speaks to the contribution that relevance of instruction can make to motivation. Damon (2008) has proposed that a sense of purpose is a major component in adolescent development and that realistic career goals contribute to such a sense. We review this research and assess its implications for career-focused education. We conclude the chapter by summarizing the findings of the Committee on Increasing High School Students' Engagement and Motivation to Learn (National Research Council & the Institute of Medicine, 2004) regarding how the practices of schools with occupational themes align with the available evidence on factors that improve motivation and engagement.

HIGH-STAKES TESTING

Educational improvement through accountability reached its apotheosis with the passage of the No Child Left Behind Act (NCLB; PL 107-110). The annual testing requirements in this legislation have the explicit purpose of closing the achievement gap between White and minority students. They are intended to combat the "soft bigotry of low expectations"[1] that does not challenge minorities to reach the same standards as Whites. Schools that do not meet the criteria of annual yearly progress established for their states are subject to a variety of sanctions, the most severe of which is closing. Independent of NCLB, 24 states have established exit examinations that must be passed to receive a high school diploma, and 2 additional states are implementing such exams but in 2009 did not withhold diplomas (Zhang, 2009). When all 26 states begin withholding diplomas, they will enroll 75% of all public high school students and 84% of students of color (Center on Education Policy, 2008). High-stakes tests have a major impact on the lives of both students and educators.

The basic assumption underlying NCLB and accountability in general is that explicit standards and tests with consequences will motivate educators and students to higher levels of performance. The validity of the assumption and the consequences, both intended and unintended, that follow from it have been debated since high-stakes testing began to play a primary role in educational reform. The controversy is reflected in the titles of this small sample of books published since NCLB became law:

- *Raising Standards or Raising Barriers: Inequality and High-Stakes Testing in Public Education* (Orfield & Kornhaber, 2001)
- *Education Myths: What Special Interest Groups Want You to Believe About Our Schools—And Why It Isn't So* (Greene, 2005)
- *Collateral Damage: How High-Stakes Testing Corrupts America's Schools* (Nichols & Berliner, 2007)

- *High-Stakes Testing and the Decline of Teaching and Learning: The Real Crisis in Education* (Hursh, 2008)
- *Unequal By Design: High-Stakes Testing and the Standardization of Inequality* (Au, 2009)
- *Correcting Fallacies About Educational and Psychological Testing* (Phelps, 2009a)
- *The Paradoxes of High-Stakes Testing: How They Affect Students, Their Parents, Teachers, Principals, Schools, and Society* (Madaus, Russell, & Higgins, 2009)

We have listed books that reflect both sides of the debate on the value of high-stakes tests, but even in these seven titles, the critics outweigh the supporters. Only two, Greene (2005) and Phelps (2009a&b), are supportive of high-stakes testing. The other five are mostly or totally critical. It would be a digression to attempt to summarize all the arguments in these books, but we will briefly present the positions of one of the most forceful proponents, Richard Phelps, and a sampling of the arguments of the critics.

Phelps has made it his mission to refute the claims that there is little evidence on the effects of high-stakes testing. He has twice assembled groups of scholars who support high-stakes tests to present their positions in books whose titles explicitly state their purpose: *Defending Standardized Testing* (Phelps, 2005a) and *Correcting Fallacies About Educational and Psychological Testing* (Phelps, 2009a). The contributors to these volumes summarize evidence that indicates high-stakes tests increase achievement and motivation without producing adverse effects on curriculum or children from minority and poor families. Phelps (2005b) quotes the conclusions of several meta-analyses that found significantly higher achievement scores to be associated with both frequent testing and high school graduation tests. He reports his tallies of surveys conducted over a 43-year period that show substantial majorities of both providers (teachers and administrators) and consumers (students, parents, and the public) believe that standardized testing has improved instruction and student motivation.

Phelps has also documented that the research summarized in the two books he edited is rarely, if ever, cited by critics of testing. In *Correcting Fallacies About Educational and Psychological Testing*, Phelps (2009a) contributed a chapter in which he provides "case studies" of how the claims of the critics regarding the limited amount of relevant research are refuted by an extensive literature base. He raises the question "What is the effect of test-based accountability?" and presents a list of 133 selected citations, "a small sample of useful, insightful, relevant, well-done studies that effectively answer the question, could have informed the design of NCLB, and have been declared by prominent researchers not to exist" (Phelps, 2009b, p. 126).

It is of interest that despite Phelps's many publications on the topic of high-stakes testing, his work is not cited in any of the books critical of testing that are listed above. In a personal communication (July 16, 2009), Phelps indicated that while he was at that date affiliated with a major test publisher, he did not take this position until September 2007 and his views and writings on the merits of standardized testing preceded that position.

Although Phelps presents a persuasive argument, a blue-ribbon committee of the National Academies' National Research Council does not support it (Sparks, 2011). The committee reported its findings from a decade-long examination of test-based incentives to improve education. It concluded that the approaches implemented so far—including high school exit exams and other testing and accountability issues—have had little or no effect and may in fact produce results opposite of those intended.

David Berliner also has a mission: to demonstrate that the past 25 years of criticisms of public education have little basis in fact. He makes his argument most forcefully in *The Manufactured Crisis: Myths, Fraud, and the Attack on the American Public School* (Berliner & Biddle, 1995). As Berliner sees it, public education has become the scapegoat for the decline of the American economy relative to its international competitors. The results of high-stakes testing are being used to undermine support for public education, but that is not his main reason for opposing such tests. In *Collateral Damage: How High-Stakes Testing Corrupts America's Schools* (Nichols & Berliner, 2007), he argues that attaching major consequences to performance on tests is inherently flawed. Central to this argument is "Campbell's Law":

> The more any quantitative social indicator is used for social decision making, the more subject it will be to corruption pressures and the more apt it will be to distort and corrupt the social process it was intended to monitor. (Campbell, 1975, p. 35)

Nichols and Berliner refer to this as a law, but in the source document, Donald Campbell refers to two laws. In his discussion of the law(s), it is clear that Campbell is sympathetic to the Nichols-Berliner position:

> From my own point of view, achievement tests may be valuable indicators of general school achievement under conditions of normal teaching aimed at general competence. But when test scores become the goal of the teaching process, they both lose their value as indicators of educational status and distort the educational process in undesirable ways. (Campbell, 1975, p. 37)

To support the generality of his law(s), Campbell draws upon research from the former Soviet Union on the distortions caused by the use of production goals to monitor factory productivity. If production was measured by monetary value, factories produced their most expensive products. If by weight, factories produced their heaviest products. If by number, they produced those things easiest to produce. Coincidentally, one of the sources Campbell cites for this research also has the name Berliner (J. S. Berliner, 1957), but it is not the same person who applied his law to high-stakes testing.

Critics of NCLB point to the distortion of its primary goal—improving the education of minority and disadvantaged students—as an example of Campbell's Law in action. Diane Ravitch (2010) argues persuasively that high-stakes testing, the core of No Child Left Behind, has been destructive and corrosive to the art of teaching: It can lead to Dickensian rote learning and memorization while igniting manipulative and unethical use of testing results and statistics. The truth in her criticism lies in the increasing list of school districts like Atlanta and Washington, D.C., where massive testing irregularities have occurred. To other critics, it is minority and disadvantaged students who are most adversely impacted by high-stakes tests. Instead of receiving a broad curriculum that encourages questioning, problem solving, and higher order thinking, students who do not score well are subjected to drill and practice focused on the content covered in the tests by which their schools are judged (Jones, Jones, & Hargrove, 2003; McNeil & Valenzuela, 2001). If these classes do not bring the students to the necessary level of competence, ways are found to exclude them from testing and, as they become older, to "encourage" them to withdraw from school (Heilig & Darling-Hammond, 2008). To radical critics, such as Au (2009) and Hursh (2008), high-stakes tests are additional evidence of the hidden curriculum of all of education: the inculcation of attitudes, values, and self-perceptions that perpetuate the economic inequalities of capitalism.

Basic to all of these criticisms is the concern that high-stakes tests undermine the goals of education. Damon (2008) has studied the importance of purpose in adolescent development, and he sees high-stakes testing as squeezing out "the real mission of schooling: developing a love of learning for learning's sake—a love that will then lead to self-maintained learning throughout the lifespan" (p. 111). He then adds:

> Every bit as important, though not often noticed, is a student's quest for meaning in the demands and activities of the school day. It is essential to ask—and young people always do—what, if any, is the relation between what a student does at school and any larger purpose that could attract his or her interest, energies, and eventual commitment.
>
> Making a connection between what students are learning academically and how they can find careers that will be meaningful to them is one of the lowest priorities at our contemporary academic institutions. . . .
>
> This "meaning gap" extends from the student's present activities to his or her future prospects; in both cases, students too often are mystified about the

relevance of their schoolwork to the knowledge skills that they will need to use. (pp. 111, 114)

The debate goes on, but our reading of the arguments we have briefly summarized leads us to conclude that, despite their proneness to distortion, high-stakes testing may have some impact on motivation. It follows that courses in which students have an interest, those which are inherently relevant, could capitalize on that motivation and increase the engagement of students who are having difficulty. In the following section, we examine research that has found, despite their negative image, that taking CTE courses is associated with high school graduation.

CTE AND HIGH SCHOOL GRADUATION

The association between CTE enrollment and high school graduation has been studied with a variety of methodologies: analyses of data from national longitudinal surveys of young people, intensive case studies, and comparisons of students admitted to and denied programs by lottery. This final method is the most rigorous because unmeasured characteristics that may influence the outcome of interest, high school graduation, are randomly distributed in the two groups. Some of these studies have found that as participation in CTE courses increases, graduation rates increase; others have not. We summarize these studies and explore some possible explanations for their contradictory results. We also present the results of a different type of analysis by Bishop and Mane (2004) on the relationship between participation in secondary occupation training and educational attainment in advanced industrialized countries.

What National Data Tell Us

Plank, DeLuca, and Estacion (2005) examined the relationship between taking CTE courses and graduation among participants in the National Longitudinal Survey of Youth 1997 (NLSY97). These analyses extended and refined similar analyses that had been reported by Plank in 2001 using an older national data set (National Education Longitudinal Study of 1988). NLSY97 tracks a nationally representative sample of 8,984 youths living in the United States who were 12 to 16 years old as of December 31, 1996. When the analyses were conducted, there were seven rounds of NLSY97 data available that included detailed information about youth labor-market, educational, and developmental experiences.

Plank and his colleagues focused on a subsample consisting of 1,628 of the oldest NLSY97 participants, those born in 1980. Their analyses of the relationship between enrollment in CTE courses and graduation were further limited to 846 of these participants for whom high school transcript data were available. The researchers employed a statistical procedure referred to as *hazard models* (or survival or event history models). No attempt will be made to provide a simplified explanation of these models beyond quoting the original report:

> Hazard models . . . are useful for describing the timing of life course events and for building statistical models of the risk of an event's occurrence over time. (Willett & Singer, 1991, quoted in Plank et al., 2005, p. 1)

The event of interest was dropping out of high school anytime after entry into the 9th grade. The analyses determined the relationship between the probability of this event and a measure of enrollment in CTE courses while controlling for other variables.

Plank and his colleagues developed several hazard models by progressively adding variables that past research has shown to be related to the probability of withdrawing from school. The model most similar to Plank's previous work included measures of race/ethnicity, gender, highest grade completed by a parent, household income, family structure, living in an urban area, score on a mathematics test, and grade point average in the most recently completed academic term. The model also included the ratio of CTE to academic credits earned in the most recently completed term and the square of this measure. Entering the square of the ratio of CTE to academic credits tests for curvilinear relationships between the independent variables and dropping out.

Generally, the results of this model paralleled those from Plank's earlier analyses, which had yielded a U-shaped relationship between the ratio of CTE to academic credits and the probability of dropping out. Plank found that students who earned no or few CTE credits had a higher probability of dropping out than did those who took a ratio of slightly more than three CTE to four academic credits (.77). As this ratio increased (i.e., more CTE than academic credits), the probability of dropping out also increased. The hazard model using a newer data set showed a flatter curve with a different low point, a ratio of one CTE to two academic credits (.54).

Plank and his colleagues did not stop with replicating the earlier work. They tested a new model that added the age at which the student entered the 9th grade while retaining all of the other measures. This variable had a strong impact, increasing the total explanatory power of the model considerably but reducing the statistical significance of the CTE-academic ratio variables. The linear variable was no longer significant and the squared variable dropped from the .05 to the .10 probability level. Clearly the age at which students entered the 9th grade had a strong association with their chances of dropping out.

To explore this association further, the researchers divided their transcript sample into students who were less than 15 when they entered the 9th grade and those who were older, 14 being the modal age for entry. Using the same model specifications with both of these groups, they found a strong curvilinear CTE-academic ratio relationship for those less than 15 and a significant linear variable, but the age at entry into the 9th grade was not significant. The low point of the curve was .54, slightly more than one CTE credit for every two academic credits. With the older students, the age at entry was significant, but the ratios of CTE to academic credits, both linear and squared, were not. "For those who are older than is normal upon high school entry, this single factor of age is a strong correlate of dropping out that swamps or obfuscates most other effects" (Plank et al., 2005, p. 25).

Here is how the researchers summarize the implications of their findings:

> If we borrow language from dosage research, we might say the following: For students who are of a normal age, or even younger than normal, at the time of high school entry, it appears that some CTE combined with core academic coursetaking is good medicine, but only up to a point. Too much exposure to CTE (concentrating on CTE to the exclusion of adequate academic coursetaking, and moving above the estimated point of inflection) implies increased risk of dropping out. For students who are older than normal upon high school entry, the received dosages of CTE and academic coursetaking do not seem to have detectable effects on dropout likelihood. It seems likely that the constellation of risk factors or challenges encountered by these older students makes them not receptive to any potential effects of coursetaking variation. At the peril of pushing an analogy too far, one can think of one set of patients who are generally healthy, and thus responsive to doses of preventative medicine; one can think of another set of patients whose immune systems are weakened to the point that they are unresponsive to that same medicine. (Plank et al., 2005, p. 25)

The evidence from this research strongly implies that for students who enter high school at the traditional age taking a combination of one CTE course for every two academic courses increases their probability of graduating. This implication holds true even after many other factors known to influence school withdrawal have been controlled statistically. Plank and his colleagues underscore, however, that their model cannot prove causality: "One thing we have not established definitively is a causal relationship between coursetaking and dropping out" (Plank et al., 2005, p. 25).

The evidence also implies that for students who are older than normal when they enter the 9th grade, simply enrolling them in CTE classes will not keep them in school. In fact, the trend line for these students (although not statistically significant) suggests that as the ratio of their CTE to academic credits increases, the less likely it is that they will graduate and it does not appear that such students lack the ability to succeed. Scores on the mathematics test used in the hazard models were not a significant predictor of dropping out, but most recent grade point averages were. These older students seem to have the ability to succeed (as reflected by their math scores) but were not applying themselves (as reflected by their grades), underscoring once again the need for instruction that engages students in what they are required to learn.

Regression analyses of a different data set found that taking CTE courses had no effect on graduation. Agodini and Deke (2004) conducted their analyses on data from the National Education Longitudinal Study that began in 1988 with initial data collection from about 25,000 students, representative of all those in the 8th grade that year. If these students made normal progress, they would have graduated in 1992. Agodini and Deke limited their sample to those who had provided information for the four rounds of data collection that were available when they did their analyses and for whom transcript data were also available. These criteria and additional data editing reduced the number used in their analyses to 10,251. Transcript data on credits earned were used to classify these students into four CTE groups[2] and a comparison group:

- *CTE concentrator:* five CTE credits, at least three of which are in the same occupational area and not enough credits in core academic subject to complete an academic program. An academic program is defined as four credits in English and three each in mathematics, science, and social studies.
- *CTE explorer:* same as a concentrator without three CTE credits in the same occupational area.
- *Extreme CTE:* nine CTE credits and a smaller number of core academic credits than a CTE concentrator. Agodini and Deke say this combination is similar to the ratio of three CTE to four academic credits that Plank's 2001 analyses found to have the best probability of reducing dropouts.
- *Integrated program:* enough CTE credits to be classified as a concentrator and enough core academic credits to complete an academic program. This combination is often referred to a "dual concentrator" (Stone & Aliaga, 2003).
- *Basic academic:* 2 CTE credits and not enough core academic credits to complete an academic program.

The CTE credits Agodini and Deke used for these classifications were limited to those from occupationally specific courses while Plank et al.

(2005) had included all CTE courses. In several respects, the analytic techniques in the two studies were similar. Both used hazard models that estimated probabilities from a defined starting point, entry into the 9th grade, and controlled for measured characteristics known to be associated with the probability of withdrawing from high school. The main differences between the analyses were how CTE participation was measured and the test for a curvilinear relationship. Plank et al. used a continuous measure, the ratio of CTE to academic courses. Agodini and Deke used the number of CTE and academic courses to create the groups defined above. Plank et al. tested if there was a curvilinear relationship; Agodini and Deke compared the basic academic group to each of the CTE groups.

While Plank et al. found their measure had a curvilinear, U-shaped relationship with the probability of dropping out, Agodini and Deke found that CTE participation had no effect, neither positive nor negative, on high school completion. This was the case even for the group Agodini and Deke labeled "integrated," those who both concentrated in CTE and completed a rigorous academic program. Stone and Aliaga (2003), who had classified such students as "dual concentrators," found their high school achievement similar to that of students who took college preparatory programs. The only significant differences between groups that Agodini and Deke found were for students who reported themselves to have no plans to attend college. Among these students, CTE concentrators were slightly less likely to drop out than CTE explorers and those in the basic academic group. In both of these comparisons, the difference was about three percentage points.

Stephen Plank suggested in a personal communication (July 23, 2009) that a possible explanation for why his findings differ from Agodini and Deke is that they did not test for a curvilinear relationship. As a result, the lower dropout probabilities associated with a one-to-two ratio may have been obscured by the higher probabilities associated with both less and more CTE relative to academic courses. Other differences between the studies have already been noted: the types of CTE courses included in the analysis and the differing data sets on which the analyses were conducted. The on-time graduation year for the students in the data used by Agodini and Deke was 1992. For the students in the Plank et al. data, on-time graduation was 1997 or 1998.

As this debate continues, ongoing analyses of national longitudinal data being conducted by the NRCCTE continue to show the power of CTE to engage students in school consistent with Plank's analyses (Aliaga, Stone, Kotamraju, & Dickinson, 2011). The analysis grouped students based on CTE standardized Carnegie units or credits earned while in high school, similar to the categories used by Agodini and Deke. For the NRCCTE analyses, the researchers used the following typology:

Group 4: Students who earned three or more CTE credits with at least one three-credit concentration in an occupational field (e.g., advanced manufacturing, culinary arts, computer technology).

Group 3: Students who earned three or more CTE credits but did not focus in at least one occupational area.

Group 2: Students who earned more than zero but less than three CTE credits.

Group 1: Students who earned zero CTE credits.

Using restricted data from the Education Longitudinal Study of 2002 [ELS:2002] (National Center for Education Statistics, 2010), the researchers conducted two kinds of analysis.

The first analysis attempted to provide an unbiased estimate of the treatment effect using propensity score matching. Using this approach, the researchers sought to explore the relationship between the treatment and the likelihood of finishing high school. In this analysis, three or more CTE credits and three-credit concentration or more was the treatment (Group 4) and the comparison group included all other students who matched the treatment group except for the treatment condition. This process provided two matched groups of 1,346 students. The logistic regression (dropout=1; non-dropout=0) showed Group 4 students were half as likely to drop out of high school compared to the matched comparison group. The statistical model used a set of covariates, of which urbanicity (or location of school), prior academic achievement (9th-grade GPA), and the last available GPA were also statistically significant predictors of finishing high school.

The second kind of analysis employed a hazard ratio model that describes the *time-to-event* in survival analysis. This is the ratio of the rate at which subjects in two groups experience events where a slower rate or lower ration suggests a longer period of event-free survival or, in this case, dropping out of high school. The researchers compared Groups 4, 3, and 2 to the omitted group (1). The results showed that while Group 2 students did not differ from Group 1, Groups 3 and 4 had a greater likelihood of surviving high school; Group 4 more so than Group 3 (see Figure 3.1). That is, students who take three or more CTE credits with and without an occupational concentration are more likely to complete high school than those who take less than 3 CTE credits when the analysis controls for early high school GPA and gender (both significant predictors of high survival) and race (not a significant predictor in this model). Please note that in this figure, the lower the bar the less likely the variable is related to the event (dropping out).

These analyses support past research that reported the positive effects of CTE on engaging students in high school. Also, this research suggests the importance of a high-intensity and articulated CTE experience—which are

FIGURE 3.1. Effect of Measured Variables on Probability of Completing High School, Hazard Ratios

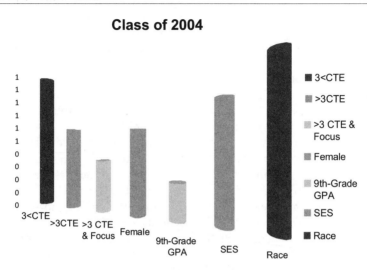

elements present in the Programs of Study design incorporated in the most recent version of the Perkins legislation.

The other methods used to examine the CTE-dropout relationship—case studies and random assignment, which we discuss next—have yielded inconsistent findings.

What Case Studies Tell Us

One of the major continuing studies of the National Research Center for Career and Technical Education when it was at the University of Minnesota was an in-depth, longitudinal examination of career-based school reform in selected high schools. This study yielded the five reports included in the References for this volume for which the senior author of each was Castellano (2001, 2002, 2003, 2004, 2007). The researchers who produced these reports used both qualitative and quantitative research methods to describe the structure and operation and assess the outcomes of three high schools. These schools were selected for study because they were implementing career-based comprehensive school reforms, served a majority of students from low-income and racial/ethnic minority backgrounds, and collaborated across middle school, high school, and community college levels.

The researchers attempted to use an additional selection criterion: The schools provided exemplary CTE with well-documented records of substantial improvements in student outcomes. They were unable to identify any schools with such records that also met their other criteria. As a result, they selected schools that were implementing career-themed reforms that met the criteria listed above and showed promise of developing good records over the 4-year period of the study. During this period, the three selected schools were implementing different reform models. We give brief overviews of the three schools here.

Academy High School (AHS), located in a large urban center in the western United States, was divided into three career academies. AHS was an Urban Learning Center, which means it was located in a single facility with an elementary school and a middle school. Only students from Academy Middle School could apply to AHS, and they were selected using a lottery process. This provided an opportunity to create a de facto random assignment design, since many of the students who were not selected to attend AHS subsequently attended the comparison school, C-AHS. In their analyses at this site, the researchers compared only the grade cohorts at C-AHS who had attended Academy Middle School to their counterparts at AHS.[3]

Pathways High School (PHS), located in an agricultural area in the Pacific Northwest, implemented career pathways across the curriculum. PHS students interested in specialized CTE instruction could attend a regional vocational skills center that served several small districts. C-PHS, the comparison school, was also a comprehensive high school that sent students to a regional skills center, and data were collected on both groups of students at these skills centers.

Vocational High School (VHS) is located in a small city in the Northeast. VHS was one of four high schools in this district. Three of the high schools were college preparatory in nature, including C-VHS, the comparison school. VHS was the district's vocational-technical high school. It had adopted High Schools That Work (HSTW) and other reforms to improve student academic performance. Over the years, VHS had gained a reputation as the appropriate destination for lower achieving and special needs students. Despite its widely acknowledged status as the district dumping ground, VHS also attracted motivated students who were interested in the concentrated CTE programs offered there.

Instruction and its outcomes were studied at the three reform-oriented schools and the three comparison high schools located near them that served similar students but were not involved in reform efforts. The researchers visited the reform schools annually from 2001 through 2004 to collect a variety of data. They collected quantitative data from school records, including student characteristics; grade point average; attendance; credits earned in science, math, and CTE; dual (college) credits; and graduation (or withdrawal). Other quantitative data came from student surveys of post-high-school expectations and from the local community college records remedial coursework taken and postsecondary credits earned. During their annual visits the researchers also collected qualitative data through interviews and focus groups with students, teachers, and administrators, and from class observations.

The most consistent finding from this mass of data, across all three sites, was that as the ratio of CTE courses to total courses increased, the probability of graduating from high school increased. A hazard model (similar to that described above for the NLSY97 data) was specified that included variables for student characteristics, and separate analyses were run for each of the three sites. Here is how the researchers reported their finding for each site:

- AHS and C-AHS: There was no difference between the schools in the likelihood of dropping out. Regardless of high school attended, taking a higher ratio of CTE classes to academic classes reduced the risk of dropping out. (Castellano et al., 2007, p. xxi)
- PHS and C-PHS: PHS students earned fewer science credits and had a higher risk of dropping out. The independent effect of taking a higher ratio of CTE classes to academic classes reduced the risk of dropping out, regardless of high school attended. (Castellano et al., 2007, p. xxiii)
- VHS and C-VHS: The odds of dropping out were much higher at VHS than at C-VHS. Here too, the independent effect of taking a higher ratio of CTE classes to academic classes reduced the risk of dropping out regardless of high school attended. (Castellano et al., 2007, p. xxv)

The data from these three schools were inconsistent in demonstrating the ability of CTE classes to engage students in their learning as measured by attendance. The data on attendance showed VHS as having a major problem, but the AHS students attended more regularly than those at their comparison school. There were no differences in attendance rates at PHS and C-PHS. Class observations at VHS found no more engagement in CTE than in academic classes, while at PHS higher levels of engagement were seen for CTE. The CTE classes at PHS were described as having significantly more independent work, more use of computers, and more hands-on learning than non-CTE classes.

Random Assignment Studies

Career magnets and career academies are two ways schools use CTE to organize the school curriculum. Because of their popularity in some school districts, they are oversubscribed, that is, more students seek to enroll than space allows. When this occurs, many school districts use a lottery system to select who is admitted. A true lottery system approximates an experimental or random-controlled-trial (RCT)—often considered the gold standard of educational research.

A study of career magnet programs (Crain et al., 1999) and a study of career academies (Kemple & Scott-Clayton, 2004) compared the outcomes of students who had been selected at random to attend these programs to those of students who had applied but were not selected. Because these assignments were made by lottery, any unmeasured characteristics that may have affected the outcomes of participation were randomly distributed in both groups. If the outcomes of the admitted students were significantly different from the nonadmitted, at accepted probability levels, it could be concluded that participation caused the difference. For the career magnet programs, being selected increased the chances of dropping out. For the career academies, admission had no significant overall effect, positive or negative, on graduation.

While these findings would appear to weaken our argument that CTE increases engagement, a closer examination of these two studies reveals that they had some weaknesses also. The career magnet study (Crain et al., 1999) was done in an area where the programs were available to students from a low-income city and a ring of older suburbs. Six out of every seven students were African American or Latino. School record data were analyzed for 59 career magnet programs to which 9,716 students had applied. Policies and practices in the schools housing the career magnet programs placed those admitted through the lottery at a distinct disadvantage. Only half the students had been admitted through the lottery. The other half had been, in the words of Crain et al., "handpicked." The programs set high standards that the handpicked students could meet, but which tended to push out the students who had enrolled through the lottery. This was especially the case for the more desirable programs and internships.

In addition to the analyses of the graduation rates of students who had won or lost the lottery, 110 interviews were conducted with subsamples of both groups. These subsamples were matched on gender, ethnicity, school achievement, and neighborhood. The interviews revealed that students who graduated from the career magnets earned one third more college credits and engaged in less risky behavior such as smoking, use of alcohol, and becoming pregnant or causing pregnancy. The study's authors attribute this to the career magnets fostering, among those who did not drop out, a career identity, a sense of becoming "really good at something" (Crain et al., 1999, p. iv.). This finding aligns well with the importance that Damon (2008) attributes to a "sense of purpose" in adolescent development and supports our argument that CTE can engage students.

The career academies study (Kemple & Scott-Clayton, 2004; Kemple & Willner, 2008) was conducted in nine cities across the United States. Care was taken in the selection to ensure that the sites studied were implementing the core components of academies: a school-within-a-school organization, an integrated academic/vocational curriculum, and employer partnerships. Two of the academies were 4-year programs and seven were 3-year. Students entered the study at the end of the 1992–93, 1993–94, or 1994–95 school years when they were completing their 8th or 9th grades. The original sample included 1,764 students who had applied to attend the academies, of whom 959 were admitted and 805 were not. Data were collected while these students were in high school and 4 years and 8 years after the years in which they would have graduated if they had made normal progress. The follow-up obtained data from 83% of those selected for the academies and 82% of those who were not.

In the analyses of the impact of the academies, all those initially accepted were included whether they enrolled or not. From the group originally selected for the academies and responding to the follow-up, 15% never enrolled and 30% enrolled but withdrew. Most of those who withdrew did not drop out of high school; instead they transferred to regular programs. Those who enrolled but withdrew attended the academies an average of 3 semesters, a little more than one third of a 4-year academy or half of a 3-year program. Consequently, estimates of the impact of the academies include in the academy group substantial numbers of students with varying degrees of exposure and many with none at all. The logic of a random assignment comparison requires that all those assigned to the treatment of interest must be included in the analyses, whether they receive the treatment or not. If those who do not enroll or withdraw were to be excluded, the problem of self-selection would cloud any differences that were observed between the treatment and control groups. With such a large proportion of students having no or limited participation, the effects of the academies would have to be quite powerful to cause the outcomes of all in the group to be significantly different from those in the nonacademy group. Academy participation was not powerful enough to produce differences in high school achievement or graduation, but as we shall discuss in Chapter 6, it did produce differences in earnings after high school. While the lack of academic effect disappointed advocates of career academies, one can also interpret these findings as evidence of the potential to expose high school students to high-quality CTE that produces an economic benefit while "doing no harm" to students' academic development.

The nonenrollment/withdrawal rates from the career academies points to a difficulty in any attempt to assess the effectiveness of secondary CTE: Students enroll in these courses to explore the nature of the occupations as least as much as they do to prepare for a specific career. As discussed in Chapter 2, there are several theories of career development (Osipow & Fitzgerald, 1996), but they all agree that the average high school student is in the exploratory stage of their development. Few high school students have formulated specific career goals. They tend to have orientations toward broad types of occupations with only a hazy sense of the skills and preparation needed. For many high school students, CTE courses provide a way of testing the match between their interests and abilities and the requirements of occupations. From the perspective of evaluating the effectiveness of a given program, withdrawal is judged a failure to achieve its intended outcome. From the perspective of the students who withdraw, participation may have provided a valuable learning experience, albeit one that increased their understanding of the requirement of an occupational area to the point that they decide to explore other possibilities.

Both of these studies highlight the methodological challenges of conducting rigorous, random-controlled-trials (RCT) of school interventions. Self-selection bias is one. Students who choose to attend a magnet or career academy are systematically different from those who do not. Thus a finding of no immediate academic difference in the career academies study may only mean that the population of applicants is more motivated and possesses other, unmeasured characteristics related to the outcomes of interest than those students who chose not to apply. A second challenge in using a lottery approach to these designs is that there are very few pure lotteries as the Craine et al. and other studies cited earlier demonstrate.

As this is written, researchers at the NRCCTE are conducting a meta-analysis of the best available published studies on the educational and labor market outcomes of participating in CTE. Their preliminary conclusion on the impact of CTE on high school completion reflects the difficulties of identifying the independent effect of CTE participation. While the effects are positive, they fail to rise to accepted levels of statistical significance, leading the authors to conclude that: "Perhaps the most appropriate conclusion is that while the evidence is promising, we do not yet know if the effect of CTE on high school graduation is positive" (Jeffrey Valentine, personal communication, June 30, 2011). The effects of postsecondary transition and labor market outcomes are substantially different and will be discussed in Chapter 6.

INTERNATIONAL COMPARISONS

Bishop and Mane (2004) take a different approach to examining the relationship between CTE participation and high school completion. They state that regression analyses are biased because students who do not like or are unsuccessful in academic courses are overrepresented in CTE courses, and it is impossible to completely control for unobserved traits that may make CTE students more prone to drop out. The analysis they conducted compared data from non-Asian countries that are members of the Organisation for Economic Cooperation and Development (OECD). The variables they examined were percent of upper secondary students enrolled in vocational and prevocational programs to total enrollments of 15- to 19-year-olds and 20- to 29-year-olds in school and college, upper secondary graduation rates, and reading and math scores on the OECD PISA examinations. They found a statistically significant relationship between the percent of upper secondary students in vocational and prevocational programs and total enrollment of 15- to 19-year-olds and high school graduation. Their equations estimate that for every 10% increase in enrollment in vocational programs, graduation rates increase by 2.6% and total enrollment of 15- to 19-year-olds increases by 1.9%. There were no significant relationships with the other outcomes. The authors conclude: "These results are consistent with the hypothesis that offering students a robust career-tech option increases upper-secondary enrollment and completion rates without lowering test scores at age 15 or college attendance rates after the age of 20" (Bishop & Mane, 2004, p. 386).

The Bishop-Mane conclusion has been reinforced by the OECD (2010) report, *Learning for Jobs*, which was discussed in Chapter 2. Most OECD member countries enroll large proportions of their upper level secondary students in vocational education and training (VET). Historically, the expectation was that graduates of these programs would enter the labor market, many with the employers that provided their technical training. In recent years OECD countries are seeing increasing numbers of their VET graduates continue their education at what most of the world refers to as the "tertiary" level. In Korea the proportion is almost three quarters.

The policies recommended by the OECD to respond to these changes include a broadening of VET instruction with greater emphasis on academics and transferable skills applicable in a range of occupations. However, the OECD recommendations stress the importance of a continued emphasis on work-based learning because of its capacity to engage the less academically inclined students and teach the employability skills sought by employers.

SUMMARY

The debate over the effects of high-stakes testing on student motivation and engagement in school is unresolved but the critics are becoming more numerous and vocal. Advocates claim that such tests motivate students and make educators accountable. Critics claim high-stakes tests distort the purpose of education and are detrimental to those students who need the most support. Our own experience in working with schools is that such a narrow focus distorts the educational process and limits the curriculum space and options for young people to take courses that might better engage them in learning. This occurs too frequently when students are pulled from advanced CTE courses, for example, so they can endure "drill and kill" courses to get them to a passing grade on one or more of the high-stakes tests. If testing has any motivational effect, courses in which students have inherent interest have the potential to enhance student engagement.

The empirical evidence on the relationship between participation in CTE and high school graduation derived from national longitudinal data has been consistently positive since the early 1990s. Taking more CTE is linked to a greater likelihood of finishing high school. Other studies using different approaches vary in the strength of the association but lean toward a positive effect.

Studies that can unambiguously claim causality, that CTE causes graduation, are difficult to implement. Regression models can control for measured characteristics, such as gender, race, socioeconomic status, and GPA, but typically have no measures of other variables, such as individual motivation and parental support, that certainly influence whether students finish high school. Approximations of random assignment experiments (possible if schools select students for programs by lottery) control for unmeasured variables, but have analytic problems of their own, especially when students who are selected for the treatment of interest but do not attend.

Overall, the preponderance of evidence strongly suggests that including CTE as part of the high school experience can benefit all students, but more so for students who are otherwise disengaged from high school and who might have dropped out. Newer evidence points toward the importance of a concentrated, focused sequence of CTE coursework as providing the most benefit. This is a lesson known for some time by our international competitors as discussed earlier. It is now, perhaps, time for this lesson to be brought home to make high school matter for more young people than just those already in a college prep trajectory.

Providing high-quality, sequential CTE with sufficient intensity enhances engagement but is insufficient to wholly preparing youth for a productive adulthood, however. As we will demonstrate in the next chapter, a truly career- and college-ready experience requires the intentional connecting of technical and academic learning as well to help youth increase levels of achievement in the core areas of literacy and mathematics.

CHAPTER 4

Developing the Skills Required in the Workplace

Students who take several CTE courses score significantly lower than students with fewer CTE credits on standardized measures of academic achievement (Silverberg et al., 2004). From the time vocational education became part of public education until late into the 20th century, differences in academic performance were accepted as a result of differences in individual ability that separate curriculum tracks were designed to accommodate. This conclusion is usually based on questionable classification schemes for identifying CTE students and using simplistic analytic techniques. Other analyses that accommodate known covariates (e.g., 8th-grade test scores) suggest the reality is more complex. For example, research conducted at the University of Arizona (McGinley, 2002) showed that when analyses control for demographics, learning style, and prior learning, the apparent differences disappeared, suggesting a selection bias that tends to distort reality.

In the last 2 decades of the 20th century, as the calls for educational reform became pervasive, pressure mounted for vocational education to contribute to the learning of academic skills. This pressure was most evident in the 1990 reauthorization of federal legislation (Perkins II), which specified the attainment of academic skills as one of the indicators by which the performance of vocational programs were to be evaluated. This requirement was progressively strengthened by the 1998 and 2006 Perkins reauthorizations.

In this chapter we explore what integration of academic and technical instruction requires, reasons why it has so rarely been achieved, and what it looks like if it is done effectively. We base our discussion on the following definition of *integration*:

> Curriculum integration is a series of conscious and informed strategies used to connect academic and vocational content so that one becomes a platform for instruction in the other over an extended period of time. (Johnson, Charner, & White, 2003, p. 12)

Johnson and her colleagues (2003) developed this definition from case studies of seven sites selected because of the quality of their integration efforts. Comparisons of findings across these sites identified three key elements that must be present for real integration to occur: planning, cross-discipline connections, and long-term commitment. When it does occur, integration takes the form of "a double-helix with academic content and instruction regularly linking vocational content and instruction" (p. 46). They qualify this analogy by noting that typically the amount of instruction from each discipline is not equal and at times there is no integration. When true integration is present, however, academic and CTE instructors have jointly examined their separate curricula and identified opportunities for drawing upon each other's contents and methods to strengthen instruction in their own areas while contributing to the learning of concepts from their counterparts' areas.

While we accept the Johnson et al. definition, we do not expect major change to occur in the academic classroom. The involvement of academic teachers is essential to assist CTE teachers to identify academic content inherent in their curriculum and to develop lessons that teach that content. When academic teachers are involved in this way, most are likely to use some of the practical applications they identify in their own classrooms (Stone, Alfeld, Pearson, Lewis, & Jensen, 2006), but that is not the main reason they need to be involved. They are needed to provide expertise in teaching academic content. Improving the teaching of academics in CTE does not require the traditional academic curriculum to change to any significant degree.

THE POWER OF CONTEXTUALIZED LEARNING

In 1999 Hoachlander summarized what he considered to be the major implications of the research on academic-vocational integration that the National Center for Research in Vocational Education had conducted during its 13 years at the University of California–Berkeley. He identified four levels of integration: (1) course-level, with the existing vocational and academic curriculum; (2) cross-curriculum, with horizontal and vertical alignment; (3) programmatic, around career clusters or industry majors; and (4) school-wide, with academies or other strategies for defining the mission of an entire school.

Research on integration continued when the renamed national research center (National Research Center for Career and Technical Education, NRCCTE) moved from Berkeley to the University of Minnesota and then to the University of Louisville. In 2010 the NRCCTE Curriculum Integration Workgroup published a report in which it made a distinction between *context-based* and *contextualized* integration.

A context-based approach provides a structure for academic instruction taught within a context that is relevant to the student. The distinction between this and a contextualized approach is found in the focus of the approach: the academic content. A context-based approach begins with the identification of academic content and situates it, sometimes literally, into a workplace setting. . . . In contrast to the context-based approach, the genesis and focus of a contextualized approach to integration is the CTE content. In other words, the process of integration begins with the CTE curriculum and the identification and enhancement of the academic content naturally occurring within it. Contextualized teaching and learning does not require the sacrifice of CTE content or the addition of artificially imposed academic content. Rather, the academic concepts resident in authentic applications of CTE support the understanding of both; rigor resides in combining CTE and academic skills as applied to real-world problems. (pp. 9–10)

As is obvious from the paragraphs quoted, our preference is for a contextualized approach that reinforces the academics inherent in the CTE curriculum. Our goal is to effect the first and most achievable of Hoachlander's levels, course-level integration of existing vocational and academic curriculum, but even at this level a major investment must be made if real change is to occur.

The Johnson et al. (2003) study underscored the importance of leadership and adequate resources for integration to be achieved. These findings parallel the extensive literature on effective schools (e.g., Fullan, 2007; Leithwood, Louis, Anderson, & Wahlstrom, 2004; Newmann, 1996). A strong commitment to integration is needed from leaders at the district and school levels. This leadership must provide professional development opportunities and, perhaps even more important, time for academic and CTE teachers to work together to plan coordinated instruction. We contacted each of the seven sites visited for the Johnson et al. report and present brief descriptions of the current status of integration efforts at four of them.

While leadership and resources are essential to all educational change, Johnson et al. (2003) also identified three structural factors that are unique to integration efforts: a single-industry theme or focus, co-location of academic and vocational instruction, and a single school setting. If these structural elements are lacking, integration can be achieved if ways are found to create situations that provide the same types of support.

Three random-assignment experiments have tested the effectiveness of integration of mathematics (Stone et al., 2006), literacy strategies (Park, Santamaria, van der Mandele, Keene, & Taylor, in press), and science (NRCCTE Curriculum Integration Workgroup, 2010). We discuss how these studies were conducted and the results they yielded. We also discuss a follow-up of the teachers who participated in the mathematics study that determined how many continued to use the methods and lessons from the experiment in the school year after it ended. We conclude this chapter by presenting the five principles that emerged from these studies and their implications for effective integration of instruction in technical and academic skills.

WHY IS INTEGRATION SO RARE?

As discussed in Chapter 1, prior to the passage of the original federal support for vocational education, the Smith-Hughes Act in 1917, the potential of using occupational context to enhance learning was extensively debated. However, the argument that CTE should focus on teaching job skills in shops or labs approximating industry settings came to dominate CTE from its inception to the latter part of the 20th century. In all areas that teach occupationally specific skills, teachers must have several years of relevant work experience to be certified. In some areas, especially the mechanical, industrial, and construction trades, most teachers have not completed a 4-year teacher education program. Instead, they receive alternative certification by completing a few courses in the basics of pedagogy. This historic separation of CTE from academic instruction has been a major barrier to curriculum integration.

The historic separation of vocational and academic education is part of the reason why integration of academic and technical content rarely occurs, but a more fundamental explanation lies in what Tyack and Tobin (1994) have labeled "the grammar of schooling" and what Elmore (1996) has referred to as the "core of educational practice." This grammar/core is a set of deeply held, largely implicit, beliefs about the teaching-learning process, what Senge (1990) refers to as "Mental models . . . that influence how we understand the world and how we take action" (p. 8). These beliefs see teachers using methods that they choose and develop (lecturing, questioning, projects, worksheets, and so on) to transmit defined bodies of knowledge (English, mathematics, auto technology, and so on) within a period of time (the class schedule) established by the school administration. Teachers teach subjects in the curricula that are driven by standards, textbooks, and tests specific to each discipline. Most teachers teach in the way that they were taught when they were students. Integration of academic and technical content does not fit the grammar/core of schooling.

The change we advocate for the classroom experience is not directed at academic teachers, but their involvement is essential if CTE teachers are to contribute to improving academic skills. The teaching of academics requires knowledge and skills that most CTE teachers do not have, nor is it reasonable to expect them to acquire these. By working with academic teachers, however, CTE teachers can learn enough of the academics inherent in their curriculum to strengthen the learning of concepts essential to the occupations they teach. Because the applicability of the concepts is intrinsic to the occupations, it is more likely that students will put forth the effort necessary to grasp the concepts. The direct application of academic concepts can also facilitate the learning of students who have difficulty with more abstract presentations of these concepts. We turn again to the OECD and Harvard studies discussed earlier to support this perspective.

An example from health occupations may help to explain what we propose. When treating patients who have been severely burned, medical professionals use what is referred to as the "rule of nines." The main parts of the body—the head, upper and lower front and back torso, each arm, and front and back of each leg—each represent roughly 9% of the total surface area of the body. To estimate the amount of body surface that is burned, the extent of burns on each of these body parts is observed and added together. A patient with extensive burns on the front of one leg would be estimated to have burns on 9% of his or her body; burns on all of one leg, front and back, 18%; and so on. These estimates are used to determine the amount of fluid replacement that is necessary and whether the patient should be transferred to a facility that specializes in the treatment of burns.

In a typical health occupations class, the rule of nines is taught largely as explained above with no attempt to examine the mathematics that were used to develop the rule. As discussed in more detail below, Stone et al. (2006) brought health and mathematics teachers together to develop lesson plans, one of which taught the geometry that underlies the rule of nines. In this lesson, the head was considered to be a sphere, the arms and legs were cylinders, and the torso was a set of rectangles. After relating the body to geometric shapes, the lesson plan introduced the formulas for calculating the surface area of each of these shapes and had students practice applying them.

To teach these geometric concepts, the CTE teachers had to obtain a full understanding of the formulas and of effective ways to present them to students. Working with math teachers to produce lesson plans developed this understanding. The team that developed this lesson then presented it to other teachers and had them critique it. Other teams prepared lessons on different concepts and presented them. After receiving the feedback from the critique and revising the lessons, the CTE teachers taught the lessons and came together again to share their experiences and discuss any problems they encountered. In this manner, the CTE teachers learned the general principles underlying the mathematics inherent in their curricula, but they were not "taught" mathematics.

The cooperation of the mathematics teachers was essential to the success of the Math-in-CTE project, but mathematics and academic teachers rarely work together in this manner. It took considerable time to develop the lessons. The teachers received 10 days of professional development, most of which was spent in group work writing the lessons and presenting and critiquing them. Five of these 10 days were in the summer and the other 5 during the school year. The research project paid for the teachers' time in the summer, and if necessary, for substitute teachers during the school year. This was time out of the classroom. If academic and CTE are to work together as they did in this study on an ongoing basis, they would need to be compensated for their time and this would add significantly to instructional costs.

Providing time for teachers to work together to improve instruction is essential if communities of practice are to emerge. On his website Wenger (2010) has defined such communities as "groups of people who share a concern or a passion for something they do and learn how to do it better as they interact regularly." This is the more general term for what are usually referred to in the United States as "professional learning communities" (Hord, 2004). The primary goal of learning communities is to improve student learning. In a true community teachers assume joint responsibility for this goal and work together to develop ways to achieve it. A leaning community defines the needs and problems of students, identifies and assembles resources to respond to these needs, and fashions and tests approaches to improve learning. The results of the tests are jointly reviewed and modifications made as needed. As one need is addressed, the process moves on to new priorities in an iterative manner (Carpenter et al., 2004; Fullan, 2007; Giles & Hargreaves, 2006; Hargreaves & Goodson, 2006; Newmann, 1996; Wei, Darling-Hammond, Andree, Richardson, & Orphanos, 2009).

Obviously, teachers need leadership, training, and administrative support to function in this manner, all of which have cost implications. A more subtle but perhaps more formidable obstacle to communities of practice is that they do not align with prevailing concepts of the grammar/core of schooling, which see teaching as an individual, not shared, responsibility. If the necessary resources were to become available, overcoming this largely implicit resistance may be the biggest challenge to expanding communities of practice.

SCHOOL LEVEL APPROACHES TO CURRICULUM INTEGRATION

Johnson, Charner, and White (2003) presented case studies of seven sites that met their definition of curriculum integration. In April 2010, as part of the research for this book, we contacted each of these sites to determine how the integration efforts described by Johnson et al. had evolved in the 8 years after they had been visited by the study team. Unfortunately, only four of the seven responded to repeated inquiries. The following updates draw upon the information presented by Johnson et al. and our follow-up interviews with representatives of the sites that responded. In this section, we also describe two local integration initiatives that were reported at the 2010 annual convention of the Association for Career and Technical Education, and a multiyear program conducted by the state of Pennsylvania to improve reading skills of CTE students.

A Career Academy Model

Apex High School Academy of Information Technology[1] is located in Apex, a suburb of Raleigh, North Carolina, close to the Research Triangle Park, a planned research park with over 140 companies, most of which are involved in some aspect of advanced technology. The high school serves a relatively affluent (median family income in 2009 of $93,505), predominantly White (79%) population (U.S. Census Bureau, 2011c). During the 2009–10 school year the high school enrollment was 2,268. Two thirds of the students plan to continue their education and obtain a 4-year college degree, and almost all the rest plan to go to community college.

The Academy of Information Technology (AOIT) is a 4-year secondary program that students must apply to enter. Preference is given to siblings of past or current students and other entrants are selected by lottery. No students are admitted after the 9th grade. AOIT was visited for the Johnson et al. report in the spring of 2002, during its first year of operation. That first class enrolled 68 9th-grade students, all of those who had applied. For the 2009–10 school year, the program received 140 applications and admitted 90, the maximum new entrants that it can serve. The increase in applications indicates that the program has developed a favorable reputation among students and parents.

Few of the students admitted to AOIT withdraw from the academy. The numbers admitted and continuing in the academy during the past 4 school years are presented in Table 4.1.

The AOIT director reported that a student rarely withdraws because of dissatisfaction. The primary reason students leave is because their families move from the school district. The director also reported that student follow-ups typically find that 90% or more of graduates continue their education, almost all in 4-year institutions. A few graduates attend community colleges, and one or two from each graduating class might enter the military.

AOIT is a member of the National Academy Foundation network. The Foundation is a membership organization that encourages and supports the development of academies in four career areas: finance, engineering, information technology, and hospitality and tourism. To become a member of the

TABLE 4.1. Enrollment and Continuation Statistics for AOIT

School Year	Admitted	Enrolled in 2009–10
2006–07	68	55
2007–08	75	68
2008–09	75	72
2009–10	90	90

network, applicants must agree to develop an academy that (1) creates small learning communities, (2) encourages active participation by local business and civic leaders, (3) connects students to the world of work through paid internships and industry-relevant coursework, and (4) motivates teachers by engaging them in school improvement efforts (National Academy Foundation, n.d., p. 5). To become a member of the Foundation network, school districts and other applicants must engage in a year of planning to develop an academy that incorporates these principles. During this year the planning group receives technical assistance from the Foundation.

The Apex AOIT fosters small learning communities by offering classes during the 9th and 10th grades that are taken only by academy students. In the 9th grade, for example, the state-mandated course of study requires English, World History, and Biology. The teachers for these three subjects and the teacher for computer applications work together to plan coordinated instruction. In the first semester of the 2009–10 school year this instruction was built around virtual trips to foreign countries. Students were divided into teams that selected countries they wanted to visit. The teams planned and budgeted their trips, read the work of writers from their countries, researched potential health threats and traditional foods, wrote blogs about their travel experiences, and made presentations after they had completed their trips. In the 11th and 12th grades, the students enroll in a variety of courses and it is more difficult to schedule AOIT-only classes, but all students have at least one such course. When feedback is obtained from alumni, one of the most recurring suggestions for program improvement is more AOIT-only classes in the 11th and 12th grades.

The AOIT stresses the "soft skills" desired by employers across the curriculum. The students receive specific instruction on working as a team, and project-based learning is used to reinforce these skills. All academy students must complete a one-semester paid internship before the spring of their senior year, and much of the training in soft skills is in preparation for these placements. Students are exposed to potential placements through guest speakers, mini job fairs, and visits to employers. In the 11th grade AOIT students prepare resumes and have mock interviews with human resource personnel from employers. Even with the high levels of unemployment during the 2009–10 school year, the AOIT was able to find internships for all its

11th-grade students. The academy director attributes the receptivity of employers to the reputation the students have developed: Employers know they
get well-trained workers who make a real contribution to their companies.

A Regional Career Center Model

In California, Regional Occupational Programs (ROPs) offer training
that individual school districts cannot provide because of too few students
or high costs. Students from several districts attend ROPs on a part-time
basis to obtain training in these specialized programs and take their academic subjects at their home high schools. The East San Gabriel Valley ROP[2]
serves seven districts in eastern Los Angeles County and enrolls a diverse
student population: Latino, 52%; White, 23%; Asian Pacific, 20%; African
American, 4%; and others, less than 1%.

The East San Gabriel Valley ROP has had initiatives since the 1980s to
integrate academic and vocational instruction. The earliest efforts took the
form of academic instruction as needed in vocational classes. These initial
efforts became more focused in 1994 when a 6-week Summer Institute for
Integration of Academic and Vocational Learning was conducted. This institute brought together academic and vocational teachers to jointly develop
lessons they could both use in their classes. Each lesson identified its academic and vocational/technical objectives and the competencies and content
standards addressed. Business people from the community and a technical
writer from the community college supported the teacher teams in the lesson
development. This institute produced 41 lesson plans for curriculum integration, and a second institute in the summer of 1995 produced 30 more.

When the ROP was visited for the Johnson et al. (2003) study, most
curriculum integration took place through Design-Based Learning (DBL;
see Nelson, 2004), and this continues to be the primary approach. DBL
combines interdisciplinary lessons, project-based learning, teamwork, and
problem solving. Students are given a challenge to design a solution to a
problem in a simulated environment. The examples given by Johnson et al.
were a never-before-seen spa for cosmetology students and a never-before-
seen wellness center for health students. The "never-before-seen" qualifier
is used to reduce students' concerns about suggesting proposed solutions,
because there are no right or wrong answers.

When the ROP was contacted in the spring of 2010, the instructional
coordinator said a DBL challenge recently used in a business algebra class
was to design a never-before-seen jungle. To structure the learning of positive and negative numbers, the teacher imposed the condition that some of
the animals in this jungle had to go uphill to find drinking water and some
had to go downhill. To provide a hands-on component to the challenge,

the students were required to make barrels to hold rainwater. The ways in which teachers and students responded to these challenges varied from creating virtual jungles within boxes to using an entire room.

Because the ROP students take their academic courses in the sending high schools, it is difficult to coordinate academic and technical instruction. However, the pressure to prepare students for the California High School Exit Exam has made some academic teachers receptive to DBL. ROP instructors have demonstrated DBL lessons in some of the sending high schools. When academic teachers observe the student engagement in these lessons, they become interested in learning more about DBL. The instructional coordinator for East San Gabriel Valley noted that principals and superintendents have a major influence on teachers' receptivity to DBL. Johnson et al. had noted that the superintendent of the ROP has been a strong advocate for curriculum integration.

An Agricultural Education Programmatic Model

Johnson County is located in the far northeast corner of Tennessee on the border with North Carolina. In 2009 the total population of the county was estimated to be 18,019, almost all of whom are White (U.S. Census Bureau, 2011d). About 2% of the population is African American, and all other racial/ethnic groups total about 3%. The median family income in 2009 was $34,513. This remote, rural area in the Appalachian Mountains has developed courses in agricultural education that have received international attention. In the 13 years since a new Johnson County High School[3] building opened for its hydroponics and aquaculture programs, it has received an average of 1,000 visitors a year who have come from 40 states and 20 foreign countries.

In the early 1990s the agricultural education program had one full-time and one part-time teacher and was struggling to attract students. On a visit to Epcot Center at Disneyworld, the teachers were impressed with the hydroponic and aquaculture facilities they observed and replicated them on a small scale in their high school. These efforts caught the attention of a state senator and representative who visited the school. With the support of these elected officials, the high school sought funds from several public and private sources to build a state-of-the-art building to house the programs. Funds were received from the Appalachian Regional Commission, the Tennessee Valley Authority, the Geothermal Heat Consortium, and a local bank that provided matching private funds. Before the new courses were started, enrollment in agricultural education was less than 100. In the 2009–10 school year, enrollment was 475 and some students had to be put on waiting lists because there were no openings in the courses they wanted to take.

The program now has four full-time teachers and two technical assistants.

Harvey Burniston, Jr., was the full-time teacher on the trip to Epcot, but his interest in academic integration preceded that experience. He reported that it began when a middle school teacher asked if she could bring her students to visit his greenhouse. Her students were studying a unit on the plant kingdom and she wanted a tour to supplement her in-class instruction. Harvey saw the potential to create interest in his programs among future students and was happy to oblige. This began a relationship that continued when the middle school teacher was promoted to curriculum director and then high school principal. In each of these positions she was a strong advocate for curriculum integration, in Harvey's words, "our biggest cheerleader. We were doing curriculum integration before we even knew what it was."

All CTE teachers at Johnson High School are required to teach at least one unit during the school year that emphasizes academic integration with the technical content of their occupational areas. Harvey's integration activities occur throughout the school year. Many opportunities for integration are inherent in the CTE curriculum and some arise upon the request of academic teachers. For example, the pH (acid-base) scale, which is widely used in agriculture, is a measure of the concentration of hydrogen ions. Teaching students to use this scale provides an opportunity to teach the chemistry of ions and the applications of logarithms. A recent example of cooperation with a biology teacher concerned cell structure. The biology students visited the greenhouse and Harvey explained how the amount of chlorophyll in a plant leaf impacts the length of time it takes to bring it to maturity and the economic implications of a longer growing period.

Harvey encourages the other agricultural teachers to initiate contact for joint teaching with academic teachers. He advises them to start with teachers with whom they have good relationships and to move from them to those with whom their relationships are more distant. Once the academic teachers see how the applications of their content areas can engage and motivate students, they often initiate the contacts. In Harvey's view, the biggest barrier to more integration is high-stakes testing. The academic teachers are reluctant to give any class time to instruction not directly related to preparing their students to pass the tests. Harvey thinks incentives are needed to encourage more integration. The many demands upon teachers' time make integration a low priority.

More than the recognition his programs have received, Harvey's main source of satisfaction is the self-confidence and self-esteem that he sees in his students. Before their new facility was built, the students at Johnson County High School had little to be proud of. Now they study in a facility that has been featured in *USA Today* (Briggs, 2000) and provide tours for visitors, many of whom are high-ranking officials from other countries. The respect that agricultural education receives has also increased, and it is attracting students who would not normally consider a CTE program. In the past 10 years about half of the graduating class valedictorians were agriculture students. Before the new facility was opened, the enrollment in agricultural education was primarily male, but that too has shifted to the point that in the 2009–10 school year almost half—200 students—were female.

A Manufacturing Education Programmatic Model

Johnson et al. (2003) described the Lansing (Michigan) Area Manufacturing Partnership (LAMP)[4] as among the most successful models of curriculum integration that they observed. There were no separate academic and occupational classes that had to be integrated. Instead the students studied manufacturing concepts that required the application of state-defined academic skills in language arts, math, science, and social studies. Much of the instruction took the form of project-based activities in which students analyzed problems, conducted research, developed proposed solutions, tested the solutions, and reported on their results. An example that Johnson et al. cite is a catapult exercise in which students designed and produced catapults for plastic golf balls. The students launched the balls, plotted where they landed, and used the information to adjust the catapult to increase accuracy. For this activity, the instructors required students to learn problem-solving tools typically used in manufacturing, such as Pareto charts, control charts, and scatter diagrams.

LAMP began in the 1997–98 school year as a partnership of General Motors (GM), the United Auto Workers (UAW) union, and the Ingham Intermediate School District (ISD), which serves 12 local districts. The program was developed to interest students in manufacturing and to provide a pipeline for future workers. During the first 10 years of its operation, senior students from any of the 25 high schools served by the Ingham, Eaton, and Clinton county regional educational service agencies could choose to attend LAMP on a half-day schedule. In its last 2 years, due to declining enrollments, the program was opened to junior and senior students, but this was not sufficient to continue its operation. The three partners decided that with the changing economic conditions there no longer was a need for the program, and after the 2008–09 school year, LAMP was closed.

Jeffrey Dole was with LAMP, first as a teacher and then as its director, for its full 12 years, and he identified three major factors leading to its closure. The primary factor was the decline of the automobile industry in Michigan. As the sale of American-made cars declined, there was decreased need for new workers, and layoffs were more frequent than hiring. Students were aware of the limited prospects of manufacturing employment and few considered it as a career option. The second factor was the elimination of the transportation stipend provided to LAMP students. The program was offered at the UAW-GM Lansing Training Center, located at a General Motors plant, and students had to provide their own transportation. During the first 6 years of LAMP, the UAW-GM training fund paid for almost all program costs, including the transportation stipend. After the 2002–03 school year, support from this fund stopped, and Ingham ISD assumed most costs, but it could not continue the transportation stipend. In the first 6 years, many students had traveled considerable distances to attend, but when the stipend stopped, enrollments came mostly from students who did not have far to travel. The third factor was increasing academic requirements. Legislation was passed in Michigan that required all students graduating after 2010 to have earned 16 credits in core academic subjects. Some local districts awarded academic credit for some of the LAMP courses, but this was an individual district decision. Student concerns about meeting the 16-credit requirement made them less inclined to enroll in LAMP.

Before the LAMP program closed, Ingham ISD had decided that the approach had merit and began to develop a similar partnership in health care. Unlike manufacturing, all projections for the Lansing area indicate growing demand for health care workers. To provide the on-site instruction that made a significant contribution to LAMP, contacts were made with the hospitals in Lansing and the surrounding area. The Capital Area Healthcare Education Partnership (CAHEP) emerged from these efforts and enrolled its first 15 students in the 2007–08 school year. In the 2008–09 school year CAHEP increased enrollment by adding 2 more sections for a total of 45 students and in 2009–10 enrolled 44 in 3 sections. The main limitation on growth of the program is the capacity of participating hospitals to provide classroom space. The program currently has a waiting list of students who cannot be enrolled because of space limitations.

CAHEP has many of the same features as LAMP. It is designed more for exploration of health-related careers rather than specific occupational preparation. It is offered on-site in two hospitals, taught by registered nurses, and open to any junior or senior in the Ingham and two other ISDs. Students must provide their own transportation. The project-based curriculum teaches academic, employability, and problem-solving skills in a health care context. Ingham ISD provides recommendations concerning the academic standards addressed, but local districts make the final decisions on the credits they will award for participation. Some award credits in math and science, and others consider it an elective.

The information obtained from these four follow-ups underscores the challenges of sustaining integration efforts. Integration does not emerge spontaneously. As the Johnson et al. (2003) definition indicates there must be "conscious and informed strategies" that receive ongoing support from administration. The two examples to which we now turn, describe in depth two such strategies. These examples were identified when the individuals responsible for these initiatives presented their experiences at the 2010 convention of the Association for Career and Technical Education (Coburn, Dooling, McGinnis, & Nelson, 2010).

Academic Integration at Washington High School

Four teachers at Washington High School in Glendale, Arizona, have combined their efforts to strengthen the literacy skills of students in business education courses. Washington is one of nine schools operated by the Glendale Union High School District. Glendale, which is directly north of Phoenix, had a population in 2009 of 249,555, of whom over one third (35%) were Hispanic or Latino (U.S. Census Bureau, 2011e). Washington's enrollment during the 2008–09 school year was 55% Hispanic (or Latino), 25% White, 11% African American, and 9% other (U.S. Department of Education, National Center for Education Statistics (NCES), 2010b). In 2009 the median family income in Glendale was $61,214, virtually the same as that for the full country ($62,363), but during the 2008–09 school year over half (61%) of the students at Washington were eligible for free or reduced price lunches.

Washington is thus serving a predominantly low-income, minority enrollment that typically scores lower on standardized testing than more advantaged students. By enhancing language arts instruction in a business context, these teachers have raised the scores of their students above the district averages on the reading and writing tests that are part of a districtwide summative assessment: 54% of the students who had received integrated instruction scored at the highly successful level compared to 39% at this level districtwide.

The approach these teachers follow could be adopted by any teachers who wish to draw upon the relevancy of CTE courses to increase student involvement in learning academic skills. Three business education teachers, Maryellen Coburn, Rebecca McGinnis, and Buck Nelson, work with language arts teacher Linda Dooling to identify activities in their curriculum where they can reinforce the learning of language arts standards. Activities they identified included freshmen final projects, resume and cover letter writing, and senior final projects, which are portfolios documenting career objectives and plans.

The freshmen final project was coordinated with the study of *Romeo and Juliet*. The students prepared a print ad using Elizabethan English and took part in a Shakespeare celebration that included games, prizes, acting, and presentations. When teaching resumes and cover letters, the business education teachers encouraged their students to "release their inner Beowulf," which they had studied in English, and not be shy about presenting their abilities. Topics such as heroism and literary analysis were reinforced. For reading assignments, the CTE teachers used Reciprocal Teaching literacy strategies taught in English: predict, clarify, summarize, question, connect. These are strategies very similar to those employed in the Authentic Literacy Study discussed below. When the seniors have developed their career portfolios, they make presentations to their classmates, staff members, administrators, and members of the community.

One of the books used in business education is *The Seven Habits of Highly Effective Teens* by Sean Covey (1998). The study of this book enables the CTE teachers to relate its content to topics covered in literature classes, such as character development. The seven habits are used to analyze the character of Shakespeare's Macbeth as ambition changes him from the savior of Scotland to a murderer.

The teachers who developed these integrated activities received a small grant from West-MEC, a joint technical district that serves 40 high schools. The grant paid for the teachers' time to meet and plan. The director of grants for West-MEC, Michele Bush, has reported that grant money can also be used to pay for substitutes to release teachers for planning time. The Washington High School teachers encourage others who want to try a similar approach to start with small projects. An academic teacher interested in the potential of integration is essential. When such a teacher is found, the standards for his or her academic area provide the starting place for identifying learning that can be enhanced in the CTE curriculum. Administrative support, primarily in providing time for joint planning, is also needed. The resources for integrated instruction developed by teachers who receive West-MEC funding can be accessed at the West-MEC website (www.west-mec.org/teachers/academic-integration).

Academic Credit at Cass Career Center

Cass Career Center in Harrisonville, Missouri has succeeded in what some CTE educators consider the Holy Grail of integration: awarding academic credit for learning that occurs in CTE courses (Tews, 2011). Cass did this by hiring "highly qualified" (meeting the No Child Left Behind definition) English and mathematics teachers to teach 4th-year skills and content in occupational context. Students have dual enrollment in their CTE programs and in the integrated English IV and Math IV courses. A Carnegie credit, equivalent to a full-year, senior-level course is awarded in English and in mathematics to students who successfully complete four semesters of CTE courses taught in 3-hour-block classes. That is, students earn one quarter of a credit in both English and math for each semester successfully completed.

Cass is located about 40 miles southeast of Kansas City, Missouri, and enrolls students from 12 sending high schools who attend for a half day and offers both block and hourly classes. Academic credit is awarded only in the block classes. The English and math teachers work with the CTE teachers to identify literacy and numeracy skills required for graduates to be ready for careers or additional education. The English and math teachers also meet with their counterparts in the sending schools to identify the essential skills and content standards to be included in the integrated curricula. The teachers then work with the instructors of eight of the technical programs taught at Cass to develop separate curricula for each of these programs and to determine when these curricula will be taught. The English and math teachers go to the CTE teachers' classrooms and teach the academic content that has been identified for each of the programs. A side benefit of this approach is that the CTE teachers are in the classroom when the English and math lessons are taught, thereby increasing their ability to reinforce this learning when the academic teachers are not present.

Making the content relevant to each program obviously requires considerable flexibility on the part of the academic teachers. But this does not mean that they must start anew for each occupational area. The essential skills, content standards, and assessments are based on those that have been adopted by Missouri for all Level 4 English and math courses and are the same for all programs. Alignment to the individual areas occurs by making the learning activities, instructional strategies, vocabulary, and resources to achieve these standards relevant to the occupations being studied.

Cass conducts pre- and posttesting of the English and math skills of the students in the dual enrollment blocks; the director of Cass, Jim Spencer, provided these test results to the authors for analysis. All students took the same English test that consisted of a grammar section and a reading section from Compass, a standardized test published by ACT that is widely used at the postsecondary level to determine if incoming students have an adequate command of English to enroll in credit courses. The math tests administered in the separate occupational areas were different, but they all were reported on the same scale, percentage of items answered correctly. This made it possible to combine the results across program areas. Table 4.2 presents the summary statistics for the combined areas and for each of the areas that had 10 students or more who took both the pre- and posttests.

The top two rows of Table 4.2 present the combined results for all programs and the posttests are significantly higher than the pretests. Cohen's *d* is a measure of effect size. It is the difference between two means as a

TABLE 4.2. Pre- and Posttest Scores in English and Mathematics by Program Area for the 2009–10 School Year at Cass Career Center, Harrisonville, Missouri

Occupational Programs	Pretest		Posttest		r	t	p	Cohen's d	n
	Mean	SD	Mean	SD					
All Programs									
English	61.16	16.60	66.09	16.39	.79	5.58	<.001	.46	144
Mathematics	46.53	18.45	61.58	20.36	.71	12.05	<.001	1.04	137
Auto Technology									
English	59.33	17.56	67.95	17.66	.92	7.27	<.001	1.21	34
Mathematics	41.32	18.64	55.59	21.91	.62	4.62	<.001	.82	34
Construction Tech									
English	56.76	12.80	58.36	10.67	.62	.54	.30	.16	13
Mathematics	49.23	16.69	69.42	16.21	.58	4.85	<.001	1.34	13
Fire Science									
English	65.13	18.89	72.67	13.75	.77	3.22	.002	.68	27
Mathematics	49.49	16.26	66.34	18.21	.69	6.52	<.001	1.24	28
Health Science									
English	67.24	15.26	71.18	14.36	.72	1.87	.04	.36	28
Mathematics	56.47	17.02	73.58	13.36	.84	9.76	<.001	1.99	28
Welding									
English	55.43	12.83	56.96	14.58	.68	.72	.24	.14	27
Mathematics	43.74	19.41	55.38	20.37	.74	3.73	<.001	.81	21
Information Systems Technology									
English	60.92	18.32	63.68	20.06	.85	1.00	.17	.26	15
Mathematics	34.19	15.36	46.15	19.91	.45	2.28	.02	.65	13

Note. Cohen's *d* was calculated on the website, www.cognitiveflexibility.org/effectsize/, which corrects for the within subject comparison using Morris and DeShon's (2002) equation 8. The results for the agriculture and CAD programs are not shown in the table because they are based on fewer than 10 students.

proportion of the pooled standard deviations of those means. The d value for math is over twice as large as that for English. These results imply that the integrated math instruction had more influence on posttest results than the integrated English, but this may be a result of the testing as much as the instruction. The math tests for each of the program areas were developed by the math and CTE teachers for these areas and thus were more aligned to the instruction than the standardized Compass test. The posttest Compass scores were significantly higher in three of the six areas while the posttest math scores were significantly higher in all six areas. Integrated instruction is obviously having an impact, but the degree varies by program area and how the impact is measured.

Pennsylvania Reading Initiative

Pennsylvania provides an example of a statewide effort to train CTE teachers to improve the reading skills of their students. This training took the form of 1-week summer workshops conducted by Temple University as part of the Governor's Institute (Wichowski & Garnes, 2004). Several of these institutes are conducted each summer in different content areas. From 2003 to 2007, institutes were offered on the topic "Integrating the Pennsylvania Standards on Reading, Writing, Speaking, and Listening." About two thirds of the participants were teachers who taught occupational skills or related academics at regional career centers and about one quarter taught in comprehensive high schools. The other participants were administrators. The teachers received training that had been especially developed to assist CTE teachers to use students' interest in the occupations they were studying to motivate and improve their ability to read and understand complex content.

The training provided in Pennsylvania covered strategies similar to those used in the Authentic Literacy study, which is discussed below. The strategies were grouped into three categories:

- Reciprocal Teaching: predicting, clarifying, questioning, and summarizing the contents of a given text
- Scaffolding: activities before, during, and after reading (e.g., previewing, note taking, summarizing) to assist students to understand and learn from text
- Journaling: reflective writing used to monitor students' understanding of the meaning of content they have read

After the five summer workshops had been completed, Wichowski and Heberley (2009) conducted a follow-up of all those who had participated in them. They were able to contact 272 out of 280 participants and 75 (29%)

completed the survey. Almost all respondents reported they had moderate (58%) or high (35%) success in implementing the methods they had learned in the workshops. Only one respondent reported no success. The respondents' ratings of the effect of the strategies on the reading achievement of their students were a little lower: moderate, 62%; high, 9%; low, 15%; and none, 3%. The questionnaire also presented the teachers with a list of tests that are administered in Pennsylvania and asked them: "Were there any increases in scores on any of the following measures that could be attributed to the use of RWSL [Reading, Writing, Speaking, Listening] strategies in your class/school?" Teachers reported gains, which Wichowski (n.d.) summarized as follows:

- There was a 12% gain on 11th-grade Pennsylvania System of School Assessment Reading Test scores.
- There was a 15% gain on student NOCTI written tests.
- There was an 8% to 20% increase in scores on teacher-made tests.
- The pass rate on a difficult publisher-made unit test increased from a long history of scores in the 40% range to the 90% range.

It should be noted that these are self-reported results obtained from a highly self-selected sample. Attending the institutes and completing the survey yielded a group of teachers who were motivated to improve the reading skills of their students and very likely to implement the methods they had learned in the workshops. Thus the survey results are almost certainly more positive than if they had been collected from all who had participated in the institutes. It seems just as certain that a random sample of all CTE teachers in Pennsylvania would not be as interested as these respondents were in improving the reading skills of their students.

These efforts in Pennsylvania and at Washington High School and Cass Career Center are examples of the type of change that we would like to see happen in all CTE programs. We propose no grand design or template that will be appropriate for all, but local efforts developed for local circumstances can have results.

THEORY-DRIVEN APPROACHES TO CURRICULUM INTEGRATION

A number of organizations work with schools to integrate academic and career and technical learning. The Southern Region Education Board's High Schools that Work and the Center for Occupational Research and Development are perhaps the two most prominent. To our knowledge, however, there have been only three rigorous tests of the claim that enhanced instruction of academics in an occupational context yields measurable increases in learning. One of these is the Math-in-CTE study (Stone et al., 2006) that enhanced instruction on the mathematical concepts inherent in the CTE curricula. The second used two different literacy frameworks to improve the reading skills of CTE students (Park et al., in press). The third is a pilot study, Science-in-CTE, that tested whether science knowledge and understanding could be influenced by instruction embedded in agricultural education courses (NRCCTE Curriculum Integration Workgroup, 2010). We discuss each of these studies in detail in this section.

Math-in-CTE

The Math-in-CTE study involved teachers from five occupational areas with quite varied content: agricultural mechanics, auto technology, business and marketing, health, and information technology. As part of the recruitment for the study, CTE teachers were asked to identify math teachers who would be willing to work with them as part of the experiment, and to obtain the approval of the principals of their schools for their participation. An honorarium of $1,500 each was offered the CTE teachers and math partners who were randomly assigned to the experimental group and $500 to the CTE teachers assigned to the control group. The study was conducted by the National Research Center for Career and Technical Education with funding from the U.S. Department of Education.

The study was conducted in two stages: a one-semester pilot test from January through June 2004, and a full-school-year treatment from September 2004 through June 2005. For the pilot test, 94 CTE teachers who had been assigned to the experimental group received 2½ days of professional development during which they worked with their math partners to identify the math inherent in their curricula and to develop lesson plans to teach that math. The professional development was specific to the occupational areas. Each of the areas met separately and worked with the facilitators who had recruited them for the study. After the initial workshop, they taught some of the lessons they had developed to their students and then came together for another 2½ days to discuss any problems they had encountered and to improve the lessons. Pre- and posttesting of students of the 94 experimental and 104 control teachers was conducted with three standardized tests of mathematics achievement: TerraNova, Accuplacer, and WorkKeys. The pilot test found significant effects from the enhanced instruction, and the U.S. Department of Education approved a full-year trial.[5]

As an incentive to continue, experimental teachers (both CTE and math) were offered an honorarium of $2,500 for the full-year study, and the control CTE teachers were offered $750. One of the requirements for continuation was participation in 5 days of professional development during the summer of

2004. Of the 94 experimental teachers in the pilot test, 11 said they had other commitments that prevented them from attending the workshops. An additional 6 did not qualify because the occupational courses they taught were only a semester or trimester in length. Nine declined because they felt participation was too much work, and 8 cited a variety of personal reasons such as retirement, a new baby, death in the family, and a move to a new school. We were unable to determine the reasons why 3 teachers did not continue. The number who continued for the full year was 57.

The characteristics of the teachers who applied but did not participate, participated in the pilot study only, and participated in both the pilot and full-year study were compared and only one significant difference was found: control teachers who participated in the pilot but not the full-year had lower self-reported income. Other measures of the teachers' gender, race/ethnicity, and math anxiety, and of the characteristics and pretest scores of their students yielded no significant differences.

While we found minimal differences between teachers with varying levels of participation, we make no claim that these teachers are representative of CTE teachers in general. The fact that they volunteered for the research defines them as atypical, but it does not follow that their students were also. CTE students do not select teachers. They choose occupations to study because of interests and career plans. Teachers with good reputations may attract students, but because of randomization such selectivity would be distributed across the experimental and control groups.

The parents of all students of participating teachers, both experimental and control, were informed of the research and given the opportunity to exclude their students by signing and returning a form. This is commonly referred to as *passive consent*, and very few parents returned the form. To encourage student participation, they were offered a $10 gift card for each of the two test administrations, pre- and posttesting.

The intervention that the experimental students received consisted of, on average, 20 hours of math-enhanced CTE instruction delivered at appropriate times during the school year. Each teacher within an occupational area was free to choose when he or she would teach each lesson, and all lessons were taught by the CTE teachers alone. The intervention did not involve team teaching. All lessons, regardless of occupational area, included the seven elements listed in Table 4.3. For the summer 2004 workshops, a standardized, two-column template was adopted for use in lesson development. The content to be covered for each of the elements was presented in the left column and teacher notes (including answers to questions posed in the left column) in the right column.

Even though the experimental students received an average of only 20 hours of enhanced math instruction, these lessons produced a significant effect. The experimental students scored 9% higher than the control students

TABLE 4.3. The Seven Elements of a Math-Enhanced Lesson

Introduce the CTE lesson.	Assess students' math awareness as it relates to the CTE lesson.	Work through the math example embedded in the CTE lesson.	Work through related, contextual math-in-CTE examples.	Work through traditional math examples.	Students demonstrate their understanding.	Formal assessment.
Explain the CTE lesson. Identify, discuss, point out, or pull out the math embedded in the CTE lesson.	As you assess, introduce math vocabulary through the math example embedded in the CTE. Employ a variety of methods and techniques for assessing awareness of all students, e.g., questioning, worksheets, group learning activities, and so on.	Work through the steps/processes of the embedded math example. Bridge the CTE and math language. The transition from CTE to math vocabulary should be gradual throughout the lesson, being sure never to abandon completely either set of vocabulary once it is introduced.	Using the same math concept embedded in the CTE lesson: Work through similar problems/examples in the same occupational context. Use examples with varying levels of difficulty; order examples from basic to advanced. Continue to bridge CTE and math vocabulary. Check for understanding.	Using the same math concept as in the embedded and related contextual examples: Work through traditional math examples as they may appear on tests. Move from basic to advanced examples. Continue to bridge CTE and math vocabulary. Check for understanding.	Provide students opportunities for demonstrating their understanding of the math concepts embedded in the CTE lesson. Conclude the math examples, return to the CTE content; conclude the lesson on the topic of CTE.	Incorporate math questions into formal assessments at the end of the CTE unit/course.

on the TerraNova posttest, and 8% higher on Accuplacer.[6] They also scored higher on WorkKeys, but the difference was not statistically significant. The 20 hours of enhanced math represented just 11% of a 1-hour class taught for the typical 180 days of a school year. And not all of this time was spent on math, because the math was taught in the occupational context in which it naturally occurred. If the academics inherent in all occupational contexts had received the type of explicit instruction that occurred in one course in the Math-in-CTE study, the tested academic skills of CTE students who received such instruction would almost certainly have exceeded students without academic enhancement by even more.

More important than the test scores themselves was the effect on students' attitudes toward mathematics. During the course of the research, math teachers who worked with the CTE teachers reported examples of CTE students who early in the year sat in the back of the classroom and avoided interaction with the teacher as much as possible but became more attentive as the year progressed. One math teacher described a CTE student who by year's end was standing in front of the class explaining a math concept he had mastered in his CTE class. While changing attitudes toward math was not the intent of the study, such anecdotes suggest another value of teaching academics in context. So too does direct testimony from students who are beneficiaries of this approach to learning.

May 8, 2009
To whom it may concern:
My name is C. J. Anderson and I am in Mr. Shamburg's afternoon Carpentry class. I've always had trouble with Math and my grades usually showed that. When I came into the Carpentry program I was worried about learning the Math part. This year I feel like I've overcome that worry at least in Carpentry. I have more faith in what I'm doing because of the Math I've learned in Carpentry. Recently I had to take my ACTs at my home high school. When it came to the Math part of the test I started to get nervous. After starting the test I realized I knew the answers to the questions because of what I've learned in my Carpentry class. I felt it was important to let you know how well I did on the Math part due to the Math I've learned through Mr. Shamburg's Carpentry class. It's so much easier to learn Math when you apply it to the real world and not just studying out of a textbook. Thank you for your time.

C. J. Anderson

The success of the math-enhanced lessons was heavily dependent on the extensive professional development that the teachers who developed and presented them received. The teachers who participated in the full-year study received a total of 15 days of professional development, 5 during the pilot study, and 10 during the full year. In addition to the 5 days during the summer of 2004, 2½-day sessions were conducted during the late fall of 2004 and the spring of 2005. During the school year, they also met with their math partners prior to teaching the lessons to review the math and obtain teaching suggestions.

In the judgment of those responsible for the study (two of whom are authors of this book), the extensive professional development was critical to the success of the study. The continuing interaction of the teachers encouraged communities of practice (or professional learning communities) to emerge. As we discussed earlier in this chapter, a recurring theme in the literature on professional development is the need for teachers to work together in learning communities. The primary goal of learning communities is to improve student learning. In a true community, teachers assume joint responsibility for this goal and work together to develop ways to achieve it. This involves defining the needs and learning problems of students, identifying and drawing upon resources to respond to these needs, and fashioning and testing approaches to improve learning. Obviously, teachers need administrative support to function in this manner.

Most discussion of learning communities assumes that they will be developed within a school with the principal playing a key role by supporting the community and providing leadership. The communities in the Math-in-CTE study were not school-based, and the teachers who volunteered to participate were drawn from many schools. However, as they worked together to identify embedded math and develop lessons, communities of practice emerged. The teachers shared a concern for improving the math skills of their students, and their interactions helped them learn how to do this better. The time and structure offered by the study provided the conditions needed for communities of practice to emerge.

In the summer of 2005, after the experiment had ended, the CTE control teachers were given the opportunity to take part in a 2½- day workshop that provided an overview of the lessons developed for the Math-in-CTE study. As in the study itself, separate workshops were conducted for each of the occupational areas. All of the control teachers, whether they attended the workshops or not, were sent copies of the lessons developed for their occupational areas.

Toward the end of the 2005–06 school year, almost a year after the Math-in-CTE study ended, a follow-up survey was conducted with all the teachers who had participated in the study (Lewis & Pearson, 2007). The questionnaires sent to the CTE teachers included two screening questions. First, were they teaching CTE courses that prepared students for employment during the 2005–06 school year? Those who replied "Yes" were asked if they included *explicit mathematics instruction,* defined as "going beyond specific occupational applications to explain the general math concepts that underlie the applications." If they answered "Yes" to this question, they were asked about the approach they used to teach mathematics and if they had taught or planned to teach any lessons from the study. The questionnaire for math teachers had similar screening questions: Were they teaching math, and if they were, did they use any of the methods or examples of applications of math from the lessons developed for the study in their classes? Table 4.4 presents the results from this survey.

Three fourths of the experimental CTE teachers who responded to the survey reported teaching explicit math, and almost all of them used the method and lessons from the Math-in-CTE study. A little more than one third of the control teachers reported teaching explicit math, and about one fourth used the method or lessons from the study. No effort had been made during the study to influence how the math partners of the CTE experimental teachers taught their classes. Although no such effort was made, focus groups conducted after the intervention ended found that many of the math teachers reported using examples of math applications developed for the lessons in their classes. Consequently, it was decided to include the math partners in the follow-up, and almost two thirds of those who were teaching math reported using the method or examples from the lessons they had helped to develop.

In light of the literature on the difficulties of sustaining change in education, we consider these to be fairly impressive findings; but are they? We could find in the literature only one study that obtained data directly from teachers on the extent to which they continued to use innovations they had tested. Lieber et al. (2010) found that 12% of 43 teachers who had tested a curriculum for at-risk preschool children continued to use the full curriculum after the intervention ended, and an additional 60% used parts of the curriculum.

We also found a follow-up of schools, not teachers, who implemented various school reform models. The Southwest Educational Development Laboratory (2003) surveyed 288 schools in its five-state service area that had received funding under the Comprehensive School Reform Demonstration program 2 years after their funding had ended. Forty percent (106) of the schools returned questionnaires with 79 reporting that they had continued all or at least half of the reforms they had implemented, and 29 reporting that they had not. This represents a 75% continuation rate, essentially the same as for the experimental teachers. If we make the same assumption about those who did not respond to the Southwest Lab survey that was made for Table 4.4—that those who did not respond were not continu-

TABLE 4.4. Use of Math-in-CTE Method or Materials During 2005–06 School Year by Experimental and Control CTE and Mathematics Teachers

Use of Method or Lessons	Percentage of Respondents		Percentage of Total Sample	
	All	*Those Teaching*	*All*	*Those Teaching*
Experimental CTE Teachers				
Taught explicit math	71.7	75.0	55.0	56.9
Did not teach CTE courses	4.3		3.3	
Used Math-in-CTE method/ lessons	65.2	68.2	50.0	51.7
Used lessons not method	4.3	4.5	3.3	3.4
Used other methods	2.2	2.3	1.7	1.7
Did not teach explicit math	23.9	25.0	41.7	43.1
Base for percentages	*46*	*44*	*60[a]*	*58*
Control CTE Teachers				
Taught explicit math	33.3	38.5	27.4	30.8
Did not teach CTE courses	13.3		11.0	
Used Math-in-CTE method/ lessons	11.7	13.5	9.6	10.8
Used lessons not method	11.7	13.5	9.6	10.8
Used other methods	10.0	11.5	8.2	9.2
Did not teach explicit math	53.3	61.5	43.8	69.2
Base for percentages	*60*	*52*	*73*	*65*
Mathematics Teachers				
Used Math-in-CTE methods/ examples	44.2	65.5	36.5	50.0
Did not teach high school math	32.6		26.9	
Used both method and examples	14.0	20.7	11.5	15.8
Used teaching method not examples	7.0	10.3	5.8	7.9
Used examples not method	23.3	34.5	19.2	26.3
Did not use examples or approach	23.3	34.5	36.5	50.0
Base for percentages	*43*	*29*	*52*	*38*

Source. Lewis and Pearson (2007), Table 3, p. 13, and Table 7, p. 18.

Note. The percentages for Total Sample are estimates that were calculated assuming that teachers who did not respond did teach and did not use the method or lessons.

[a]Questionnaires were sent to three experimental teachers who had volunteered to continue for the full year but were dropped because their courses were only a semester or trimester in length.

ing—the percentage of those continuing the reforms drops to only 27%. If we make the less draconian assumption that half of the 182 who did not return questionnaires were not continuing, the number continuing increases to 59%. We repeat: This was a study of schools, not teachers, and of whole school reform models, not instructional methods.

In addition to the mail survey, personal interviews were conducted with the CTE teachers who reported they were teaching explicit math and with the math teachers who were using the method or examples from the study. These interviews were designed to verify the mail responses by reviewing how the teachers had used material from the study and any difficulties they encountered in sustaining this approach when the support provided by the study ended. In these interviews, some of these teachers reported that their participation had influenced or changed their approach to teaching. They had internalized the seven-element pedagogy to the extent that they approached virtually all their teaching from this perspective. Such a change was not true of all teachers, of course. About one fourth of the experimental teachers did not continue to use the pedagogy or the lessons, with the most common reasons given being lack of time and lack of fit between the lessons and their curriculum. Lack of fit was especially true of health teachers, since the health lessons had been designed for the first-year core curriculum and in the year of the follow-up many of these teachers were supervising 2nd-year students in internships.

It bears repeating that the rates of continued use of the experimental materials were achieved with teachers who responded to recruitment and participated for the full duration of the study, both pilot and full-year trial. These teachers were self-selected and in all likelihood more open to change and motivated to improve their teaching than teachers who did not volunteer. The teachers who participated in the next study we discuss were also self-selected and willing to try different methods for improving the reading skills of their students. Like the teachers who taught enhanced math, these CTE teachers found that explicit emphasis on improving their students' ability to understand the reading materials essential to their classes produced higher scores on a standardized measure of reading skills.

Authentic Literacy in CTE

As noted above, students who earn three or more credits in related occupational courses score significantly lower on reading tests than students with fewer CTE credits (Silverberg et al., 2004). CTE students often find, however, that the material that they need to read in their career areas is more difficult than that encountered in the typical academic classroom. The International Center for Leadership in Education (2009) contacted employers and collected over 2,400 documents that employees use in their jobs. The reading complexity of these documents was analyzed using Lexile® software. A Lexile measure of text ranges from BR (Beginning Reader) to 2000. The method of scoring is proprietary, but MetaMetrics, the company holding the copyright, states on its website (http://www.lexile.com): "A Lexile text measure is based on two strong predictors of how difficult a text is to comprehend: word frequency and sentence length." A novel widely ready in high school English is *To Kill a Mockingbird* by Harper Lee. The MetaMetics's website indicates that this book has a Lexile text score of 870.

The report of the 2,400 documents analyzed by the International Center for Leadership in Education does not provide summary information on their Lexile text scores. To estimate this information, we averaged the first score listed on the 48 pages that present these scores. The average score was 1270, and the range was 870 to 1680. The lowest score, the same as *To Kill a Mockingbird,* was for a manual for clerical duties and the highest was for the National Electrical Code. Some CTE students may elect occupational courses to avoid reading, but if they are to succeed in their chosen careers, they will need to be able to read and understand complex text.

The Authentic Literacy study (Park et al., in press) tested whether it was possible to use students' interest in the occupations they study to enhance their reading skills. It did so by training teachers to apply established methods of improving reading skills to printed materials inherent in CTE courses. The general design of this study paralleled the Math-in-CTE study in several ways: (a) It consisted of a pilot test that led to a full-year trial; (b) CTE teachers were recruited from several occupational areas and randomly assigned to experimental and control groups; (c) experimental teachers received professional development in implementing the interventions, and the control teachers were asked to continue their previous practices with regard to reading; and (d) pre- and posttesting was conducted using a standardized measure of reading achievement (Gates-MacGinitie). However, the Authentic Literacy study did not pair CTE teachers with English teachers or other reading specialists. The research team for the study delivered the professional development received by the teachers in the experimental groups.

During the first year of this project, focus groups were held with CTE teachers to identify the types of reading difficulties their students encounter. Analysis of the teachers' responses and the results of the pilot study led to the selection of two approaches to improve the reading skills of students that were tested during the full-year study: MAX Teaching (Forget, 2004) and the Ash framework as embedded in Adolescent Literacy Support Framework (Education Alliance at Brown University, 2011). The MAX acronym is derived from Motivation, Acquisition, eXtension (Forget, 2004). Both MAX and the Ash framework employ similar strategies to help students understand content by leading them through a sequence of activities before, during, and after reading. Park et al. (in press) summarized the basic strategies of each method that were most applicable to CTE content in two tables that are reproduced below as Tables 4.5 and 4.6.

The professional development provided to the experimental teachers prepared them to use the strategies in the two tables to structure and guide their students' reading assignments. The strategies were explained and modeled and the teachers worked collaboratively to identify how they could use them in their own curriculum. Within each of the approaches, teachers chose which of the strategies they would use and when they would use them. The impact of the interventions was pilot testing in a random assignment experiment during the spring of 2009. Teachers who volunteered to participate were randomly assigned to one of two treatment groups or a control group. The students received the interventions during April and May 2009, and despite the short period, those in the treatment groups scored higher on the Gates-MacGinitie than students without such exposure. These results led to a decision to conduct a full-school-year test of the two approaches during the 2009–10 school year.

During the summer of 2009, CTE teachers in New York and South Carolina (states with universities that are part of the NRCCTE consortium) were recruited and randomly assigned to the MAX Teaching, Ash Framework, or control groups. A stipend of $750 was offered to attract volunteers. A total of 116 were recruited and assigned, but 20 did not continue through the full experiment. The most frequent reason, accounting for six teachers, was failure to collect and submit pre- and posttest data from their students. The next most frequent, four teachers, related to administrative matters such as schedule changes or moves to new schools. Three teachers gave no reasons, two said they were too busy, one obtained only four informed consent forms from parents, and one reported his students "gave up" and would not do the assigned reading. The number of teachers who continued and provided test data from their students were MAX = 28, Ash = 25, and control = 28. An additional group also participated: 17 teachers who had been in the MAX group in the pilot study were invited to continue for the full-year study and 15 did so.

As noted in connection with the Math-in-CTE study, the teachers who participated in the Authentic Literacy study are not representative of all CTE teachers. They volunteered to participate, which in itself defines them as different. In all probability, they were more motivated than the average teacher to seek and use new ways to improve their instruction. But these characteristics were randomly assigned to the experimental or control conditions. Consequently, any significant effects found for the students of the experimental teachers can be attributed to the treatments that they expe-

TABLE 4.5. MAX Teaching Strategies with Phases of Engagement and a Brief Introduction to the Strategy

Strategy	MAX Phases	Brief Introduction to Strategy
Anticipation Guides	Motivation Acquisition eXtension	Prior to reading, students indicate which statements will be supported in text. Class discusses predictions. Individual silent reading. Groups discuss validity of original predictions, reach consensus. Students use evidence from text to support arguments.
Previewing Nonfiction Text	Motivation	Teacher leads students through a systematic and thorough text preview. Focus on: title, introduction, subtitles, bold print and italicized words, pictures, charts, maps, graphs, summary and review questions (those found in the text used).
Cornell Note Taking	Acquisition eXtension	Draw a vertical line 2–3 inches from left edge of paper. Write only main ideas in the left column. Students record the details concerning main idea in the right column—easy review notes.
Cubing	Motivation eXtension	Students divided into groups of less than six. Students follow directions to build cube. One student in each group responds to the text by: Describing, Comparing, Associating, Analyzing, Applying, or Arguing for or against the specified topic.
GIST	Acquisition eXtension	Achieve class consensus on the definition of "summarizing." Explain benefits of the skill in reading. Model the skill. Set a limit on the number of words used in summarizing.
Guided Reading Procedure	Motivation Acquisition eXtension	Using title, students predict reading topic. Students read for x minutes and remember information. Close books, record one fact per student, allow students to correct facts. Students review text for x minutes. Correct ideas and add new.
INSERT	Acquisition eXtension	During the reading, the student is responsible for making decisions about their reaction to the text. The insert marks are written lightly down right on the text. This monitors students' comprehension and allows the teacher to see their reactions.
Paired Reading	Acquisition eXtension	Paired students read same text silently simultaneously. They close books and paraphrase what they have read. Students have two roles—listener and teller—and students take turns with each role.
Student-Generated Graphic Representation	Motivation Acquisition eXtension	Students preview text; groups hypothesize which graphic representation best portrays content. Each student then reads individually, gathering information into graphic representation. Small groups meet to discuss and construct meaning and make large poster graphic representation; then they present to class.
Three-Level Study Guides	Acquisition eXtension	Structured 3 statement levels: statements directly from text, statements implied from text, statements beyond text. Students read text and check statements they agree with, giving evidence for agreement. Then they share with each other.

Source. Park et al. (in press)

TABLE 4.6. Ash Content Area Reading Framework Reading Strategies

Strategy	Description
Guided Reading of Text	
Directed Reading-Thinking Activity	Students sample text by reading the title, a few lines, pictures. Ask the students to make predictions. Students read the text to confirm or correct predictions.
Anticipation Guides	Have students write whether they agree or disagree with the statement. While reading, students reassess answers and provide evidence. After reading, groups of two or three discuss and come to a consensus. Come back to whole class in order to discuss and come to a consensus.
I-Charts	Students are given a chart to complete with a number of sources. There are questions in columns across the top. Each row corresponds with a particular source. The last row is a general summary of each question.
Direct Instruction of Comprehension Strategies	
Asking Questions	Teacher creates questions to help students predict and anticipate what might occur next in the text, solve problems, and clarify understanding.
Question-Answer Relationships (QARS)	Students are guided through the text by 4 levels of questions which are: In the text—right there / In the text—think and search / In my head—author and me / In my head—on my own
Generating Interactions Between Schemata and Text	Assign a segment of the reading to be summarized. Students read to themselves silently. Groups work to summarize. Repeat steps 1–3 for another reading and continue until complete. Students share their work and reflect on what they have read.
Word Study	
PreReading Plan (PreP)	Students brainstorm and write down their thinking about the subject. Students share what they wrote by writing their ideas on the chalkboard. Students reflect on initial associations and are asked to give rationale. Students divide into groups, consider how they would organize terms. Teacher leads a class discussion to narrow thinking of the groups.
List-Group-Label	Students list key words from a reading section. Have them group words into logical categories based on shared features. Have them label the categories with clear and descriptive titles.
Vocabulary from Context	Students decipher vocabulary by reading the word in a sentence and using context.
Peer-Led Discussion of Text	
Reciprocal Teaching Plus	Making and revising predictions Asking questions Clarifying different points and vocabulary Summarizing material and critical evaluation of text, identifying author's perspective and analyzing points of view that were left out

TABLE 4.6. Continued

Peer-Led Discussion of Text	
Literature Circles	Allow students to choose their own reading materials. Divide them into small, temporary groups based upon book choices. Have each group read their selected book. Have groups meet on a regular schedule to discuss the reading. Encourage notes to guide reading and discussion while facilitating. Observe students while reading (students complete self-evaluation). When students are finished reading, each group shares with the class.
Jigsaw	Divide the reading among students. Have each student read their section individually. Have them reconvene and teach each other the reading they completed.
Purposeful Oral Reading and Text Production	
Readers' Theatre	Students read an entertaining and informative script about a subject without costumes, props, and sets. Students do not memorize lines but should act with enthusiasm.
Role, Audience, Format, Topic (RAFT)	Think about the concepts or process that you want students to learn as they read a selected passage. Consider how writing in a fun way may enhance students' understanding of the topic. Brainstorm possible roles students could assume in their writing. Decide who the audience would be as well as the format for writing. After students have finished reading, identify the role, audience, format, and topic (RAFT) for the writing. Assign the same role for all students, or let them choose from several different roles.
Inquiry Learning	
Investigative Reporting	Students should have a set of questions that they need to answer by interviewing various people and by research, in a sense "investigating" a situation.
Multimedia Literacy Projects	Have students create and develop projects about a given subject using various types of media, then create a presentation for the class.

Source. Park et al. (in press)

rienced. The broader question is whether less motivated teachers can be persuaded to learn and use the methods that were tested in the study. This question can only be answered by attempts to disseminate information about these methods and to train teachers in their use.

During the summer of 2009 the teachers who had volunteered for the full-year study received 4 days of professional development. This was an extended version of the preparation provided to the teachers in the pilot study with additional time for demonstration and modeling, collaboration with other teachers, and microteaching with peer feedback. The experimental intervention took place from September 2009 through mid-April 2010. Pretesting was conducted with the 7th- to 9th-grade version of the Gates-MacGinitie Form S and posttesting with Form T. The 7th- to 9th-grade version of the test was used even though most of the students were in the 11th and 12th grades to accommodate students with below-grade-level reading

TABLE 4.7. Pre- and Posttest Total Raw and Extended Scale Scores on Gates-MacGinitie Reading Test

Group	Pretest Mean	SD	% of Control	Posttest Mean	SD	% of Control	Effect Size	r	N
Raw Scores									
Control	60.24	18.37		56.53	21.27			.70	547
MAX	63.36	16.40	1.05	61.80	18.74	1.09	.26	.69	436
Ash	61.07	19.19	1.01	61.28	20.78	1.08	.23	.71	588
MAX2	62.19	19.03	1.03	65.87	17.97	1.17	.48	.72	323
Extended Scale Scores									
Control	544.16	37.86		538.50	42.01			.69	547
MAX	549.02	34.06	1.01	548.04	37.34	1.02	.24	.66	436
Ash	545.04	38.53	1.00	548.02	42.02	1.02	.23	.73	588
MAX2	547.24	37.82	1.01	556.57	38.42	1.03	.45	.69	323

Source. Park et al. (in press)

Notes. Ash and MAX present the statistics for the students of the teachers who participated in only the full-year study. MAX2 presents the statistics for the students of the teachers who participated in both the pilot and full-year study.

Effect size is Cohen's *d* calculated at http://cognitiveflexibility.org/effectsize/ effectsizecalculator.php

skills, of whom there are many in CTE classes. On the pretest, the average number of correct responses was 61.6 out of a total of 96 items, a little less than two thirds (64%) correct, which implies that the 7th- to 9th-grade-level test was challenging for most students.

Several different statistical analyses were conducted by Park and his colleagues, most of which indicated that the experimental students scored higher on the posttests than the control students. When these analyses are reported as Extended Scale Scores (ESS), the differences between the groups are modest, albeit statistically significant. When they are reported as raw scores, they are more substantial. The ESS scale ranges from 74 to 714 and was developed to allow comparisons across grades. Raw scores can range from 0 to 96. Although the final technical report of the Authentic Literacy study is not yet published Travis Park, the principal investigator for the study, shared with the authors data that allowed us to calculate the results presented in Table 4.7 for the total raw and ESS pre- and posttests.

The mean scores, especially the raw scores, indicate that except for the students of the teachers who continued from the pilot to the full-year study (MAX2), the experimental interventions did not increase the posttest performance of their students. Instead the interventions prevented the scores from dropping. Scores dropped in the control group, stayed about the same in the classes of the MAX and Ash experimental teachers who participated only in the full-year study, and rose for the students of the MAX2 teachers who participated both in the pilot and full-year study. This pattern resulted in the posttest mean raw scores of the students in the experimental group being 8%, 9%, and 17% higher than the mean of the control group. The percentage differences for the ESS are more modest, because of the wide range of that scale. The increase in the scores of the MAX2 students implies that teachers who received additional professional development and had more experience in using the reading strategies were able to improve the reading skills of their students, not just prevent their skills from dropping.

Science-in-CTE

The Science-in-CTE study was designed to test the effectiveness of enhancing the science that naturally occurs in CTE curricula. Following the successful efforts to integrate mathematics and CTE, Donna Pearson, Associate Director of the NRCCTE, and her colleagues tested a similar approach for science. They randomly assigned teachers of agricultural education who volunteered for the study to the experimental or control groups, conducted professional development in which the agriculture teachers worked with science teachers to identify science concepts inherent in the agriculture curriculum, and developed lessons to enhance the teaching of those concepts. The experimental teachers taught those lessons and the control teachers taught their regular curriculum. The TerraNova CAT Survey was administered as the pretest in the treatment and control classrooms at the beginning of the term, before the implementation of the enhanced lessons. The TerraNova CTBS Survey Plus Level 21/22 Form A was administered as the posttest at the end of the term. There were data for 363 students and 29 classrooms available for the analysis, with an average of 13 students per classroom.

Analyses of test data from the pilot study showed that science integration works differently from math integration. Overall, the treatment had no significant impact on students' science achievement. When the researchers disaggregated the data by quartiles based on pretest scores, however, they had an interesting finding. The effects of the treatment were inconsistent across levels of pretest science achievement. That is, the treatment had no effect on posttest science achievement for those in the first quartile, but a substantial positive effect for those in the second, third, and fourth quartiles. As shown in Figure 4.1, the magnitude of this effect increased for each quartile increase in pretest science achievement. The effect measures (Cohen's d) were .15 for those in the second quartile, .30 for those in the third quartile, and .45 for those in the fourth quartile, intervention effects of small to moderate impact. The negligible result for students in the first quartile seems counterintuitive in relation to the upward trend in the high-

FIGURE 4.1. Pre- and Posttest Mean Scores on TerraNova Standardized Tests of Science Achievement by Pretest Quartiles

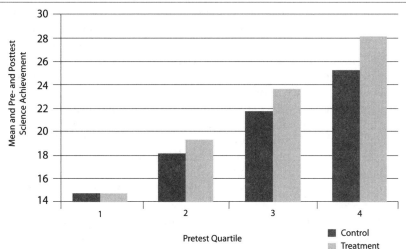

er quartiles and cannot be explained with the available data. The research team concluded from the maps developed for the CTE curriculum that there was sufficient embedded science content to warrant a more extensive test of an integration model.

The research team reexamined the seven-element pedagogic framework that had been adapted from the Math-in-CTE model. An assumption made in the pilot study was that science integration could be treated in the same manner as math integration. However, findings from the pilot invalidated that assumption. The transfer of learning so evident in the Math-in-CTE study was not evident in the adaptation for teaching of integrated science. As a result, the research team sought assistance from the advisory group including science professors, leaders from the science education community, and research experts, and undertook a revision of the framework.

The changes were substantial; seven elements were revised into six elements. They revised the first two elements to more clearly situate the lesson in CTE content and the real-world context. Moreover, they rewrote elements 3–5—the transfer of learning elements of the previous framework—to reflect the recursive nature of science learning. The new elements 3–5 now afford students opportunities to engage in field-based and laboratory activities that support learning of the explicit science embedded within the CTE content. The framework retains the formative and summative assessment elements. At the time of the publication of this book, the research team is field-testing the newly revised model.

Research Informing Policy

While the benefits of contextualizing academics in the teaching of career and technical content is valuable, moving research to policy is often a challenge. The Math-in-CTE model is beginning to show some movement in this direction. In the 2008 Washington state legislative session, a bill (SB-6377) was introduced and passed that included a provision to "allocate grant funds to school districts to increase the integration of and rigor of academic instruction in career and technical courses. Grant recipients are encouraged to use grant funds to support teams of academic and technical teachers using a research-based professional development model supported by the National Research Center for Career and Technical Education." As a result of this legislation, Washington has used the Math-in-CTE model to coordinate and promote integrated science, technology, engineering, and mathematics (STEM) across the state.

The Denver Public Schools have adopted the Math-in-CTE model starting as far back as 2004. After taking part in the initial Math-in-CTE research study, Denver schools have continued to implement the model with 18 different CTE/ Math teacher teams in 7 program areas in 10 different schools.

Since 2006, the Oregon Department of Education has supported specific professional development on elevating the level of mathematics instruction in CTE. The Math-in-CTE project, which started as a single workshop provided in collaboration with Lane Education Service District, now helps CTE teachers from other school districts partner with math teachers to identify the math that naturally occurs in CTE courses.

In the 2005–06 school year, the state of Michigan embarked on a pilot project to create Career Cluster Resource Guides for each of the 16 career clusters. These resource guides were designed to be available on the Internet and provide teachers and administrators with sample lessons integrating academics into the CTE programs. The Math-in-CTE model's seven-element lesson plan was adopted by the state.

CORE PRINCIPLES

Analysis of qualitative data collected as part of the Math-in-CTE study yielded five factors that the authors labeled "core principles" and considered critical to its success. The Authentic Literacy study provided further support for these practices and led to a slight modification in their wording to broaden them from a focus on math to include all academic subjects. These are the revised core principles:

1. Develop and sustain a community of practice among the teachers.
2. Begin with the CTE curriculum, not the academic curriculum.
3. Understand that academics are essential workplace knowledge and skills.
4. Maximize the academics in the CTE curriculum.
5. Recognize that CTE teachers are teachers of academics in CTE, and not academic teachers. (Stone et al., 2006, p. 69, as modified by Pearson et al., 2010, p. 45)

The order in which the principles are listed reflects their importance. In the math study we found that CTE and math teachers working together within the same occupational area and focused on the improvement of instruction was essential. The Authentic Literacy study underscored the importance of peer support, but the teachers were from several occupational areas. The strategies that they learned and tested were applicable to any content area. In math, however, the applications had to be inherent in the occupational tasks, for example, the cylinder displacement of an internal combustion engine or the ratio of herbicide to water for treating a given acreage. This leads directly to the second principle: Begin with the CTE curriculum. If CTE is not the starting point, integration will, in all likelihood, be forced. Starting with CTE also signals the value of its content. In a good CTE program the curriculum responds to the labor market—the skills taught are those students will need if they enter the occupations they study. Among these skills are reading, writing, and computing, which is the third core principle. Academic skills are not needed just to pass tests; they are required to perform jobs.

The fourth principle encourages teachers to reinforce academics whenever it occurs. After a lesson on a particular strategy or concept has been presented, opportunities to apply it will emerge several times. Teachers can use these occasions to remind students of the concept and its application in multiple settings. The auto technology teachers who participated in the Math-in-CTE study reported that they taught a lesson on conversion of English to metric measurement early in their programs because their curriculum often involves such conversions. Each occupational task that required a conversion provided an opportunity to reinforce the underlying math.

The final principle speaks directly to the Johnson et al. (2003) definition of integration. The CTE curriculum is a platform for instruction in an academic skill, but it does not attempt to replace academic instruction. In the best of all worlds, the academic curriculum is also a platform for instruction in the skills it teaches that are needed in the CTE curriculum. A few of the high schools studied by Johnson et al. had such dual platforms, but they are rare. In most high schools, if any integration takes place, it occurs in the CTE classroom.

In the three studies the NRCCTE has conducted, the approaches they used affected academic classrooms only indirectly. Two thirds of the math teachers who had worked with the CTE teachers to develop the lesson plans told us that they had adopted examples of the application of mathematics from those lessons for their classrooms. This is not the planned, systematic approach that Johnson et al. (2003) define as true integration, but it is perhaps the most that can be achieved without threatening the grammar/core of schooling (Elmore, 1996; Tyack & Tobin, 1994) to the point that there is little chance that the innovation will continue.

TWO UNDERUTILIZED PEDAGOGIES

Beyond the classroom, quality CTE programs have two other pedagogic opportunities. As called for in both *Learning for Jobs* (OECD, 2010) and *Pathways to Prosperity* (Symonds et al., 2011), actively involving employers in the training and education of youth is a necessary part of preparing youth for a successful adulthood. Another pedagogy unique to the American system of education is the career-technical student organization (CTSO).

Work-Based Learning

Most high school instruction is still based on the behaviorist assumption that knowledge can be taught independent of context and that such learning can be evaluated using nonauthentic/nonperformance methods. Modern cognitive science research finds the opposite. As Grabinger (1996) points out, "knowledge learned but not explicitly related to relevant problem-solving situations remains mostly inert, meaning the learner is unable to use it for anything practical when the opportunity arises and thus such knowledge quickly disappears" (p. 69). Algebra, for example, is a mathematical procedure for solving many practical problems but is taught and evaluated in a noncontextual abstract form. One of the "quiet" equity issues in U.S. schools is that classes taught in these decontextualized abstract modalities are effective only for a relatively small number of intellectually blessed students. As we have argued earlier, for most students, skills and knowledge are best learned within realistic contexts where students have the opportunity to practice and master outcomes that are expected of them.

The debate over costs and benefits of adolescent employment has raged for some time. Stone (2011) summarized these and discussed the many issues attendant to the marked decline of youth working in the United States. The key in making work benefit youth is linking it to education.

The OECD (2010) report *Learning for Jobs* shows that beyond smoothing the transition from school to the workplace, work-based learning (WBL) offers a powerful tool for increasing more transferrable soft skills critical to workplace success and largely ignored in more conventional school-based learning. Studies of employer preferences here and elsewhere in the world show they strongly value soft skills such as the ability to work in teams, communication skills, problem solving, entrepreneurship, and work discipline. But perhaps the most important value work-based learning provides is the opportunity to increase the basic literacy and numeracy skills learned in a practical environment, an appealing alternative to the many youth not inclined toward the more abstract pedagogies commonly used in school-based learning. In an analysis of over 37,000 students enrolled in High-Schools-That-Work sites, Bottoms, Han, and Murray (2008) found high-quality CTE and WBL linked to improved reading scores. Finally, and perhaps most germane to the education debates in the United States, research by Bishop and Mane (2004) and others shows that countries where high percentages of youth engage in intensive CTE and WBL, such as apprenticeship, perform better on traditional academic achievement outcomes (e.g., school completion, tertiary education, reading and math literacy) than in nations where such participation is low, like the United States. There is also evidence on the effect of WBL on higher education participation and success. Swail and Kampits (2004) found that students who participate in high school work-based learning activities achieve at the 4-year postsecondary level as well or better than students who do not participate in these activities. Further, their finding that WBL students (defined as those who participate in two or more WBL activities) enroll at the postsecondary level and do as well as other students has implications for admissions and recruitment practices. They also found that almost three quarters of all postsecondary students believed they learn better through hands-on projects. This is precisely the kind of experience provided by WBL.

Today's high schools have several WBL pedagogies they could employ, with a variety of features. We describe several of these here:

- *Cooperative education* is a structured method of instruction whereby students alternate or coordinate their high school or postsecondary studies with a job in a field related to their academic or occupational objectives. Written training and evaluation plans guide the instruction, and students receive course credit for both their work and classroom experiences.
- *Job shadowing* is a career exploration activity for middle school and early high school students. Students follow an employee in a work setting for one or more days to learn about a particular occupation or industry.

- *Workplace mentoring* includes instruction in general workplace competencies, including development of positive work attitudes and employability skills. It includes broad instruction, to the extent practicable, in all aspects of the industry.
- *School-based enterprises* are enterprises in which goods or services are produced by students as part of their school program. Stern, Stone, Hopkins, McMillion, and Crain (1994) refined this definition by focusing on production of goods and services for sale to or use by people other than the students involved.
- *Internships* are situations where students work for a specified period of time for an employer to learn about a particular industry or occupation. Workplace activities may include sample tasks across different business units or may focus on special projects or on a single occupation. Internships may or may not include financial compensation.
- *Apprenticeships.* Registered apprenticeships are contracts between an employer and employee during which the paid worker, or apprentice, learns an occupation in a structured program. Many apprenticeships are jointly sponsored by employers and labor unions. The contract specifies increasing wage levels as the apprentice learns additional skills. Youth apprenticeships are typically multiyear combinations of school- and work-based learning in a specific occupational cluster designed to lead directly into either a related postsecondary program or a registered apprenticeship. Unlike registered apprenticeships, youth apprenticeships may or may not include financial compensation.

Obviously, all of these approaches require the cooperation of employers, and in the United States it has been difficult to find enough employers to make WBL available to large number of students (Lewis, 1997; Silverberg, Bergeron, Haimson, & Nagatashi, 1996). The School-to-Work Opportunities Act of 1994 (P.L. 103-239) provided federal funding to encourage increased employer involvement, but had limited impact. This act had been passed with a sunset provision, because it was intended to provide seed money that would lead to lasting, structural relationships between schools and employers. When the federal funding ended in 2001, most of initiatives dependent on this funding faded away. If WBL is to be made available to more students, it will require more than appeals to the goodwill of employers. Employers will have to see direct benefit to their firms from assuming an increased role in the preparation of young people for the workforce. We discuss the difficulties of encouraging employer involvement at greater length in Chapter 5.

Career-Technical Student Organizations

Almost all successful CTE programs have an active student organization. CTSOs are cocurricular with some activities taking place during regular classes and others outside of school hours. Because of their integration of rigorous academic and technical content and focus on preparation for a career, CTSOs complement many elements of the programs of study required under the 2006 reauthorization of the Perkins legislation.

FFA (formerly Future Farmers of America) was the first CTSO established in 1928, one decade after the Smith-Hughes Act began to provide federal support for vocational education in the public schools. Organizations for students with other career interests gradually emerged as preparation for additional occupations became eligible to receive federal funds. Today there are eight such organizations recognized by the U.S. Department of Education.[7]

The mission statement of FFA reflects the general goals of each: "The National FFA Organization is dedicated to making a positive difference in the lives of students by developing their potential for premier leadership, personal growth and career success through agricultural education" (National FFA, 2009). Local chapters are organized at the school level with a teacher from the occupational area acting as adviser. State-level advisers, usually from the CTE unit of the state department of education, assist schools in establishing local chapters and provide coordination for statewide events, such as skill competitions. National offices establish policy and guidelines and provide curriculum and other support to state and local chapters.

Zirkle and Connors (2003) attempted to identify sound research documenting the benefits claimed for CTSOs and found little. This literature review and discussions with national leaders of these organizations led staff of the National Research Center for CTE, when it was at the University of Minnesota, to identify four major activities of CTSOs that are likely to influence educational outcomes: leadership development, professional development, competitions, and community service. Alfeld et al. (2007) hypothesized that participation in these activities would affect students' achievement, transition to postsecondary education and training, and employability through a variety of moderating variables, such as achievement motivation, engagement in school, and career self-efficacy.

To determine the independent effect of CTSOs on these outcomes, Alfeld et al. (2007) designed a quasi-experimental study that compared three groups of students: those in CTE classes that included a CTSO, those in CTE classes without a CTSO, and those in general classes (non-CTE classes such as English and social studies). Because involvement in extracurricular activities, volunteering, and part-time work have also been found to affect the outcomes of interest, the study controlled for participation in these activities among all three groups of students. The study compared the groups on results from surveys administered at the beginning and end of the 2004–05 school year. Findings were based on the responses of 1,797 students who took the survey at both time points in order to gauge the effect of CTSOs over one academic year.

Students in classes with CTSOs scored higher on most of the moderating variables and outcomes at the beginning of the school year, but did not increase as much during the year as the CTE students who were not in CTSOs. At the end of the school year, the CTSO students remained higher on academic engagement, civic engagement, career self-efficacy, and employability skills, but the differences between them and the CTE-only students had narrowed. CTSO students were higher than the general (non-CTE) students only on career self-efficacy in the fall, and increased less than the general students during the school year.

These findings reflect the basic problem in research on CTSOs: self-selection. Students choose to join CTSOs or not to do so. When comparisons are made between CTSO participants and nonparticipants, any differences between them may be due to the personal characteristics that underlie the decision to join or not to join rather than due to participation in the CTSO itself. Indicators of self-selection in the Alfeld et al. (2007) study were the high pretest scores of the CTSO members on variables that CTSOs attempt to influence. Despite the absence of strong evidence documenting their effects, CTSOs remain popular with students and CTE educators and provide experiences that extend learning beyond the classroom.

SUMMARY

On average, CTE students score lower on standardized tests of academic achievement than students taking college preparatory curricula. For most of CTE's history these lower scores were accepted as a result of individual differences in academic ability that curriculum tracks were designed to accommodate. In the final decades of the 20th century, pressures grew to increase the performance of all students, and CTE is now expected to contribute to academic learning, especially as the academics are expressed in the workplace. Curriculum integration has the potential to enhance academic learning, but this potential has rarely been realized. The historic divisions between vocational and academic learning reflect what some scholars have referred to as the "grammar of schooling" or "core of educational practice"—the division of instruction into disciplines each delivered by an individual teacher. Integrated instruction does not fit this grammar/core and targeted efforts are necessary if it is to be achieved.

This chapter presents brief follow-ups of four sites that were identified in 2002 as making such special efforts. Three of these sites were found to be continuing, but one had been closed because the market demand for its students had declined. Three other efforts to enhance academic instruction in CTE courses, two at the local and one at the state level, are discussed. The chapter also summarizes the Math-in-CTE, Authentic Literacy, and Science in CTE studies that experimentally tested the effects of enhanced academic instruction in several occupational areas. These studies found meaningful, statistically significant differences on standardized tests of mathematics and reading comprehension between students who had received the enhanced instruction and those who had not. The results of the pilot study of Science-in-CTE found increases in science knowledge for all students except those in the lowest quartile on the pretest. These studies demonstrate that CTE can build academic skill alongside occupational and technical skills under specific conditions. Much of the success of these studies was attributed to the development of communities of practices that emerged among the teachers who delivered the experimental interventions. The chapter concludes with brief descriptions of WBL and CTSO, two pedagogies that provide opportunities for the kind of learning that is rarely experienced in a classroom and add value to the high school experience.

We have shown that CTE can increase student *engagement*, the likelihood of students completing high school. We have also shown that experimental studies have demonstrated the potential for CTE to increase traditional academic *achievement*. In the next chapter, we explore the research on CTE and student *transition* to postsecondary education and the workplace.

CHAPTER 5

Transitioning to Successful Adulthood

Even in an age of high-stakes testing, the real measures of a high school education come after students leave school, either through graduation or withdrawal. Are they prepared to successfully continue their education or to obtain rewarding employment? This is the essential dilemma American youth confront in the era of college and career readiness. As discussed in Chapter 2, the simple truth is that the nearly 3 decades of focus on sending all youth to college has produced a system that works reasonably well for less than half of those who start 9th grade.

From its origins at the beginning of the 20th century until its last 2 decades, CTE focused on preparing students for entry-level employment in occupations that require specialized skills below those usually obtained at the baccalaureate level. In Chapter 1, we discussed the emergence of the global economy and the frequent claim that a high school education is no longer sufficient to prepare the highly skilled workers our nation needs to compete in world markets (e.g., Achieve, 2004; National Association of Secondary School Principals, 2004; National Center on Education and the Economy, 2007). The association that represents CTE educators has, in effect, endorsed this position by publishing a position paper in which the first recommendation is "Establish postsecondary preparation and expectations for all" and the second is "Develop education systems that integrate all levels" (Association for Career and Technical Education, 2007, p. 1).

Since 1990, federal legislation for CTE has authorized the use of funds for Tech Prep programs that link secondary and postsecondary instruction and enable students to earn postsecondary credits while in high school. The 2006 reauthorization of federal CTE legislation (Perkins IV) requires all recipients of funds provided under this act to offer at least one program of study (POS) that includes 2 years of instruction at the secondary level that are articulated with 2 years at the postsecondary level. In this chapter, we review the evidence on the effectiveness of previous initiatives to link secondary and postsecondary CTE programs and identify changes that are needed to strengthen these linkages.

In addition to Tech Prep, there have been three other major initiatives to facilitate secondary-postsecondary transition: career cluster/pathways, youth apprenticeships, and dual enrollment courses. Studies have compared the outcomes of students who took part in these initiatives with similar students who did not on such measures as postsecondary enrollment, credits earned, and attainment of degrees or credentials. Often there were no statistically significant differences between participants and nonparticipants, and when significant differences were found, they were typically in the range of 4% to 5%. We summarize the studies that have produced these findings and assess their implications for the implementation of the POS required by the 2006 legislation. The National Research Center for Career and Technical Education (NRCCTE) is currently conducting three studies that are examining POS, and each of these is briefly described and their preliminary results presented.

PREVIOUS EFFORTS TO LINK SECONDARY CTE AND POSTSECONDARY EDUCATION[1]

The economic prospects of young people who do not continue their education after high school have been on a steady decline since at least the middle of the 1970s. *The Forgotten Half*, a report from the W. T. Grant Foundation Commission on Work, Family and Citizenship (1988), was instrumental in raising awareness of this decline. During the 1990s there were a number of policy responses, including the School-to-Work Opportunities Act, but the problem continues (Berlin, 2007; Halperin, 1998). In 2006, Perkins IV required high schools and postsecondary institutions that wanted to be eligible for the funds it authorized to cooperate in POS designed to encourage students to continue their education beyond high school. This requirement is new, but the components that POS must include are not, with the exception of the requirement of an industry credential (see below). Perkins IV specified that states were to submit plans on how they intended to implement its provisions, including a description of

A. the career and technical programs of study, which may be adopted by local educational agencies and postsecondary institutions to be offered as an option to students (and their parents as appropriate) when planning for and completing future coursework for career and technical content areas that
    i. incorporate secondary education and postsecondary education elements;
    ii. include coherent and rigorous content aligned with challenging academic standards and relevant career and technical

content in a coordinate, nonduplicative progression of courses
that align secondary education with postsecondary education
to adequately prepare students to succeed in postsecondary
education;

iii. may include the opportunity for secondary education students
to participate in dual or concurrent enrollment programs or
other ways to acquire postsecondary education credits; and

iv. lead to an industry-recognized credential or certificate at the
postsecondary level, or an associate or baccalaureate degree.
(P.L. 109-270. Sec. 122(c)(1)

Each of these components had been introduced into federal vocational
education legislation by the Tech Prep title of P.L. 101-392, Perkins II, which
was passed in 1990. Tech Prep had been proposed by Parnell in his 1985
book, *The Neglected Majority.* The "majority" Parnell identified consisted
of students in the middle two quartiles of academic ability, those who complete high school, but rarely obtain 4-year degrees. Tech Prep was designed
to serve these students by linking the last 2 years of high school with 2 years
of postsecondary education through articulation agreements. High school
graduates could earn postsecondary credits for courses they had studied in
high school by continuing their education at institutions that had signed the
agreements.

The major difference between Tech Prep and POS is that all recipients
of Perkins funds must offer at least one POS. Tech Prep was and remains
voluntary, but states may, if they choose, combine the funds provided under the Tech Prep title of Perkins IV with their basic state grants. The
language for POS also stresses rigorous content aligned with challenging academic standards and relevant career and technical content. The
adjectives "rigorous" and "challenging" do not appear in the Tech Prep
language.

The requirement for POS in Perkins IV represented congressional endorsement of a reorientation that CTE has undergone in the past quarter
century. From its start in 1917, the focus of high school vocational education was on equipping young people with the skills needed for entry-level
employment. In the 1970s the value of a high school diploma began to
decline. Berlin (2007) has examined why the economic growth enjoyed by
all sectors of society in the post–World War II era ended: "Unexpectedly,
the up-escalator economy ground to a halt after 1973. Output per worker
slowed to less than 1 percent a year, and wages and earnings fell" (p. 19).
When the economy recovered, those with a high school diploma or less
did not share in the growth. Shifts in the skills needed in the labor market
rewarded those with postsecondary training and the real, inflation-adjusted

wages of those whose education stopped with high school graduation actually dropped. Globalization, technological change, the offshoring of manufacturing jobs, and the decline of unions all contributed to this drop.

The convergence of the declining economic value of the high school diploma and calls for increased rigor in all of education caused CTE educators to examine their high school programs to determine if they remained appropriate in the emerging global economy. This rethinking of the purposes of secondary CTE resulted in efforts to broaden programs and to link secondary and postsecondary instruction. The broadening took the form of organizing related occupations by the types of products and services they produce into career clusters, such as manufacturing, health services, and architecture and construction. Within each cluster, the introductory courses provide instruction that is applicable across a range of occupations from those that can be entered directly after high school to those that require extensive postsecondary preparation. Career pathways link secondary and postsecondary instruction by providing guidance as to the knowledge and skills—both academic and technical—that must be acquired to prepare for occupations at varying levels within each career cluster. The background and rationale for these changes are presented in two position papers published by the Association for Career and Technical Education: *Reinventing the American High School for the 21st Century* (2006) and *Expanding Opportunities: Postsecondary Career and Technical Education and Preparing Tomorrow's Workforce* (2007).

Seen from the perspective of the changes during the past 2 decades, POS are not a new federal mandate imposed on the field. Instead, they represent an expansion of initiatives that have been in existence for several years. In the following section, we examine what is known about the effectiveness of these previous initiatives. Tech Prep, career pathways, and youth apprenticeships were all designed to have the four characteristics required of POS: secondary and postsecondary elements, alignment of academic and technical content, opportunities to earn postsecondary credit while in high school, and the goal of attaining a postsecondary degree or certificate. Studies that examined the implementation of these designs often found major discrepancies between what was intended and what was achieved (Hershey, Silverberg, Owens, & Hulsey, 1998; Silverberg et al., 1996). Even those programs that were implemented largely as intended, however, often fell short of producing the desired outcomes. The evidence we present in this section comes from programs that were studied because they were judged to be good examples of their type. They were programs that incorporated the features that Tech Prep, career pathways, and youth apprenticeships should have. We also review studies of the effects of dual/concurrent enrollment upon transition to and success in postsecondary education.

Tech Prep

A good Tech Prep program, one that incorporates all the components originally specified in Perkins II, is a POS. Bragg and her colleagues (2002) have assessed the effects of participating in good Tech Prep programs. Their study followed students in eight selected consortia from high school to college and into employment between January 1998 and December 2001. The eight consortia that were studied had begun planning their programs before or shortly after Tech Prep was authorized by Perkins II and were enrolling students at the secondary and postsecondary level by the mid- to late 1990s. The consortia were from urban, suburban, and rural locations and demonstrated a strong commitment to Tech Prep as a primary vehicle of educational change that in the judgment of state personnel and members of the study's advisory panel reflected preferred policies and practices. The programs were of high quality, but not so unusual as to be unrepresentative of other consortia.

To study the effects of participating in these consortia, Bragg and her colleagues selected a total of almost 4,600 students for follow-up, with roughly equivalent numbers of Tech Prep and nonparticipants in each group. A systematic random sampling procedure was employed within each group to ensure that the students in each were similar, based on high school academic performance as measured by cumulative grade point average (GPA) and/or class rank percentile (CRP) at the time of high school graduation. The sampling yielded groups that were similar on GPA, but family income and parental education were somewhat lower among the Tech Prep participants. Tech Prep participants had many of the characteristics that placed them at risk of noncompletion at the college level, including first-generation college enrollment and part-time enrollment combined with part-time or full-time work (Tinto, 1996). Transcripts were collected for the selected students and two follow-up surveys were conducted

Over 80% of the Tech Prep participants in six consortia attended 2-year colleges, and the percentages in the nonparticipant group were close to that or higher in five consortia. Enrollment of Tech Prep participants tended to exceed nonparticipants, but the differences were small, reaching statistical significant in only two sites. While many students enrolled at the college level, few earned sufficient credits to obtain a certificate or degree. Most enrollees were required to take developmental, noncredit courses. The study found that from 40% to nearly 80% of Tech Prep participants took some college-level course work, with a slightly wider range (nearly 30% to 76%) among nonparticipants. Relatively few who enrolled in 2-year colleges received degrees (AA, AS, or AAS) or certificates, regardless of Tech Prep status. By 3 to 4 years after high school graduation, the median percentage of students that earned some credential was only 10.5%. The percentage of students that completed postsecondary programs ranged from 8.5% to 19.0%. These results were consistent across sites for both study groups.

Stone and Aliaga (2003) analyzed data from the National Longitudinal Survey of Youth 1997 to determine the effects of Tech Prep on the academic achievement of young people who were in Grades 9 through 12 during the period from 1997 to 1999. These data are based on a nationally representative sample, but they rely upon students' self-reports of both the kinds of courses they took and their GPA. Regression analyses found no significant relationship between Tech Prep participation and GPA.

A Congressional mandated evaluation of Tech Prep (Hershey et al., 1998) had a formative rather than summative focus, but it also included case studies of 10 consortia selected because of the reputed quality of their programs. These case studies included follow-up interviews with 486 former Tech Prep students conducted approximately 18 months after they should have graduated from high school, but did not include similar non-Tech Prep participants against which the outcomes of the participants could be compared. Enrollment in postsecondary education or other types of formal occupational preparation from these 10 consortia was 61%, but only 15% reported that their programs awarded credits for the articulated courses they had taken in high school. Over one third (37%) of those attending community colleges had not started programs leading to degrees. They were taking developmental and general education courses.

These results were not encouraging, but the evaluation found evidence of implementation efforts that led them to provide a strong endorsement for the types of POS mandated by Perkins IV:

> The conclusions presented here are drawn from detailed examination of the *implementation* of Tech-Prep, not of its impact on students. Whether Tech-Prep, in any of its forms, improves student outcomes is a question that still remains to be addressed; this study was not designed to answer that question. However, our five-year evaluation suggests that prospects for Tech-Prep to change educational pathways and success of students in the ways framers of the Tech-Prep legislation anticipated will be enhanced if federal and state education agencies renew their emphasis on developing structured, focused programs of study with a strong career theme, meaningful integration between technical and academic curricula, and a close link between high school and postsecondary stages of the program. (Hershey et al., 1998, p. 130)

Career Pathways

At the same time Tech Prep consortia were being organized, other initiatives were being implemented to align high school preparation more closely with the changing needs of the labor force. One of these was the development of career clusters and career pathways. The traditional organization of occupational instruction at the secondary level was created by federal legislation. In 1917 the Smith-Hughes Act limited the kinds of occupations eligible for federal funding to those in agriculture, trades and industry, and home economics, which evolved into family and consumer science. Later legislation expanded these categories to include distributive/marketing, health, and business occupations. For most of the 20th century, secondary vocational education was delivered within this structure and aimed primarily at teaching the skills needed for entry into occupations. In the last 2 decades of the century, however, changes in the skills needed for success in the labor market caused an increased emphasis on academics and preparing students to continue their occupational preparation at the postsecondary level. This emphasis led to efforts to more closely align academic and technical instruction and secondary and postsecondary education. Career clusters and career pathways emerged from these efforts.

Career clusters have evolved into the primary way of organizing secondary occupational instruction, but their evolution was anything but smooth. Ruffing (2006) wrote a short history based on interviews with individuals who had played key roles in the projects that led to the adoption of the 16 current clusters. As she described these events, in the 1990s the U.S. Department of Labor and the U.S. Department of Education recognized the overlap in the projects they had funded to develop occupational skill standards and the need for a common system of classification. The two departments agreed to jointly fund the Building Linkages project that contracted with three consortia to conduct pilot projects in retail and banking, health, and manufacturing. In each of these sectors, the consortia examined existing academic and technical standards and attempted to develop integration models. In two of the sectors—health and manufacturing—these efforts were successful and laid the foundation for career pathways that specified the academic foundations and technical skills that must be acquired to enter occupations at different levels within these sectors. The retail and banking sector was terminated after it was determined that the sector was too narrow and did not provide sufficient opportunities for high-wage employment.

After one year, the U.S. Department of Education assumed responsibility for funding and oversight of the efforts that had been started by the Building Linkages project. The Office of Vocational and Adult Education (OVAE) selected three additional sectors for development: information technology; transportation, distribution, and logistics; and arts, audio/video technology, and communication. By 1999 the two clusters that had emerged from the first pilot projects and the three new clusters were deemed sufficiently developed for OVAE to adopt a classification system consisting of the 16 clusters presented in Chapter 1.

To develop the remaining 11 clusters, OVAE issued a request for proposals and selected the National Association of State Directors of Career Technical Education Consortium (NASDCTEc) as the successful bidder. When the grant was awarded, states within the consortium volunteered to develop the clusters in which they had particular interest and expertise. The tasks carried out by the states were identical across clusters: convene national advisory committees, define their specific cluster, identify the skills and knowledge needed for occupations at various levels within their clusters, create pathways, and validate their work. The project director and four consortium coordinators supported and monitored the work of the separate states to ensure consistency and quality. The NASDCTEc board of directors and a national advisory consortium with representatives from all major stakeholders provided oversight. In September 2002 the tasks listed above had been accomplished and the resources for the 16 clusters were made available for adoption.

The original contract with NASDCTEc called for a second phase in which curriculum, assessments, and certifications would be developed. OVAE decided not to fund this second phase and shifted the funds that had been budgeted to the College Career Transitions Initiative, which will be described below. NASDCTEc decided to continue the work that had started under the second phase by establishing the States' Career Clusters Initiative. With initial funding from the consortium and states, this Initiative has become self-sustaining from the sale of its products and revenue from its annual Career Clusters Institute. In 2006 OVAE provided additional funding to improve the Initiative's products and to develop additional pathways for the 16 clusters.

In the summer of 2007 NASDCTEc surveyed its members on the implementation of career clusters and POS. Questionnaires were returned by 47 states, the District of Columbia, Puerto Rico, and Guam. Of these 50 respondents, 26 or more provide programs within 15 of the 16 career clusters, and 36 or more provide programs in the most popular 7 clusters. Many states reported working to ensure that the pathways being offered within these clusters meet the definition of POS set forth in Perkins IV.

The College and Career Transitions Initiative (CCTI), an OVAE-funded project administered by the League for Innovation in the Community College, worked with community colleges to encourage career pathways within career clusters. CCTI began in 2002 by inviting community colleges to submit proposals describing how they would develop partnerships with high schools and employers to design and implement career pathways. The definition of career pathway adopted by CCTI was developed in cooperation with the National Clearinghouse for Career Pathways at CORD and other interested parties:

> A Career Pathway is a coherent, articulated sequence of rigorous academic and career courses, commencing in the 9th grade and leading to an associate degree, and/or an industry-recognized certificate or licensure, and/or a baccalaureate degree and beyond. A Career Pathway is developed, implemented, and maintained in partnership among secondary and postsecondary education, business, and employers. Career Pathways are available to all students, including adult learners, and are designed to lead to rewarding careers. (Hull, 2004, p. 6)

This definition differed from traditional Tech Prep by starting the pathways in the 9th grade and placing more emphasis on rigor comparable to that in a college preparatory curriculum.

From among the community colleges that responded to its request for proposals, CCTI initially selected 15 to receive funding to create pathways that would serve as models for other institutions. The initial experiences in developing partnerships and enrolling students in the 15 original colleges were positive and CCTI decided to open its network to any community college in North America that wanted to adopt its goals and draw upon its resources. When accessed on July 14, 2011, the CCTI website (www.league. org/league/projects/ccti/nclist.cfm) continued to list 174 colleges as members. Almost 2 years previously, on October 29, 2009, however, Laurance Warford, who had directed CCTI, indicated in a personal communication that when the federal funding of the network ended, the League for Innovation no longer had staff to provide support for the network.

Kempner and Warford (2009) presented data on the experiences of the original 15 community colleges in the CCTI network. In 2004 the 40 high schools that had joined in partnerships with the 15 colleges enrolled 2,853 students in 15 different pathways based on 5 separate career clusters. By 2007 the number of high schools had doubled, the number of students had increased to 22,178, and they were following 176 pathways based on the 16 OVAE clusters. The original 15 CCTI colleges provided yearly outcome data on 1,124 students who participated in pathways, graduated from high school in the spring of 2004 through 2007, and enrolled in these colleges in the fall of their graduation years. Kempner and Warford reported the national average for enrollment in community colleges directly from high school at 29%, the same as that for CCTI. This CCTI percentage, it should be noted, is based on graduates who enrolled in the same pathways they had studied in high school and in the community colleges that were the postsecondary partners in those pathways. The national figure is for *any* community college enrollment and is derived from two longitudinal studies conducted by the National Center for Education Statistics. Kempner and Warford reported remediation rates for students following CCTI pathways into the original 15 community colleges were 40% for mathematics, 27% for English, and 25% for reading. They also cited sources documenting that nationally about two thirds of students entering community colleges require remediation in these subjects. These differences imply that the CCTI stress on rigorous academics and career courses may reduce the need for remediation at the postsecondary level.

To find additional evidence of the impact of career pathways, we conducted an ERIC search (http://www.eric.ed.gov/) using the keywords "career," "pathways," and "outcomes" for documents published in 1990 or later. This combination yielded 82 hits, but only a handful presented any evidence on the outcomes of career pathways. Three that reported some data were conducted by the NRCCTE. We shall discuss each of these and then summarize the three others we identified.

In the discussion of Tech Prep, we noted that Stone and Aliaga (2003) analyzed data from the National Longitudinal Survey of Youth 1997 to identify students who had participated in different types of CTE programs. Regression analyses did not find Tech Prep participation to be related to high school GPA, but career pathways (also referred to as "career majors" in the data collection) were. Students' reports of enrollment in career pathways/majors had a significant positive relationship with final 12th-grade GPAs, and this relationship remained significant when measures of student characteristics, including their 8th-grade GPAs, were added to the equation. In the full equation, career pathways had a beta weight (the relationship with GPA holding other variables in the equation constant) of .079 compared to a beta of .401 for 8th-grade GPA.

Castellano and her colleagues (2007) studied three selected high schools that were engaged in comprehensive school reform based on one of three models: career academies, High Schools That Work, or career pathways. All students at the third high school followed career pathways, and many whose pathways included CTE courses took them at a regional center that served several districts. The experiences of these students were compared to those of students in a similar comprehensive high school that had not adopted career pathways. Many students at the comparison school studying CTE courses took them at a different skill center from the pathway students.

The career pathways model did not improve graduation rates, but the pathway graduates outperformed their nonpathway counterparts on many measures of transition to postsecondary education. More pathway students had post-high-school plans than nonpathway students, and equal numbers were accepted to 4-year universities. Pathway graduates who attended the main community college serving their area outperformed their comparison group counterparts. For each academic subject, fewer pathway than non-pathway students were required to take remedial courses; however, 60% still needed remediation. More pathway students participated in Tech Prep than did their counterparts, and at the end of 1 year of college, pathway students had earned significantly more credits.

A study by Lekes et al. (2007) reversed the sample selection from the secondary to the postsecondary level. This study chose one community college that had been identified by the National Dissemination Center for Career and Technical Education as having exemplary transitional programs and a second community college that had received a Star of Education award from the NASDCTEc. At the first college, two health career pathways (Emergency Medical Technician and Patient Care Assistant) were examined, and at the second the focus was on pathways for Information Technology/Computer Information Science (IT/CIS). For the secondary component of the study, students following these pathways were matched with similar nonpartici-pants from their same schools. The high schools that were studied had been selected so that they varied in the degree to which they were engaged in career pathways. The postsecondary component relied primarily on analysis of transcript data from the second community college.

Like the Bragg et al. (2002) Tech Prep study, Lekes and her colleagues (2007) studied transition initiatives that were recognized as among the best to be found. Their findings also parallel Bragg et al. (2002) in that few differences were found between the students who had participated in pathways and those in comparison groups who had not. The pathway students were more likely than nonparticipants to have experienced the components recommended for pathways, such as contextualized learning, mentoring, and work-based learning. In most comparisons, however, these experiences were not associated with differences between pathway and nonpathway students in outcomes such as graduation, GPAs, or postsecondary enrollment. The pathway students did have an advantage in postsecondary credits earned, in part because of the dual credit courses they had taken in high school. This advantage appears to have increased their chances of earning a certificate or degree: 21.3% in the IT/CIS pathway earned a credential compared to 17.2% for the nonpathway students.

In our search, we identified three other published reports on career pathways that included any information on outcomes. Rudy and Rudy (2001) compared the academic performance of students in Berrien County, Michigan, prior to and after pathways in six broad career areas were implemented for all students. Over a 5-year period, they found improvement on these measures: high school attendance rates, mean high school GPA, scores on statewide testing, enrollment in dual credit courses, and the percentage of graduates enrolling in postsecondary education. These were all county-wide indicators, and no data were available from a comparison group for the same period.

Another report was from the Austin (Texas) Independent School District (Oswald, 2002), which offers 29 career pathways in 8 career clusters. This report classified students who took any CTE—about 60% of all high school students in the district—into three groups:

- *Elective*—those who took an incidental CTE course
- *Coherent*—those who took a sequence of CTE courses focused on developing occupational skills and knowledge within a given career pathway
- *Tech Prep*—those who met the coherent definition given above in pathways that include state-approved articulation agreement (college credit) courses

Comparisons were made across these three groups and with high school students who took no CTE courses. The comparisons are less precise than desired because of difficulties in classifying the CTE students. The plans and the courses students take change as they progress through high school, and it may not be possible to classify them until they have completed all their courses. The comparisons that were possible yielded a mixed pattern. Those classified as Coherent had the lowest attendance rates, while those classified as Tech Prep had the highest. Students in all three groups were more likely to pass statewide tests than those without any CTE courses, but those in the Coherent group had to take the test more times than those in other groups in order to pass all sections. Students taking CTE courses were more likely than non-CTE students to earn adequate credits to move to the next grade level. In the 9th grade, however, students classified as Coherent were the least likely of the four groups to earn enough credits to be promoted to the 10th grade.

The third study (McCharen, 2008) examined the extent to which students in Oklahoma who had studied health careers in high school continued on pathways within that cluster to obtain certification or 2- or 4-year degrees. The study used archival data to track 4,754 students who completed high school health programs in Oklahoma's 29 career-technology centers during the 2000–01 to 2004–05 school years. The records of these same 29 centers were searched to find how many of these 4,754 students enrolled in and completed postsecondary certificate programs in health care. The same search was made of the records of the Oklahoma State Regents for students who continued into 2- or 4-year degree programs. The tracking found that 19% of the high school completers continued in programs at the 29 centers leading to certification in a health care field, and over three fourths (78%) of those who started these programs completed them. Over half (54%) of the 4,754 students enrolled in health-related 2- or 4-year degree programs, but when the Regents records were searched, only 2% of the enrollees had completed their programs. Information was not reported on the percentage that was still enrolled.

The most recent evidence on the effect of CTE participation on transition to postsecondary education comes from unpublished analyses being conducted at the NRCCTE (Jeffrey Valentine, personal communication, June 30, 2011). These analyses were noted in Chapter 3 regarding the relationship between CTE participation and graduation from high school. The researchers have assembled the best available studies of the effects of CTE on educational and labor market outcomes. Meta-analyses of these studies suggest strong, positive relationships. Contrary to much conventional wisdom, participation in CTE appears to have a large, statistically significant effect on enrollment in postsecondary education as well as earnings after high school.

Obviously, all of these studies have many limitations. CTE independent of career pathways or Programs of Study adds value to the high school experience of participants. To the degree that POS are the same as career pathways, however, the collective results of the studies imply that POS have a definite potential to impact achievement and transition. We shall examine this potential in a later section in which we discuss the challenges to implementation of POS.

Youth Apprenticeships

The 1990s saw a surge of interest in youth apprenticeships as a means of facilitating the transition between school and work. The German dual system of combining paid employment and academic studies linked to the employment was seen as a model with much potential for the United States. Today, youth apprenticeships have largely faded from the scene. Why did youth apprenticeships generate so much interest, and why did they fade so rapidly?

Stephen Hamilton and his wife, Mary Agnes Hamilton, were key players in generating the interest shown in youth apprenticeships during the 1990s. Stephen Hamilton became a college professor after having taught in a vocational education high school. To overcome the transition problems experienced by students who do not continue their education after high school and the inherent limitations of school-based occupational training, Hamilton (1990) proposed that elements of the German dual system be adopted. He not only proposed a model, he and his wife tested it in Broome

County, New York (Hamilton & Hamilton, 1993). The model had all the components of POS. It articulated the last 2 years of high school with 2 years of postsecondary education. It had rigorous academic and technical standards and integrated academic and technical content. The goals of the Hamiltons' youth apprenticeships were for students to earn associate degrees and nationally recognized skill certificates once the program became registered with the New York State Department of Labor. The Hamilton model differed from POS, however, in that it placed the responsibility for skill training on employers.

The students in the Hamiltons' program were not registered apprentices. Registration requires written contracts between apprentices and sponsors (unions or employers), which are filed with the Office of Apprenticeship, U.S. Department of Labor. Relatively few skilled workers receive their training as registered apprentices. The U.S. Department of Labor (2008) reported that in 2007 there were 468,108 apprentices receiving registered training. In response to the criticism that "apprenticeship" should be reserved to registered apprentices, the Hamiltons responded as follows:

> Our vision of youth apprenticeships is wholly consistent with the Federal Committee on Apprenticeship's definition, but it applies to occupations that are not now apprenticeable and incorporates groups that are underrepresented in traditional programs. It also makes stronger connections between school and work than does traditional U.S. apprenticeship. Completion of most traditional apprenticeships is based on hours served whereas youth apprentices earn their credentials by demonstrating the competencies that they have acquired. (Hamilton & Hamilton, 1993, p. 2)

The Hamilton model aligned well with the political climate of the 1990s. In the year before his election to the presidency, Bill Clinton (1991) wrote an article for the *Vocational Education Journal*, the primary publication of the American Vocational Association (now the Association for Career and Technical Education), in which he described the advantages of apprenticeship and endorsed their expansion. In his initial State of the Union address, Clinton proposed a federal initiative to encourage youth apprenticeships.

As interest in youth apprenticeships grew, the W. T. Grant Foundation asked six leading scholars, including the Hamiltons, to prepare papers that could serve as a conceptual foundation to guide future efforts (Rosenbaum et al., 1992). Earlier, this foundation had convened the Commission on Work, Family and Citizenship to examine the declining employment opportunities being experienced by young people who did not continue their education beyond high school. The 1988 report of this commission, *The Forgotten Half*, recommended an expansion of apprenticeships and did much to create the climate that was so receptive to youth apprenticeships.

Rosenbaum and his coauthors (1992) saw the potential of youth apprenticeships to address many of the problems related to the transition from education to employment, but they also recognized the difficulties of large-scale adoption. The potential lies in demonstrating to young people the relevance of what they study in school, thereby increasing motivation and the learning of both academic and technical skills. Apprenticeships can also socialize young people to the realities of the workplace by requiring the performance of tasks that have economic consequences. For these benefits to accrue, however, the authors discussed the many challenges that must be met if schools and employers are to work together. The most significant of these is encouraging employers to assume a greatly expanded role in training young people. When such employers are identified, students must be recruited and matched with employers, teachers and workplace mentors must be trained and given time to work together to create and modify curriculum for both for the classroom and the workplace, and school and work schedules must be aligned.

In 1994 the School-to-Work Opportunities Act (P.L. 103-239) was passed to bring about systemic changes that would ease the transition to which its title refers. Its primary strategy was to encourage the involvement of employers in the planning and delivery of instruction. The act called for school-based learning, work-based learning, and connecting activities. Youth apprenticeships were a perfect fit with this legislation, and the act provided funding for many state and local efforts to establish programs.

Youth apprenticeships even reached the level of scholarly debate in *Educational Researcher*, the flagship publication of the American Educational Research Association and a journal that rarely concerns itself with the role of education in preparing young people for careers. In 1993, however, it devoted most of one issue to an article by Thomas Bailey (1993a), the director of the Institute on Education and the Economy, Columbia University; a rejoinder from Stephen Hamilton (1993); and a response to Hamilton by Bailey (1993b). Bailey (1993a) doubted if youth apprenticeships would ever enroll a significant number of young people. He cited, as among the reasons for his pessimism, the high job mobility of young people. Most are in the exploratory stage of their career development and frequently change jobs as they seek the best match for their interests and abilities.[2] This mobility makes employers reluctant to offer serious training to those in their late adolescence and early twenties. Bailey also questioned the pedagogy of work-based learning. Such learning is often job- and even employer-specific and does not teach skills applicable in a range of settings. His third major concern was the likely inequities in the availability of apprenticeships. There are inequities in the educational opportunities available to minorities and the poor, but these are less severe than the inequities in employment opportunities.

In his rejoinder, Hamilton (1993) argued that while young people in the United States have high rates of job mobility, the same is not true of their counterparts in countries that have extensive apprenticeship systems. In Hamilton's view, the labor market "floundering" experienced by young people who do not continue their education after high school is the result of the disconnect between education and employment. Frequent job changes are due to the lack of true career opportunities, not the inability of young people to make career commitments. Hamilton acknowledged that employers train only to the degree that it is in their own self-interest. The changes that are occurring in the nature of the work, Hamilton contended, will redefine self-interest. The need for highly skilled, flexible workers will make employers willing to offer apprenticeships.

Bailey (1993b) concluded the exchange by recommending that work-based learning be incorporated into the broad educational reforms that were started by *A Nation at Risk* (National Commission on Excellence in Education, 1983). This would require greater employer involvement in education, but still keep the primary responsibility with the schools. This approach became federal law with the passage of the School-to-Work Opportunities Act of 1994.

Even with broad political support and start-up funding from the School-to-Work Opportunities Act, however, Bailey's doubts about the widespread adoption of youth apprenticeships proved prescient. Some of the programs begun during the 1990s, including the one started by the Hamiltons, continue, but they enroll few students. During the 4 years that the Hamiltons directed the program, it enrolled a total of 100 students (Hamilton & Hamilton, 1999). That program continues now as one of the options offered by the Broome-Tioga Counties Bureau of Cooperative Educational Services, a career center that provides skill-training programs for 15 school districts. Enrollment in the youth apprenticeships offered by this center for the 2008–09 school year was 32 (S. Watkins, personal communication, July 15, 2009).

What is striking about the literature on youth apprenticeships is the absence of any studies that compare the achievement and postsecondary experiences of students who participated in apprenticeships to those who did not. After all the interest and investment following their emergence in the 1990s, most youth apprenticeship initiatives faded away. The closest approximation we found to an outcome evaluation was a study by Schug and Western (1999) in Wisconsin. The results of this study are of special interest because Wisconsin was a national leader in the implementation of youth apprenticeships. Schug and Western found that between 1992 and the 1996–97 school year, only 1,150 students had participated in apprenticeships and only 347 had completed them. These 347 represented about one tenth of 1% of the number of students in Wisconsin high schools during the 1994–95 school year.

While we found no outcome evaluations of youth apprenticeships, we found an extended formative evaluation that identified the main problems involved in establishing youth apprenticeship programs (Silverberg et al., 1996). In 1990, as the interest in youth apprenticeships began to build, the U.S. Department of Labor funded six demonstration projects. In 1992 it extended grants for 5 of these 6 and issued 10 more. Data on the implementation of these 15 programs were collected for more than 4 years. These data showed that the amount of work-based leaning varied widely across the 15 sites. Some provided only job shadowing, while others provided 2 full days per week at the work site. Only 3 came near the goal of evenly dividing the time spent in school-based and work-based learning.

Despite the variability in their work-site exposure, most students who participated in youth apprenticeships were positive about their experiences. From interviews and focus groups, the evaluators identified three categories of favorable comments made by the participants: project-based learning, program requirements, and premium workplace experience. Under project-based learning were comments about learning in the context of job requirements, the direct relevance of mathematics, working in groups, and problem solving. All of these were much preferred to the traditional academic classroom. Students saw the requirements for entering and staying in the apprenticeships—earning a specified GPA and maintaining high rates of attendance—as motivating them to work harder in school. The comments classified as premium workplace experiences included the skills students reported learning, which they perceived as giving them an advantage in the labor market. Those who worked for well-known companies thought this would add value to their resumes. A study of the attitudes of youth apprentices in Wisconsin yielded very similar findings (Scribner & Wakelyn, 1998).

Even though the students who participated in the apprenticeships perceived them favorably, the evaluators reported that the programs had difficulty recruiting both students and employers. These are the five major implementation challenges that the study identified:

- Recruitment of students
- Recruitment of employers
- Changing how students learn at school
- Ensuring students are learning on the job
- Reducing costs (Silverberg et al., 1996, p. 16)

Most programs were unable to meet these challenges to the degree that youth apprenticeships became available for large numbers of students. For all but a few, youth apprenticeship is an initiative whose time came and went. It required too much change both by schools and by employers. It was hard to recruit students and even harder to recruit employers who were willing to go beyond minimal types of work-based learning such as site tours and job shadowing.

School-to-Work

The School-to Work Opportunities Act (STWOA) of 1994 did much more than provide support for youth apprenticeship. This legislation had very ambitious goals that, if they had been achieved, would have caused major structural changes in education, especially at the secondary level, and in the relationships between schools and employers. Among the purposes of the act were the following goals:

- Offer opportunities for all students to participate in a performance-based education and training program that will
    i.   enable the students to earn portable credentials;
    ii. prepare the students for first jobs in high-skill, high-wage careers; and
    iii. increase their opportunities for further education, including education in a 4-year college or university;
- Facilitate the creation of a universal, high-quality school-to-work transition system that enables youths in the United States to identify and navigate paths to productive and progressively more rewarding roles in the workplace;
- Utilize workplaces as active learning environments in the educational process by making employers joint partners with educators in providing opportunities for all students to participate in high-quality, work-based learning experiences. (P.L. 103-239 Sec. 3(a) (1), (2), and (3))

While the act set ambitious goals, it provided relatively little funding to achieve them: $300 million for the 1995 fiscal year and "such sums as may be necessary" for each fiscal year 1996 through 1999. The act refers to the federal funds as "venture capital" meant to encourage the development of state and local systems of educational institutions and employers that would receive future funding from multiple sources. To reinforce the temporary nature of the funding, the act included a sunset provision (Section 802) that scheduled its own expiration in 2001.

Hughes et al. (2001) synthesized 132 studies that examined the implementation and effects of initiatives funded by the STWOA. They concluded that on most measures of school engagement, career development, and educational plans and aspirations, these initiatives were achieving their objectives. Students who participated in school-to-work took challenging courses and maintained their grades, remained in school, and were prepared for college. The jobs held by school-to-work participants were different and of a higher quality than those they would have normally obtained. School-to-work helped students prepare for the world of work, plan for the future, and work toward their goals. Employers were satisfied with the work of their student employees and reported their firms benefited from hiring them.

Despite these positive results, STWOA did not create self-sustaining systems capable of providing work-based learning for large numbers of students. When federal funding ended, most of the programs supported by these funds ended also. The act never produced the systemic change envisioned in its language. Even at its peak, relatively few students were involved, and the overarching purpose of the act, connecting school-based learning with work-based learning, rarely occurred. From its inception, STWOA had been the target of attacks from conservative critics who claimed it was an attempt to produce compliant workers who would be willing to accept assignments to positions in a planned economy (e.g., Schlafly, 1997). This opposition and the focus on high-stakes testing as the crucial measure of educational effectiveness undermined support for a broadened concept of how a high school should function and what it should accomplish.

EARNING POSTSECONDARY CREDITS WHILE IN HIGH SCHOOL

Perkins IV states that POS "may include the opportunity for secondary education students to participate in dual or concurrent enrollment programs or other ways to acquire postsecondary education credits" (Sec 122 (c)(1)(A) (iii)). This language encourages but does not require POS to include such opportunities. It reflects a growing interest in expanding dual enrollment beyond its traditional function of providing challenging educational experiences for high-achieving students. Dual enrollment is seen as a means of both increasing the efficiency of education by reducing the time and cost of obtaining postsecondary degrees and also increasing the rigor of high school instruction, thereby reducing the need for postsecondary remediation. Reindl (2006) discussed the tensions inherent in this expansion in his summary of a 2006 conference that addressed the broad issues of "accelerated learning." Krueger (2006) provided a synthesis of the evidence on the extent and effectiveness of dual/concurrent enrollment.

In this section, we focus on only one of the many issues related to dual enrollment: Does acquiring postsecondary credits in high school facilitate secondary to postsecondary transitions? We address only dual, concurrent enrollment courses, not Advanced Placement (AP) and International Baccalaureate (IB) courses. The full IB curriculum and 35 of the 37 AP courses are academic and designed as college-level courses for high school students, not actual college courses. We could find no studies that addressed the participation of CTE students in such courses. We first examine studies of dual enrollment/credits for CTE students, in general, and then the more structured approach of middle/early college high schools in more depth.

Dual Enrollment

Waits, Setzer, and Lewis (2005) reported that during the 2002–03 school year, 71% of public high schools offered courses in which students could simultaneously earn both high school and college credit. Almost all (92%) of these schools offered dual credit academic courses and half (51%) offered dual credit CTE courses. While dual credit courses were available in a majority of high schools, students taking these courses represented only 8% of the total high school enrollment during the 2002–03 school year.[3] Students taking CTE courses made up 36% of all dual credit students or 3.1% of total high school enrollment. These are the most recent national data available, but the growing interest in dual enrollment, as reflected in the conference reported by Reindl (2006), suggests that current figures are probably higher.

Dual credit courses vary on several dimensions beyond their content. Students may take individual (cafeteria-style) courses or defined sequences, which may be taught by high school or college faculty. The courses may be offered in high schools or on college campuses, and may enroll only high school or both high school and college students. The courses may be targeted to high-achieving or underserved students. Questions have been raised concerning the level of the courses: How qualified are the high school instructors who teach most of these courses as adjunct college faculty? Are the courses really at a postsecondary level or are they "adjusted" to accommodate high school students (Dougan, 2005)? With such variability in delivery, it is difficult to estimate the effect of earning dual credits on secondary to postsecondary transition, but there have been attempts to do so. One of the more rigorous of these was conducted by the Community College Research Center with funding from the NRCCTE (Karp, Calcagno, Hughes, Jeong, & Bailey, 2007). We present the method and findings of this research in some detail.

Karp et al. (2007) analyzed student records from Florida and from the City University of New York (CUNY). The Florida records were for 299,685 students who should have graduated during the 2000–01 and 2001–02 school years. The records included data on courses taken in high school and college, dual enrollment courses and grades, final high school

GPA and semester averages in college, and demographic information including age, gender, race/ethnicity, English language proficiency, and citizenship. The researchers added information on high school and neighborhood characteristics from the U.S. Department of Education Common Core of Data and the 2000 Census. CTE students were defined as those who took three or more courses that provided preparation for employment in a given occupational area. The data in New York were for 2,303 students who graduated from one of the city's 19 vocational high schools and enrolled in any of the CUNY community or 4-year colleges in 2001 or 2002. Information on these students included dual enrollment courses and grades, high school grades, credits and grades earned for all CUNY courses attempted, and demographic, high school, and neighborhood characteristics. The manner in which the New York sample was defined excluded records for non-CTE students.

The data from Florida yielded a number of advantages associated with earning dual credits while in high school. Logistic regressions that controlled for measured student, high school, and neighborhood characteristics yielded increased probabilities for dual credit students on the following outcomes:

- Graduating from high school: 4.3% increased likelihood for the full sample, 1% for CTE students
- Enrolling in postsecondary education: 16.8% increased likelihood for the full sample, 18.1% for CTE students
- Enrolling in a 4-year college: 7.7% increased likelihood for the full sample, 8.6% for CTE students
- Enrolling full-time: 4.5% increased likelihood for the full sample, 4.7% for CTE students
- Persisting to the second semester: 4.5% increased likelihood for the full sample, 4.2% for CTE students
- Persisting to the second year: 5.4% increased likelihood for the full sample, 5.2% for CTE students

Ordinary least squares (using the same independent variables as the logistic regressions) was used to estimate the effect of dual enrollment on the continuous variables GPA and total credits earned at the postsecondary level. These analyses yielded the following net increases associated with dual enrollment:

- First year GPA: .22 for the full sample, .26 for CTE students
- Second year GPA: .21 for the full sample, .26 for CTE students
- Cumulative GPA: .20 the full sample, .24 for CTE students
- Total credits earned: 15.2 for the full sample; 15.2 for CTE students

The results for the full sample are based on more than 127,000 records (students who enrolled in public colleges in Florida) and the results for CTE students are based on more than 18,000. These large numbers reduce the error estimates and thus increase the chances of finding significant relationships in the data.

The CUNY data had far fewer student records—2,303—and all of these students had enrolled in one of the colleges of the CUNY system. As a result, it was not possible to test the effect of dual enrollment on high school graduation or postsecondary enrollment. The advantage of the CUNY data is that all of the dual enrollment courses were through College Now, a cooperative program of CUNY and the New York City public schools. College Now has standardized eligibility and application procedures and monitors curriculum and instruction. This coordination across high schools reduces the variability in dual enrollment experiences, thereby enhancing, in the language of research methodology, the "fidelity of the intervention."

Among the CTE graduates who enrolled in one of the CUNY colleges, those who had taken College Now dual enrollment courses differed from those who had not in the following ways:

- 9.7% more likely to pursue a bachelor's degree
- .13 higher GPA in their first semester in college
- 10.65 more credits earned, 3.5 years after enrolling

Although several of the CUNY analyses did not reach statistical significance, the effects estimates were all in the expected directions. If the number of student records had been as large as in Florida, many of these may have reached accepted levels of significance. The CUNY data did not find the relationships with persistence in college or the continuing effect upon GPA as found in Florida, but they did yield intensity effects. CUNY students who took two or more dual enrollment courses had higher first- and fourth-semester GPAs and earned significantly more credits than those who took only one course. The Florida data had also been analyzed for intensity effects, with a variable that ranged from one to five or more courses, but had not yielded significant relationships.

Kotamraju (2005) also analyzed state-level data to determine the relationship between participating in the Minnesota dual enrollment program and GPA at the postsecondary level. Kotamraju selected students who met the following criteria: took dual enrollment courses during the 1999–2000 or 2000–01 school years, graduated in the spring of 2001, and enrolled as full-time students in the same 2-year colleges that had offered the courses in which they had taken their dual enrollment courses anytime between the fall of 2001 and the spring of 2004. All of these colleges were part of the Minnesota State Colleges and Universities System. When these students were identified, they were matched with similar students who had also graduated in 2001 and entered these 2-year colleges during the same time period. The matching was based on gender, ethnicity, and high school cumulative GPA. The final sample included 3,639 students, of whom 461 had taken dual enrollment courses. Those who had taken such courses were classified into those who had taken only Liberal and General Study courses (45%); those who had taken only CTE courses (13%); and those who had taken both (43%). The restrictive criteria used by Kotamraju to define his sample resulted in students with similar characteristics who had similar exposure to postsecondary education but entered with or without having experienced dual enrollment.

During the 3 years of postsecondary experience that Kotamraju examined, students who had taken dual enrollment courses in high school had a cumulative mean GPA of 2.92 compared to 2.53 among those who had no dual enrollment. Students who took any CTE courses at the postsecondary level were classified as "participants," "concentrators," and "completers."[4] Only among participants was there a statistically significant difference in GPA between those who had taken dual enrollment courses—2.55—and those who had not—1.88. Kotamraju concluded that the dual enrollment courses appear to give students a head start on succeeding in college courses, but that this effect declines as postsecondary exposure increases.

The overall results from these two studies, the most rigorous we were able to find, are positive. Using the best methods, short of random assignment of students, to assess impact, it appears that dual enrollment is achieving many of its objectives. Unfortunately, these methods cannot control for the self-selection of students into dual enrollment courses. These courses are more demanding than typical high school courses and students choosing this extra work are, by definition, different from their classmates. The largest effect associated with dual enrollment in the Florida analyses was for entry into postsecondary education: 16.8% for the full sample, 18.1% for CTE students. These effect estimates are three to four times as large as any of the others, except enrollment in a 4-year college. These results strongly imply that students who had firm plans for continuing their education were more likely to take dual enrollment courses. The researchers who conducted these studies were fully aware of these problems, as reflected in the following caution:

> It is important to recognize that other unmeasured factors, such as student motivation or parental encouragement and support, are likely correlated with participation in dual enrollment and are also likely to generate a positive effect. By not controlling for important factors affecting a student's decision to participate

in dual enrollment, it is possible that our models may generate what appear to be positive impacts when in fact there are no such impacts or there are negative impacts. (Karp et al., 2007, p. 20)

Self-selection and admission practices are also inherent problems when attempting to estimate the effects of middle/early colleges, to which we now turn.

Middle/Early College High Schools

Middle/early colleges are, at their core, intensive dual enrollment programs targeted to students who are underserved and often deemed "at risk" in the traditional high school. Some middle college programs are located in technical colleges such as the programs in Washtenaw Technical College in Michigan, Ozarks Technical Community College in Missouri or Durham Technical Community College in North Carolina. Following the traditional middle college high school model, students combine high school and college work but also have the opportunity to begin advanced work in technical and occupational education. The available research literature, however, does not distinguish between traditional middle college high schools and those with an occupational focus. We found no examples of "early college" programs with a CTE focus.

Is there a difference between a "middle college" and an "early college"? Middle college is by far the older term. The New York City Board of Education and LaGuardia Community College established the first middle college as a charter high school located on the college's campus in 1974 (Lieberman, 2004). This first school inspired many others, all of which have the goal of providing challenging educational experiences combined with a supportive environment. College-level courses are taught either by faculty of the college or high school teachers. In these courses, students both satisfy high school graduation requirements and earn college credit.

The original middle college served as a model for many others that were established across the country. In 2002 the concept provided the foundation for the Early College High School Initiative. This initiative is funded by several major foundations, including Bill & Melinda Gates, Ford, Carnegie Corporation, and W. K. Kellogg, and is coordinated and supported by Jobs for the Future. The use of "early" rather than "middle" to label this initiative appears to reflect an intention to indicate that it differs from its predecessors.

Our reading of the literature about the two types indicates that early colleges differ from middle colleges primarily in where they are located and their expectations regarding credits to be earned. Early colleges may not be

located on a college campus, but middle colleges must be. The first principle
of the Middle College National Consortium (http://www.mcnc.us) is that
middle colleges must be on a college campus. Janet Lieberman, a professor
at LaGuardia Community College, is credited with being the originator of
the first middle college. In a paper she prepared for the Early College High
School Initiative, she stated, "The early college high school design sees non-
integrated space as a temporary accommodation, with the eventual hope of
situating the high school on the college campus" (Lieberman, 2004, p. 3).
The second difference is the extent of articulation between the high school
and postsecondary curriculum and the goal for students in early colleges to
earn 60 postsecondary credits (an associate degree or 2 years of transferable
credits to a 4-year institution) by the time they graduate from high school.
Middle colleges typically do not have as articulated a curriculum or such
specific credit goals. The emphases on providing challenging content in a
supportive environment to underserved students are common to both.

When accessed in the summer of 2011, the Early College High School
Initiative reported on its website (http://www.earlycolleges.org) that its
partners "have started or redesigned more than 230 schools in 28 states
and the District of Columbia." The implementation of Early College High
Schools is being evaluated by the American Institutes for Research (AIR)
and SRI International. These organizations jointly issued five reports (AIR/
SRI, 2004, 2005, 2006, 2007, 2009) that assessed how the various parties
involved in implementation have carried out their roles and the extent to
which their performance reflects the Initiative's core principles. The implementation findings of the AIR/SRI reports are sobering for anyone concerned about improving education, especially for underserved populations.
The Early College High Schools Initiative appears to have all the components necessary to have a significant impact on student performance. Most
educators would endorse the approach that the Initiative has adopted, especially the emphasis on the "new 3 Rs": rigor, relevance, and relationships.
The Initiative also provides high levels of support through intermediary organizations. These organizations are intermediary in the sense that they act
for the funding foundations to foster early college high schools within the
geographic areas they serve. These intermediaries provide support beyond
anything available from a typical school district.

Despite the soundness of the approach and the support being provided,
it is clear from the five evaluation reports that implementing the core principles of the initiative is difficult. Assisting students who are typically underrepresented in postsecondary education to do college-level work while
in high school is a formidable task. There is a continuing debate among
schools in the initiative about how selective they should be. Officials of
some schools contend that it does little good to admit students unable to

meet the demands of rigorous curriculum; as a result, these schools have established selection criteria. Others respond that such criteria are antithetical to the goals of early college. Few of the Early Colleges have been able to implement the second core principle of graduating students with an associate degree or 60 credits transferable to a 4-year institution. They have modified this principle in various ways, including lowering the number of credits to be earned, giving high school credit for grades below B and college credit for B and above, and in at least one case, substituting the goal of preparing students to be college ready for that of earning actual college credits (AIR/SRI, 2007, p. 17). In the AIR/SRI 2009 report the average number of college credits earned by Early College students who had graduated during the 2006–07 school year was 23.

The 2007 and 2009 reports from AIR/SRI examined some outcomes for students participating in Early College High Schools, but their comparison group is all students in the districts from which the Early College students are drawn. Without some controls for self-selection of students, these comparisons provide little useful information. In 2010 the evaluation focus of the Initiative shifted from implementation to its impact on students. AIR (2011) published a one-page overview of the approach that will be followed. AIR will track the experiences of students who applied to be admitted between the 2003–04 and 2007–08 school years at about 25 Early College Schools that use a lottery to select those who will attend. Those who are not admitted typically attend other high schools in the same districts that offer the Early College option. AIR will collect data from school and district records on the characteristics, graduation, and college enrollment rates of those admitted and not admitted to the Early College High Schools. AIR will also survey a sample of students for whom they obtain records to determine their college enrollment, credit transfer, and expected degrees and majors. The follow-up of students selected by chance to attend or not attend Early College High Schools will provide a rigorous test of the effects of these schools.

We are aware of two other studies that used random selection to evaluate the effects of middle/early college high schools: Dynarski, Gleason, Rangarajan, and Wood (1998) and SERVE Center (2010). The Dynarski et al. study was part of a larger evaluation that examined the effectiveness of 16 middle school and high school dropout prevention programs. The middle college study included 395 students who applied to attend an alternative high school operated by Seattle Public Schools in cooperation with Seattle Central Community College. At the time it was evaluated, the high school enrolled about 300 students and its core academic curriculum focused on two modules—math/science and integrated humanities. Study participants were generally older students who were overage for grade (the average was just under 18) or had previously dropped out of school. Because more students applied to the middle college than could be admitted, a lottery was used for admission. Students not admitted (i.e., those assigned to the control group) were free to participate in other regular and alternative education programs in the community, and most did.

The original study sample of 516 students was comprised of two cohorts. Cohort 1, drawn from students who applied to the middle college at the beginning of the 1992–93 school year, included 199 students who were admitted and 123 students in the control group. Cohort 2, drawn from those who applied for the 1993–94 school year, consisted of 123 students who were admitted and 71 students in the control group. A follow-up survey was administered 2 years after random assignment; 244 intervention group students and 150 control group students responded, response rates of 76% and 77%, respectively. Results were reported for each cohort and for both cohorts combined.

Because this experiment was part of a larger dropout prevention evaluation, the outcome measures were limited to dropping out, graduating, or earning a GED. For Cohort 1, the only significant finding was that more control students earned a GED by the end of the 3rd year than middle college students (37% vs. 24%) resulting in an effect size of -.38. When both cohorts were combined, 36% of students in the middle college group had dropped out of school, compared with 33% of control group students. The researchers also found that 40% of students in the middle college group had earned a high school diploma or GED certificate 2 years after random assignment, compared with 38% of control group students. Neither difference was statistically significant or substantively important. Even conceding that the Dynarski et al. (1998) study is from only one city and over a decade old, its methodological rigor requires that its findings be considered carefully.

The SERVE Center (2010) study examined 9th-grade outcomes of students in eight Early College High Schools in North Carolina that used lotteries to determine who would and would not attend. Data on courses taken, test results, absences, and suspensions were obtained from the Department of Public Instruction for students attending the Early College schools and those who applied but were not admitted. Surveys were also conducted with these students. Analyses of these data found that Early College students did significantly better on many of the measures. Eighty-one percent of Early College students successfully completed algebra I by the end of 9th grade compared to 67% of the control group. This is at least partly due to increased course access. Virtually all (97%) Early College students had taken algebra I by the end of 9th grade compared to 76% of control group students. These results also showed a reduction in performance gaps. In the Early College schools there was a two-point difference in the percentages of minority and nonminority students successfully completing algebra I and no difference for English I. Among the students who were not admitted to the Early College schools, these differences were 14 percentage points for algebra and 9 points for English.

The surveys administered to the admitted and nonadmitted students were designed to assess self-reports of engagement and the relationship component that Early College High Schools attempt to foster. The Early College students scored significantly higher on almost all of these measures and many of the differences were quite substantial. On the measure of academic and social support, for example, the effect size was .95, indicating that almost all the Early College students reported higher levels of support than almost all of the nonadmitted students. The other effect sizes were not as large, but still quite meaningful: for example, high expectations, .66; rigorous instruction, .52; and relevant instruction, .43.

It should be noted that all of the differences between admitted and nonadmitted students are based on the experiences of all students who were admitted to the Early College High Schools, whether they attended or not. Statisticians refer to this as "intent to treat." In an experimental design, once a subject is assigned to the experimental group (in this case the Early College High Schools) they remain in that group for all outcomes analyses. Additional analyses of data from the North Carolina Early College schools were reported by Edmunds et al. (2011). These analyses indicated that 9.8% of those admitted did not attend, and 2.2% of those not originally admitted eventually did attend. To the extent that Early College schools actually produce differences in the outcomes of students, these cross-overs decrease the estimates of these effects.

The results from the SERVE Center (2010) report provide an encouraging contrast to the several AIR/SRI evaluation reports from 2004 to 2009 regarding the difficulties of implementing Early College High Schools. In North Carolina, the Early College schools receive extensive support from an intermediary organization, the New Schools Project. This support, which includes extensive professional development for teachers, appears to be assisting the Early College schools to achieve their objectives, at least in the 1 school year for which results are available.

Middle college high schools already exist that provide a CTE focus. While we could find no examples of Early College schools with this focus, the model could also be adapted to this end.

CURRENT RESEARCH ON PROGRAMS OF STUDY[5]

Perkins IV charges the NRCCTE to carry out research and evaluation that will develop, improve, and identify the most successful methods for addressing the education, employment, and training needs of participants in

CTE programs. Perkins IV also requires eligible recipients of the funds it authorizes to offer POS. This requirement created a need for information about how best to design and implement such programs, and the NRCCTE responded by initiating three studies that are examining POS from different perspectives. The first of these, referred to as "Rigorous Tests," is studying POS in three large districts, each of which offers several programs. Two of these districts use a lottery to select students for their POS, which allowed the study team to design randomized control trials of the effects of participating. In the third district, a quasi-experimental study is being conducted using propensity score matching to select students for a closely matched comparison group. In all three districts, data are being collected on program implementation and from student cohorts that are being followed from entry into POS through the first year of postsecondary experience.

The second study, referred to as "Mature POS," identified eight sites that appeared to have had most of the components of POS, especially good secondary-postsecondary articulation, well before they were required by Perkins IV. Visits were made to each of these sites to gather information about the structure and development of their POS. From the information gathered, three have been selected as most closely aligned with the legislative requirements, and these three are being studied longitudinally to better understand the factors underlying their development and operation and the outcomes of their students

The third study, referred to as "Personal Pathways," is tracking the implementation and impact of the Education and Economic Development Act, which was passed in South Carolina in 2005. This act established a statewide education reform policy that requires career majors for all students across the high school curriculum. This project is tracking the implementation and impact of this policy in eight high schools that were selected to represent diversity in the degree of implementation as well as in size, location, demographics, and the level of school and community resources in the areas that they serve. Site visits have been conducted to each of these schools to develop baseline data on their respective implementation of the mandated reform policy. Other data on the selected high schools come from state student records that will track selected cohorts from middle school through high school and from questionnaires developed in cooperation with study teams of the other two projects. The study will continue to follow the selected cohorts for 3 years.

In addition to these three longitudinal studies, the NRCCTE conducted a descriptive study of the status of implementation in six selected states during the first half of 2010. Neither the states nor the local districts visited in each were randomly selected. Rather, they represent a purposive sample chosen based on their geographic and administrative heterogeneity, the recommendations of individuals who were knowledgeable about the implementation of programs of study and the opportunity to conduct a rigorous, scientifically based evaluation. The progress these states have made and the challenges they are encountering are summarized below together with the findings from the other three studies. The initial data from these four studies cause us to be cautiously optimistic about the potential for POS. At this early stage, we offer the following preliminary observations about the implementation of the four components of POS.[6]

Incorporate Secondary and Postsecondary Education Elements. Efforts to align secondary and postsecondary instruction were evident at each of the sites studied. Sites with established methods to facilitate communication across institutions and partners, such as joint technical skill committees (which bring together secondary and postsecondary faculty with business and labor partners), appear to have achieved better alignment than sites without such methods. Good relationships among the various partners foster alignment. Although this may sound like a tautology, it is unlikely that alignment would emerge if there were no or poor relationships. All four studies found that the Perkins IV programs of study mandates have increased the attention paid to aligning secondary and postsecondary programs.

Include Coherent and Rigorous Content Aligned with Challenging Academic Standards and Relevant Career and Technical Content in a Coordinated, Nonduplicative Progression of Courses. When integration of academic and CTE content occurs, it happens primarily in CTE courses. Individual teachers typically initiate any integration that does occur. In one of the states in which the Rigorous Tests study's schools are located, relevant academic skills must be embedded in CTE programs; these skills are measured as part of the state's technical assessment system. Although integration of academic and CTE content is a requirement in the South Carolina legislation being examined, researchers found inconsistent evidence that it is occurring. When it was observed, it was primarily in the form of integration of academic standards and content into CTE courses. All sites were developing POS that offered sequences of courses that began with broad introductions to career areas and became more focused on specific occupations as students advanced in their pathways.

May Include the Opportunity for Dual or Concurrent Enrollment Programs. All of the POS being followed in the three longitudinal studies offer opportunities for high school students to earn postsecondary credits through dual or concurrent enrollment. However, student awareness of these opportunities varied widely across schools. Relative few students who successfully complete dual credit courses have the credits they earned added to their transcripts at the postsecondary level. Most often they must satisfy certain requirements, such as enrolling in the college that offered the course and presenting documentation, before having the credits added to their transcripts. The requirements of programs of study course sequences, Advanced Placement (AP), and dual credit courses often conflict and students must make difficult choices among them.

Lead to an Industry-Recognized Credential or Certificate at the Postsecondary Level, or an Associate or Baccalaureate Degree. Some of the POS in the NRCCTE's three longitudinal studies offer opportunities to earn industry-recognized credentials at the secondary level, but others have been unable to make the commitments of time, personnel, and funding required to establish and maintain programs that offer such credentials. Data on the transition from secondary to postsecondary are available only from the Mature Sites study, and what is available implies that few graduates continue their postsecondary studies in the same programs of study they had followed in high school.

The sites for the Rigorous Tests and Mature Sites studies were specifically selected because they were implementing POS, but the South Carolina and Six States studies provide a more diverse sample of state and local efforts. Our overall judgment to date is that all sites are actively implementing programs of study that incorporate the components required by Perkins IV. While many challenges remain, the trend is in the right direction, and those developing programs and providing technical assistance are aware of most of the issues that need to be addressed.

Across all four studies, it was frequently noted that initiatives similar to POS have been going on for many years, but Perkins IV made the efforts more tangible and concrete. Instead of just written articulation agreements, real connections are emerging between high school and college faculty and between course content at all levels, and relationships have developed that are encouraging a spirit of collaboration. Business interests are more actively connected to program development and instruction, and efforts to define meaningful certification and evaluation of student knowledge and skill are serious, rigorous, and ongoing.

Areas that appear to require additional effort on the parts of the states, districts, and schools involved are the coordination of rigorous academic and CTE content, and increasing awareness and participation in dual enrollment courses. Specific challenges researchers identified include:

1. Misalignment between high school and postsecondary missions; between academic and CTE programs; and between state and local entities

2. Time and resource demands. Designing and implementing true programs of study require resources that are often difficult to obtain in an era of education funding cutbacks.

3. Real-world school and occupational pathways are not always linear. Not all students move directly from high school to postsecondary education. Some career pathways require experience to move from one level to the next. As some high school students obtain valuable industry credentials, they move directly into the workforce (Schumer & Digby, in press).

4. Guidance and counseling, especially career counseling, has emerged as an important theme in the Center's research. Students cannot arrive in high school and be expected to make informed decisions about career pathways or POS absent sufficient career information and career development opportunities. Stipanovic and Stringfield (in press) found that school counselors need to play a large role in providing career development, but that CTE teachers and the CTE curriculum and activities also play important roles in providing career development opportunities. Based on their analysis, they argued for intentional and comprehensive career development services and the support to engage with students in exploring a full range of career options.

It is too early to say whether these efforts will result in increased numbers of students continuing in the same POS from the secondary to the postsecondary level and earning industry-recognized credential or degrees. The NRCCTE research continues and more will be learned in the coming years.

SUMMARY

Beginning in the late 1980s, there have been five major initiatives involving CTE that were designed to improve the transition of young people from high school to postsecondary education: Tech Prep, career clusters/pathways, dual/concurrent enrollment, youth apprenticeships, and school-to-work. These initiatives shared many of the same components as POS. Studies of these initiatives that provided data from comparison groups have found statistically significant differences on indicators of postsecondary performance such as enrollment, percentage required to take development courses, persistence to the second year of programs, total credits earned, and degree or certificates earned. Where there are such differences, however, they tend to be fairly small, mainly of a magnitude of 4% or 5% in favor of the participants. The exception to these small differences is the number of credits earned by students who earned postsecondary credit through concurrent or dual enrollments in high school. These students averaged about 15 more postsecondary credits than students who had no dual enrollment courses. This is equivalent to a full semester of credits. Middle/early college high schools attempt to provide dual credit instruction in a supportive, small-school setting to students who are traditionally underrepresented in postsecondary education. Studies of their implementation have identified many challenges, but a rigorous study of 9th-grade students attending Early College High in North Carolina has found positive effects. Preliminary findings are also presented from four NRCCTE projects that are examining POS. These projects have identified several areas that will need improvement if POS are to yield higher levels of postsecondary success than their predecessors. The kinds of changes that are needed to improve the chances for successful transitions are discussed in Chapter 7.

CHAPTER 6

Jobs and Earnings: Credentials Matter

Automation and information technology continue to eliminate jobs that can be reduced to a set of rules for repeating the same tasks in the same ways. As computing power increases and software becomes more sophisticated, more such jobs will be eliminated (Levy & Murnane, 2004). More recently two economists have argued that humans are losing the "Race Against the Machine" as technology is displacing more and more workers (Brynjolfsson & McAfee, 2011). Some economists have expressed concern that the jobs most impacted by these trends are in the middle of the skill distribution, those below professional and managerial but above low, unskilled positions. Autor, Katz, and Kearny (2006) applied the term *polarization* to this bifurcation of the workforce into low- and high-skilled jobs with declining numbers in the middle. Other economists concede that there has been a decline, but cite data from the U.S. Bureau of Labor Statistics (BLS) that show approximately half of all jobs continue to be in the middle-skill category (Holzer & Lerman, 2009). In this chapter, we present each of these positions and describe middle-skill jobs in more detail.

In this chapter, we also review evidence that high school occupational training, without additional formal preparation, yields an earnings advantage in the labor market. We present findings from several studies that show students who took occupationally specific courses had higher earnings than similar students without such training. Postsecondary degrees confer an additional advantage, but many who earn a bachelor's degree find that it does not yield the earnings or satisfaction they had anticipated. For many years, community colleges have been reporting an increasing number of graduates of 4-year institutions enrolling to obtain technical training (Yang, 2006). Many of these "reverse transfers" are seeking to learn skills that they hope will give them an advantage in the labor market that their bachelor's degrees did not deliver. As noted in Chapter 2, Gray and Herr (2006) have shown that there are "Other Ways to Win" and CTE is a major part of these other ways.

We conclude this chapter by evaluating the charge that CTE disproportionately enrolls young people from economically disadvantaged and minority backgrounds and prepares them for dead-end jobs. Oakes (2005) is the scholar most visibly associated with this charge, but she has coedited a book, *Beyond Tracking: Multiple Pathways to College, Career, and Civic Participation*, that includes a role for a curriculum that looks very much like CTE in providing options for students (Oakes & Saunders, 2008).

MIDDLE-SKILL OCCUPATIONS

Is the workforce becoming polarized? Autor is the economist most associated with the concept of polarization, and he has marshaled an array of data to document the decline in middle-skill jobs. In a 2010 paper prepared for the Center for American Progress, Autor presents statistics from the past 30 years to demonstrate these conclusions:

- Since the late 1970s, the rise in the educational level of workers has not kept up with the demand for skills.
- Employment has expanded in high-wage, high-skill occupations and in low-wage, low-skill occupations.
- Employment has contracted in middle-skill, middle-wage white- and blue-collar jobs.

The occupations declining most are white-collar clerical, administrative, and sales jobs and blue-collar production, craft, and operative positions. Autor notes that polarization is not unique to the United States but widespread across industrialized countries. He concludes that the main causes of the decline in middle-skill jobs are the automation of routine tasks and, to a lesser degree, the international integration of labor markets through trade and the offshoring of jobs. There is some evidence that these factors are also influencing higher skilled jobs in the financial industry, data modeling, and actuarial analysis (Crawford, 2007).

In 2009 Holzer and Lerman had questioned the extent of polarization, and at the request of the Center for American Progress, Holzer (2010) prepared a response to Autor's paper. Holzer conceded that there has been a decline in middle-skill jobs. Even with this decline, however, an analysis conducted by Holzer and Lerman found that in 2006 middle-skill jobs accounted for about half (48%) of all workers; high-skill jobs, 35%; and low-skill jobs, 17%. This distribution is far from the hourglass shape implied by the word *polarization*.

A key issue, of course, is how middle skills are defined. Holzer and Lerman defined middle-skill jobs as those in which most of the workers have education or training beyond high school but less than a bachelor's degree. In one of Autor's analyses (2010, p. 3, Figure 1), he defined skill level (actually rank) of 326 occupations by the average wage of workers in these occupations in 1980. Holzer questions this definition and cites studies that indicate average wages reflect "industry wage premia" for some sectors such as manufacturing and transportation, as well as skill differences. Holzer also points out that not all of Autor's analyses (using the wage definition of skill level) supported polarization. In the period 1999 through 2007, all of the increase in relative share of employment was in occupations ranking in the lower one fourth of the skills distribution. This was in sharp contrast to the previous 2 decades when almost all of the increases in share of employment were in occupations in the upper half of the distribution.

Whether the workforce is polarizing or not, jobs involving nonroutine tasks and services are the least likely to be automated or offshored (Crawford, 2007). Jobs such as these are what CTE is all about. In the 2009 projections from the BLS (Lacey & Wright, 2009), the occupation with the most job growth between 2008 and 2018 is registered nurse, which is projected to add 581,500 workers. The preparation for this job is typically an associate degree and the median wage is in the upper quartile of all occupations. Table 6.1 presents the occupations classified by Lacey and Wright in the top 30 of projected growth, in the upper two quartiles of wages, and not requiring a bachelor's degree.

The projections in Table 6.1 were the most recent produced by the BLS, when this book was written. Farr and Shatkin (2009) used the previous set of projections (published in 2007) and other data from the Occupational Employment Statistics program and O*Net to select what they labeled the "300 best jobs without a 4-year degree." They identified these jobs by ranking 484 jobs that do not require a bachelor's degree on three measures: earnings, projected growth, and projected annual job openings to 2016. They then summed these three rankings to calculate a total score for each job. Farr and Shatkin's top ranking job was the same as in Table 6.1, registered nurses, but the others in their list differ substantially. Truck drivers rank 48; bookkeepers, 55; executive secretaries, 10; carpenters, 37; first-line supervisors of office staff, 53; licensed practical and vocational nurses, 23; and maintenance workers, 89.

Obviously, with a list of 300 occupations, there is far more variability than in a list of only 8. The variety is reflected in the eight occupations in the Farr-Shatkin ranking that lie between the occupations ranked first and tenth in their list and do not appear in Table 6.1:

- Sales representatives, wholesale and manufacturing, technical and scientific products
- Dental hygienists

TABLE 6.1. Occupations with the Largest Projected Job Growth 2008–18, in the Upper Half of Median Earnings That Do Not Require a 4-Year Degree

Occupation	Employment (thousands)		Change 2008–2018		Quartile Rank by 2008 Median Wage	Most Significant Source of Postsecondary Education or Training
	2008	*2018*	*N*	*%*		
Registered nurses	2618.7	3200.2	581.5	22.2	VH	Associate degree
Truck drivers, heavy trucks and tractor-trailer	1798.4	2031.3	232.9	13.0	H	Short-term on-the-job training
Bookkeeping, accounting, and auditing clerks	2063.8	2276.2	212.4	10.3	H	Moderate-term on-the-job training
Executive secretaries and administrative assistants	1594.4	1798.8	204.4	12.8	H	Work experience in a related occupation
Carpenters	1284.9	1450.3	165.4	12.9	H	Long-term on-the-job training
First-line supervisors/managers of office and administrative support workers	1457.2	1617.5	160.3	11.0	H	Work experience in a related occupation
Licensed practical and licensed vocational nurses	753.6	909.2	155.6	20.7	H	Postsecondary vocational credential other than associate degree
Maintenance and repair workers, general	1361.3	1509.2	147.9	10.9	H	Moderate-term on-the-job training

Source. Lacey and Wright (2009), Table 5, pp. 93–94.

Note. Quartile rank: VH = highest median pay quartile, H = second highest median pay quartile. Most significant source of postsecondary education or training indicates the level needed by most workers to become fully qualified for the occupation.

- Criminal investigators and special agents
- Immigration and customs inspectors
- Police detectives
- Police identification and records officers
- Vocational education teachers, postsecondary
- Paralegal and legal assistants

The top six of these occupations had median annual earnings (as of May 2007) of $60,000 or more, which helped push them to the top of the rankings. There is a considerable drop-off in median earnings for the next two occupations, to about $45,000 each, but both of these were expected to grow almost 25% and have about 20,000 annual openings. One of the Farr and Shatkin tables present, the 100 jobs with the highest annual earnings. These jobs range from $112,930 for air traffic controllers to $44,780 for electricians. The top 23 occupations in this list pay $60,000 or more. The occupation in the middle of this list (insurance appraisers, auto damage) had median earnings of $51,500. Another table presents the 100 jobs with the most openings. At the top of this list are office clerks for which there were 765,803 projected annual openings. At the bottom are paralegal and legal assistances with 22,756.

While the middle of the occupational distribution will continue to be the major source of employment, Carnevale, Smith, and Strohl (2010) were less sanguine than Farr and Shatkin about the prospects for rewarding employment among those without postsecondary education. Carnevale et al. modified the BLS forecasts to provide a more pessimistic projection of the coming years. Carnevale et al. foresaw the effects of the recession that began in 2007 to be long-lasting. They referred to it as the "Great Recession" because of the magnitude of job loss and the time it will take the economy to return to full employment. The numbers of jobs lost in the worst months of the 2007 recession were more than double the worst months of the recessions that began in 1990 and 2001. Since the economy began to grow again, as measured by gross domestic product, there has been little increase in employment. This is because the recession accelerated automation and offshoring of low-skill, repetitive jobs. Their pessimistic assumptions about economic growth caused Carnevale et al. to estimate the total number of job openings to be created by 2018 at 46.8 million, 4.1 million fewer than the BLS projection of 50.9 million.

Of more consequence than the total number of job openings, however, are the revised estimates of openings by educational level. Carnevale et al. (2010) assert that the BLS underestimates the demand for workers with postsecondary education because of deficiencies in its methods. First, the BLS projection models treat all jobs equally. Low-skill jobs have many more

TABLE 6.2. Total Number of Job Openings in the Period 2008 to 2018 by
Educational Level of Workers in These Jobs as Projected by the Bureau of
Labor Statistics and the Center on Education and the Workforce

Source for Projections	High School or Less	Associate or Some College	Bachelor's or Higher	Total Projected Job Openings
		Projected Job Openings in Millions		
Bureau of Labor Statistics	34.0	5.3	11.7	50.9
Center on Education and the Workforce	17.0	13.8	16.0	46.8

Source. BLS: Lacey and Wright (2009), Table 3, p. 88; Center on Education and the Workforce: Carnevale, Smith, and Strohl (2010), Figure 2.1, p. 13

part-time workers and higher rates of turnover than higher skilled jobs. BLS methods count all job openings the same, however, and thus overestimate the demand for low-skilled workers. Second, the BLS classifies all of the 755 occupations for which it makes projections by "the most significant source of postsecondary education or training among workers in the occupation" (Lacey & Wright, 2009, p. 88). This implies that all workers in a given occupation have the level of preparation by which it is classified when the reality is that almost all occupations have workers with several levels. Third, the classifications assigned in the year from which projections are made (most recently 2008) are assumed to continue for the next 10 years, with no adjustment for skill changes within occupations. The methods used by Carnevale and his colleagues adjust both for differences in levels of preparation and skill trends within occupations. When the BLS and Carnevale et al. methods are applied to projections made in 1998 for the educational levels of workers in 2008, the BLS underestimated the actual number of workers with associate degrees or better by 47% and the Carnevale et al. methods overestimated the number by 4%. Table 6.2 compares the BLS and Carnevale et al. projections for the period 2008 to 2018.[1]

The two methodologies yield widely different projections. If the methods used by Carnevale et al. (2010) are the more accurate, there will be half as many openings for those with a high school diploma or less than BLS has projected. The prospects for rewarding employments for those without postsecondary education are further diminished by employers' training practices. Carnevale et al. estimate that when measured by dollars spent, colleges and universities represent only 35% of the total postsecondary education and training system. Almost all of the remaining 65% is provided by employers through formal and informal means. Unfortunately for those with a high school diploma or less, employers are more likely to train those who have postsecondary education. Eck (1993) reported that questions asked in the January 1991 Current Population Survey found that only 4.9% of high school dropouts compared to 22.9% of college graduates received formal training to improve their skills from their current employers. The percentages receiving informal training were not so disparate, but still favored those with college degrees, 10.2% to 17.2%. Carnevale et al. conclude that the opportunities for rewarding employment for those with a high school diploma or less will continue to decline and that postsecondary education is no longer the *preferred* route to middle-class status and earnings, it is the *only* route.

We find the Carnevale et al. (2010) critique of the BLS projections convincing and anticipate that it will cause the methods used by the Department of Labor to be reviewed. Future projections are likely to show a larger demand for workers with postsecondary preparation than has been true in the past. We do not agree, however, that postsecondary education has become the only route to good-paying jobs We have presented information about many jobs that do not require postsecondary education that pay well above the median for all jobs. In the next section we discuss the earnings advantages that are associated with obtaining occupational training while in high school.

THE IMPACT OF CTE ON EARNINGS

The real test of any program that teaches occupational skills occurs in the labor market. Do students who participated in CTE learn skills that give them more stable employment and better wages than those of similar students who did not participate? Many studies have been conducted to answer this question, and the most frequent answer on earnings is "yes," but the results with regard to employment are more mixed. High employment levels are found for all graduates regardless of high school program, and while some studies find CTE graduates have more stable employment than similar nonparticipants, others do not. With regard to earnings, the evidence is more consistent and the more rigorous the studies, the more clearly they indicate the earnings benefits of occupational training.

Since 1976, each reauthorization of the federal legislation governing CTE (prior to 1999, vocational education) has mandated an independent assessment of the implementation and effects of the legislation. The results of the most recent assessment completed to date were published in 2004 (Silverberg et al.). One of the effects examined was the impact of participating in CTE upon earnings. The assessment reviewed existing studies and commissioned additional analyses of relevant databases, such as the National Education Longitudinal Study (NELS:88) that followed a representative sample of approximately 25,000 young people from 1988, when they were in the 8th grade, until 2000, 8 years after on-time graduation. The review of the available evidence yielded the following conclusion:

> Vocational education has important short- and medium-run earning benefits for most students at both the secondary and postsecondary levels, and these benefits extend to those who are economically disadvantaged. (Silverberg et al., 2004, p. xvii)

The federal legislation requires that CTE be evaluated on several outcomes, in addition to its effect on employment. The findings on earnings were the only ones that Silverberg and her colleagues judged to be consistently positive. Since the 2004 report in which this conclusion was presented, four other studies have been published that support its validity. We discuss each of these in some depth.

The first of these three (Bishop & Mane, 2004) was discussed in Chapter 2 regarding the contribution that occupation courses make to retaining students in high school. In the same paper, Bishop and Mane also presented their analyses of the NELS:88 data that had been used for the Silverberg et al. (2004) report, and found even larger effects of CTE participation on earnings. Their analyses differed from those commissioned for the national assessment in several ways including different measures of CTE participation and an extensive array of control variables for characteristics of the students (as measured when they were in the 8th grade), the schools they attended, the states in which they resided, extent of participation in postsecondary education, and certificates or degrees received. The authors used all these measures to minimize, to the extent possible, self-selection biases that underlie students' choices of the courses they study in high school.

All of the Bishop-Mane regression models yielded statistically significant results indicating higher earnings were associated with taking occupationally specific courses while in high school. The net effect of the occupational courses (holding the effects of all other variables constant) varied by how the courses-taking measures were specified and the period after graduation that was covered. The measures of occupationally specific courses included the total number of credits earned and three combinations of credits from occupationally specific courses, computer courses, and academic/personal interest courses. The periods covered were 1 and 7 years after graduation. The range of the net effects on annual earnings varied from $248 to $2,640. The lowest was found the year after high school and indicated the net relationship between earnings and number of occupationally specific credits.

The highest was found 7 years after high school and indicates the net relationship between earnings and a combination of two occupationally specific courses, two computer courses, and two fewer academic courses.

These analyses included all graduates who had earned between 15 and 32 Carnegie credits while in high school. The analyses did not include students who dropped out or earned a GED, but they did include all students who continued their education after high school. Earnings of graduates who were students (full- or part-time) in the year following graduation were, of course, lower than those who entered the labor market. Measures of postsecondary participation were included in the regressions, and these indicated that almost all of the earnings advantages in the year after graduation were realized by former CTE students who were not students. The net annual earnings advantages of these CTE graduates ranged from $861 to $1,675 when the mean for all graduates was $5,427, quite substantial differences. In 2000, when almost all those included in the analysis had completed their education, mean annual earnings had increased to $26,535. Nevertheless, those who had taken occupationally specific CTE courses still realized net earnings advantages regardless of their level of educational attainment. The authors summarized their findings as follows:

> those [graduates] who devoted about one-sixth of their time in high school to occupation-specific vocational courses earned at least 12% extra one year after graduating and about 8% extra seven years later (holding attitudes and ability in 8th grade, family background and college attendance constant). This was true both for students who did and did not pursue post-secondary education. Computer courses had particularly large effects on earnings eight years after graduating. (Bishop & Mane, 2004, p. 381)

The second of the four studies appearing since the last national assessment is by Meer (2007), who also examined the relationship between CTE participation and earnings in the NELS:88 data. Meer extended previous analyses by applying a model designed to control for the self-selection of students into different curriculum tracks. Meer reviews research indicating that most students who enroll in several CTE courses have characteristics different from students in a college preparatory curriculum. He quotes Kulik (1998) regarding these differences:

> It is important to note that the groups being compared differ profoundly in educational aspirations at the start of high school. Students usually follow college-prep programs because they intend to go to college; students often follow vocational programs because they do not intend to go to college. The goals of the two groups seem almost by definition to be non-overlapping. (Kulik, quoted in Meer, 2007, p. 561)

When groups being compared differ markedly on an outcome, (e.g., attainment of a 4-year degree), it is likely that many of the factors underlying the observed difference are unobserved and consequently not controlled by regression analyses. To account for these unobserved differences, economists have developed a procedure that was employed by Meer, a multinomial logit selection model. His model estimated the likelihood of students with measured characteristics choosing a specified track, defined as academic (college preparatory), general, technical, or business. The general track included students who earned at least 12 Carnegie credits but did not meet the criteria of the other tracks. The technical track included students who had earned three or more credits in agriculture, technical, trade, or health courses. The business track included students who had earned three or more credits in business or office, marketing, and occupational home economics. Meer then used the results from his selection model to predict "counterfactual estimates": conditional means of the logarithm of 1999 annual income that indicate what students who chose one curriculum would have earned had they chosen a different one.

Meer's analyses found that without the correction for self-selection, technical students earned 11.4% less than academic students. When the selection model results are included, however, they show that the technical track was actually the best choice for the students who chose it. If technical students had taken the academic track they would have earned 3.7% less than they actually earned. If technical students had taken the general track, they would have earned 3.8% less; and in the business track, 10.9% less. Those who followed the business track, however, would have earned 10.1% more if they followed the academic track and 7.1% more if they had been in the general track. Nevertheless, the business track was a better choice for its students than the technical track in which they would have earned 11% less. Students who took the general track would have realized 9.5% higher earnings if they had followed the technical track. Meer concluded that the academic and technical students had made the correct choices given their career interests and abilities. General students would have benefited from studying technical skills and business students from increasing their general cognitive skills in the academic or general tracks.

The third study of earnings to be published since the last national assessment (Fletcher & Zirkle, 2009) analyzed data from the 1997 National Longitudinal Study of Youth (NLSY97). Unlike NELS:88, which sampled students attending randomly selected schools, NLSY97 selected its participants from a national sample of households. Extensive screening and oversampling of traditionally underrepresented demographic groups was carried out to ensure a representative sample. Initial interviews were conducted with 8,984 young people born in the years 1980 to 1984. Fletcher and Zirkle analyzed data on annual earnings in 2005 that were collected in 2006 from 83% of the original sample. When contacted for the 2006 follow-up, the NLSY participants were in the age range 22 to 26.

Self-reported data on courses taken and credits earned were used to classify the NLSY97 participants into four curriculum tracks:

- CTE—students who earned three or more credits within defined occupational pathways
- College preparatory—students who earned credits in math, science, English, and foreign language consistent with college entrance requirements at 4-year colleges and universities
- Dual—students who met both the CTE and college preparatory definitions
- General—students who did not meet either the CTE or college preparatory definitions

Fletcher and Zirkle (2009) constructed a relatively simple statistical model to explain curriculum choice, educational attainment, and earnings. Their model included measures of mothers' and fathers' educational attainment, the students' gender, race/ethnicity, and household income. This model proved quite accurate at explaining curriculum choice while in high school, relatively good at explaining educational attainment, but weak in explaining earnings. Multinomial logistic regression was used to analyze curriculum choice and educational attainment, and multiple linear regression was used to analyze earnings. The model explained 86% of the variance in curriculum choice, 31% of the variance in educational attainment, but only 8% of the variance in earnings.[2] The relationships of the socioeconomic variables (parental education levels and family income) were in the expected direction. Students from higher income families whose parents had college degrees were more likely to have followed a college preparatory curriculum and have higher educational attainment than students from the other curriculum tracks.

The unadjusted means earning in 2005 for the four curriculum tracks were as follows: general, $20,907; college preparatory, $22,183; dual, $22,653; and CTE, $22,732. The regression analysis provided estimates of the net earnings advantage realized by those who had not followed the general curriculum. When other variables in the model are held constant, those who had taken the college preparatory curriculum earned $1,386 more than those in the general track. The net advantage for those in the dual track was $2,754, and for those in the CTE track, $3,279. At the time the data were collected for this follow-up, a significant portion of the NLSY97 respondents was still enrolled in school. As these respondents complete their postsecondary education and become more established in their careers, it is likely that those from the college preparatory curriculum will have higher earnings than those who followed a CTE pathway. For the period 4 to 8 years after high school, however, the CTE track was associated with higher earnings.

The studies we have summarized to this point all used the same methodology for determining the effect of high school CTE on earnings: regression analyses of large data sets. Such analyses cannot provide the kind of evidence produced by randomized controlled trials, because they cannot control for unobserved variables that may create systematic differences between groups. A longitudinal, randomized control trial of career academies that was conducted by MDRC did control for unobserved variables. This study has been reported in a number of publications, most recently in Kemple and Willner's (2008) analyses of follow-up data collected 4 and 8 years after scheduled graduation. These data were collected from former students, all of whom had applied to be admitted to nine career academies at various locations across the country. Approximately half of these students were selected at random to enroll in the academies and half were not. Those who were not admitted to the academies constituted the study's control group and attended regular high school programs. The follow-up data reported by Kemple and Willner indicated that admission to career academies caused an 11% advantage in average earnings over a full 8 years following scheduled graduation from high school. The difference between the two groups did not decrease during the follow-up period. In a trend chart that depicts the average earnings for each month of the 8-year period, the gap between the academy and nonacademy students is wider during the second 4-year period than it was during the first (Kemple & Willner, 2008, Exhibit 2, p. 15). The advantage for young men was especially large at 16% over the 8-year follow-up period.

The implications of this earning advantage assume even more importance when the actual extent of participation in the career academies is examined. Not all those who were admitted to the academies attended, and not all those who attended completed their programs. Kemple and Snipes (2000) report that 15% of those admitted never enrolled, and an additional 30% enrolled but withdrew after completing, on average, less than half of the scheduled semesters. To provide an unbiased estimate of the effects of the academies, those who were selected to attend are counted in the experimental group regardless of the extent of their actual participation in the academies. With large proportions of students having no or limited participation, the effects of the academies on earnings had to be quite powerful to cause the average earnings of all in the experimental group to be significantly higher than those in the nonacademy group.

The most recent data examining the relationship of high school CTE and employment are from the meta-analysis being conducted by the National Research Center for Career and Technical Education. In these analyses, we find strong significant effects of participation in high school CTE and employment. Effect sizes are on the order of 1.49 (Jeffrey Valentine, personal communication, June 30, 2011).

Reverse transfers, holders of bachelor's degrees or higher who enroll in community colleges, provide an additional example of the advantages of having skills that are in demand in the labor market. There are actually two types of reverse transfers identified in the literature, undergraduate and postgraduate. Undergraduate transfers are students who initially enroll in a 4-year college or university and transfer to a 2-year college prior to obtaining a degree. Postgraduate transfers are those who have completed 4-year degrees and pursue additional education at 2-year institutions. Postgraduate transfers typically enroll in 2-year colleges for career reasons, supporting our position that occupational skills can be more important than a bachelor's degree in the competition for good-paying jobs.

We are unaware of any national data on postgraduate reverse transfers; what we know about them comes from studies conducted in individual states or institutions.[3] Most estimates of the extent of postgraduate transfers range from about 10% to 20% of the total number of community college students. A study in California found that over one fourth of the 2001 graduates of that state's 4-year public institutions took community college courses in the 3-year period following their graduation, but fewer than 5% earned 16 credits or more. This 3-year follow-up period probably yielded underestimates, because most studies find that the average age of postgraduate transfers is in the late 30s. There are consistent gender differences in the programs that postgraduate transfers enter with males primarily in technology, most often information technology, and females in health occupations.

The studies that examine the reasons 4-year degree holders enroll in community colleges continually find career goals are the most frequent. But there are no dominant patterns as to the degrees held by reverse transfers or the types of jobs they held prior to enrollment. There is little support for the stereotype that the typical reverse transfer is a liberal arts graduate who could not find financially rewarding employment. Quinley and Quinley (1999) conducted telephone interviews with a sample of 38 holders of 4-year degrees who had completed 15 hours or more at a community college serving a large urban area in North Carolina. Even in this limited sample, there was considerable variability in their reasons for attending the community college. Quinley and Quinley reviewed the respondents' answers to a number of questions and classified their primary career goals into these categories: new career, 21; personal interest, 9; update skills for current jobs, 4; supplemental income, 3; and career exploration, 1. They concluded the report of their study with the following summary statement:

> The study's results have helped dispel the long-accepted notion that a higher level of education is an automatic ladder to more money and career status. Changes in our society and the increasing value of lifelong education suggest that educational consumers throughout their lifetimes will return to various types of educational institutions to meet their personal and career circumstances. PRTSs [postbaccalaureate reverse transfer students] are not going down a level in education; they are going to the right level of education. (p. 44)

The findings we have reviewed are consistent with human capital theory. Students who learn skills for which demand exists in the labor market should realize higher earnings than similar students without such skills, and the evidence indicates that they do. This evidence, in itself, should refute the charges that CTE primarily serves low-income and minority students and prepares them for low-paying jobs with little career potential. In the concluding section we examine these charges in the context of the radical critique of education in general.

AN ALTERNATIVE TO THE DROPOUT TRACK

For much of its history, especially after the majority of students began to pursue postsecondary education, CTE has been burdened with the "dumping ground" label. Students who did not perform well in academic courses chose, or were assigned, vocational courses.[4] This is in stark contrast to our European competitors where their VET system is a first choice for large percentages of youth, and in several countries for the majority of youth.

The typical comprehensive high school may not have specific curriculum tracks, but it does have courses designed for those who plan to continue their education and those who do not, and enrollment in these courses is heavily influenced by performance in academic subjects (Powell, Farrar, & Cohen, 1985). Performance in academic subjects, in turn, is to a considerable extent explained by the socioeconomic circumstances into which children are born and raised. Most children of the middle class do well; most children of the poor struggle. As noted in Chapter 3, No Child Left Behind attempted to address this "soft bigotry of low expectations" (Bush, 2004). This unofficial tracking has also been the focus of many school reform efforts such as High Schools That Work led by the Southern Region Education Board. Despite these efforts, many youth are still shunted off into curriculum tracks and sometimes schools (e.g., alternative schools) where expectations are lower.

The high correlation between school performance and socioeconomic status has been the basis of the repeated claim that education does not open opportunities to poor children, but instead restricts them. Radical critics charge that in capitalistic economies schools are designed to perpetuate the structural inequality of society by inducing beliefs and self-perceptions among the children of the poor that cause them to accept the prevailing social order (e.g., Apple, 2004; Bowles & Gintis, 1976; Giroux, 1983). The arguments of these radical critics leave us—the best word is "uncomfortable." We are uncomfortable because on most issues we agree with the radical critics. We too decry the huge disparity in wealth in our nation and the attempts to discredit public education and promote privatization. But we are advocates for CTE and, as such, furthering the oppression that radical critics see occurring in most schools.

Like anyone involved with education, we do not dispute that academic performance is highly associated with social class and that schools are structured to prepare students for a world where middle-class values dominate: respect for authority, attendance, cooperation, responsibility. Everyone also knows that how students do in school has a major influence on the opportunities open to them after school. Students who do well in academic classes are encouraged to prepare for college, the completion of which is essential to enter many high-income, high-status occupations. Students who perform more poorly set lower goals, and CTE serves many of these students. These are the realities of education in a country with a diverse population and wide disparity in wealth and opportunities.

Unlike the radical critics, however, we think the sorting and socialization for future occupations is useful to society. Every society must have methods for allocating its members to the work to be done, and the methods used to select those who will have access to preferred jobs must be accepted by all segments of society as fair and reasonable. Public schools as well as higher education perform this function, with or without intentionality. Inducing young people to accept the legitimacy of this sorting, the radical critics contend, is the means of oppression. According to Apple (2004), Giroux (1983), and others who share their ideology, the primary thing learned by children of the poor is that they cannot meet the standards set by society and the fault is their own. Poor children become poor students who internalize a conception of the world that explains their place in society: If they were smarter or had studied harder, they would have been able to get good jobs. Their failure in school makes them willing to accept the low-paying, undesirable jobs that need to be filled. Inculcating such beliefs, the radical critics contend, is the hidden curriculum of education in capitalistic economies.

Although we endorse the educational philosophy of John Dewey especially as it supports curriculum integration, we also recognize that schools
perform a sorting function, intended or not. While in most other countries
this sorting function is based on tests given at different stages of education,
in the United States it is much more subtle and primarily based on academic
performance. Unfortunately, circumstances of birth cause much of the differences in academic performance that underlie the informal sorting that
occurs. To create a more equal society, it is these circumstances that must
be addressed. This is evident in the youth development policies of western
European and many Asian nations. This involves extensive parental training, early childhood education, social support, and continuing intervention
throughout the student years for those who need it. Just such an approach is
being implemented in Harlem by Geoffrey Canada (Tough, 2008). It is too
early to know the extent to which this approach is succeeding, but it delivers
in a feasible package the types of interventions that expert opinion agrees
are needed. A prominent example of such endorsement is the website (www.
heckmanequation.org) that disseminates information on the economic return to early childhood education based on the research of Nobel Laureate,
James Heckman.

Within this approach to a more just society, we see CTE playing a role
by providing an option for those many students who do not find joy or
purpose in academic classes. CTE provides an alternative in which they can
learn in ways more compatible with their abilities and interests. In 1970
Peter Schrag published "Growing Up on Mechanic Street," an essay that
portrays the lives and feelings of many of the students who enroll in CTE
better than any research report:

> Material things respond; theory is applicable and comprehensible—either the
> thing works or it doesn't; it never prevaricates or qualifies, while words and
> social behavior, metaphors and politics remain cloudy, elusive, and distant. You
> see them wiring an electric motor or turning a lathe, or fixing a car: pleasure,
> engagement, or better, a moment of truth. . . . The instrument of oppression is
> the book. It is still the embodiment of the Great Mystery; learn to understand
> its secrets and great things will follow. Submit to your instinctive and natural
> boredom (lacking either the skills to play the game or the security to revolt),
> and we will use it to persuade you of your benighted incompetence: "I didn't
> want to write a term paper, but the teacher said it would be good if I did; when
> I handed it in she made fun of it; so I quit school." (pp. 60, 61)

If oppression is occurring in the typical high school, it is in academic
much more than CTE classes.

This theme of the joy in the acquisition of a manual skill as a viable option in life, one that can be both intellectually and financially rewarding, has

more recently been advanced by Matthew Crawford (2009) in *Shop Class as Soulcraft: An Inquiry Into the Value of Work.* While offering a broad critique of American values, he argues that we have lost an appreciation for how to transfer "craft" knowledge from employee to employee and as a consequence downgraded nonprofessional, or blue-collar work and increasingly white-collar work as well. White-collar work is now subjected to the same kind of intellectual and skill degradation where the cognitive elements of the job are extracted from the work and replaced by a "system." Manual skills are not without an intellectual component, he argues. Whether playing a piano or repairing a motorcycle, skills have to be learned. If one plays a piano poorly, no one will listen; if you repair the motorcycle poorly, someone could die.

Oakes's 1985 book, *Keeping Track*, received far more attention from educators and policymakers than most of the writing of the radical critics, but her charges were much the same. In this book, she devoted a chapter to how CTE (then called vocational education) acted to limit the expectations and attainment of students from poor, predominantly minority families. She reviewed evidence that showed no economic benefit from participating in vocational education and presented her analysis of the types of CTE courses made available in predominantly White, non-White, and mixed schools. Oakes found no evidence that school with mainly non-White populations offered more CTE courses, but she did find that the substance of their courses differed. Schools with mainly White students had more business and fewer trade courses than schools with mixed and mainly non-White populations. She found additional distinctions in the content of the courses. The business courses in the White schools emphasized managerial and financial aspects while those available to non-Whites taught clerical and retail sales. Oakes cited similar differences in the trade course with White schools offering marine technology and aviation while non-White schools offered building maintenance and commercial sewing.

In 2005 Oakes published a second edition of *Keeping Track*, but the chapter on vocational education had no changes. She did not update her discussion of the earnings of CTE students with the more recent findings published by Silverberg et al. (2004) and Bishop and Mane (2004) of substantial advantages. Nor did she discuss the many changes that began in the 1980s toward an expanded concept of CTE that stresses preparing students for both employment and postsecondary education. The chapter on vocational education in the second edition repeats the same conclusion as the original:

> Expanded vocational emphasis is likely to continue to sort students along racial and economic lines. In view of our findings, school people and policymakers should seriously reconsider the appropriateness of vocational training in secondary schools. (p. 170)

While the second edition of *Keeping Track* made no mention of the changes occurring in CTE, Oakes has been involved in examining how occupational context can be used to enhance instruction. Oakes and Saunders (2008) coedited *Beyond Tracking*, a book of research essays that examines the potential and challenges of implementing academically rigorous, career-focused curriculum. The label given to this approach is "multiple pathways," and these pathways are being promoted by the James Irvine Foundation as a way to increase the proportion of California young people who complete high school prepared for college and careers.[5] Multiple pathways have many similarities to the career pathways discussed in Chapter 4. They differ in that multiple pathways are a total school approach, a level four in the Hoachlander (1999) hierarchy of approaches to integration while career pathways are a level three, programmatic.

In the final chapter of *Beyond Tracking*, Oakes and Saunders draw upon the topics discussed by the several scholars who contributed to the book to assess the prospects for multiple pathways. In that chapter they comment on the changes that have occurred in CTE, but hold little hope that these are sufficient to provide real opportunities for educational and career success. The research on earnings advantages associated with CTE, which we have reviewed, is not cited. For Oakes and Saunders, and for most of those who contributed chapters, the only approach that avoids the evils of tracking is teaching all students a level of academics that prepares them to do college-level work. Occupational context is seen as a means to increase relevance and engagement, but the objective is to teach academics.

From the perspective of its critics, therefore, even the broadened concept of CTE that we propose is unacceptable. Socialization for future occupational roles is not a legitimate function of schools. There should be no occupational training at the secondary level. Obviously, we disagree. We think there is a sizeable proportion of students for whom CTE classes provide more appropriate, comfortable, and engaging settings than traditional academic classes. For many of these students, this means the difference between staying in school and dropping out. The evidence we have reviewed indicates that those CTE students who learn skills needed in the labor market realize an earnings advantage. As more students forego occupational training to prepare for college, we expect the earnings advantage of secondary occupational training to increase.

In the best of all worlds, circumstances of birth would not be a major determinant of educational outcomes, and there would be no distinction between a college preparatory and a CTE curriculum. The probability of achieving such a world is nil. Career education in the 1970s and school-to-work in the 1990s attempted to infuse career themes into academic education and both had meager results. Our goal is to increase the academic rigor of CTE, not to transform the high school. If that means we endorse tracking, we plead guilty. But this is a more just track than the one imposed by the default dropout track.

SUMMARY

Trends in the automation of routine tasks and the offshoring of jobs have resulted in a decrease in the proportion of jobs in the middle range of skills, those requiring more than a high school diploma, but less than a baccalaureate degree. Nevertheless, these middle-skill jobs still represent about half of the projected total workforce in the next decade. Many of these jobs offer earnings much higher than the median for all jobs. Many of these jobs also involve trades, such as those in construction, or services, such as those in health care, that are largely immune to automation and offshoring. Reverse transfers indicate that many college graduates have found that a 4-year degree did not result in the type of career that they had anticipated. Follow-up studies conducted in the 1980s and later consistently find that students who followed a CTE concentration realized earnings advantages when compared to similar students with no CTE.

Radical critics of education contend that all of education is designed to perpetuate the class inequalities inherent in a capitalistic economy. CTE is often cited as playing a primary role by lowering the occupational aspiration of young people from low-income and minority families. Family circumstances obviously have a strong influence on educational outcomes, but the schools must deal with the students that our society produces. CTE provides for many students a preferred option to the academic classroom.

CHAPTER 7

Building the System and Delivering the Curriculum

In the preceding chapters we have argued that for many young people simply requiring more academic courses will not teach the skills needed for rewarding careers or success in college. More such courses, as typically taught, may have just the opposite effect: less learning and more dropouts. We have discussed how career and technical education (CTE) can contribute to improved academic achievement, high school graduation, and transition to postsecondary education and employment. In this we have sought to make the case that CTE engages many youth who would otherwise be indifferent, if not alienated, to traditional academic classes; CTE can prepare more youth to be truly career and college ready. We have described rewarding occupations that can be entered directly from high school, or from postsecondary certification or associate degree programs. And we have reviewed evidence indicating that students who learn occupational skills while in high school have higher earnings than similar students who did not study these skills.

We acknowledge that much of what we have discussed concerning CTE and academic achievement is more potential than reality, and major changes will be needed if CTE is to accomplish what we believe it can. In this chapter we describe the kinds of changes that are needed and present a scenario of how these changes could be implemented. We hasten to note that everything we propose here is being done somewhere in the United States today. But not everything we propose here is being done with the coherence or with the focus we propose.

We present a scenario written from the perspective of the year 2017 that focuses on organizing schools to provide more opportunities for students to begin the process of becoming productive adults. This scenario proposes a framework for how schools can be organized to provide more effective and academically rigorous CTE programs. These systems changes are not large; rather, they require the realignment of existing systems structures and functions. The scenario focuses on those students who take several CTE courses, because it is these students for whom the emphasis on more academic courses will likely be least successful. These students need to improve their academic skills, but more traditional courses are unlikely to produce the result desired.

The alternative approach we recommend will not be easy to implement. It will require cooperation between academic and CTE teachers and this means time to meet and plan. One of the major differences between American teachers and their counterparts in countries with the highest scores in international comparisons is the amount of work hours spent in professional learning and collaboration (Wei et al., 2009). American teachers spend almost all of their time in the classroom. Teachers in high-scoring countries spend less than half of their workday in direct instruction. There is an emerging consensus that a key to improving instruction is developing a sense of community among teachers. We review the evidence supporting this consensus and suggest steps that can be taken to encourage a learning community to emerge.

We conclude the book by repeating that we are not trying to change all of secondary education. We think the typical college preparatory curriculum has much room for improvement, but that is not what we are trying to change. Our concern in this book is those many students for whom the academic class is a poor fit. Since its origins, CTE has served these students, sometimes well, sometimes poorly. Our goal is to use the pedagogy inherent in CTE to improve and reinforce the skills that will be essential for success in a labor market that is certain to experience continuous economic and technological change.

BUILDING A CAREER AND COLLEGE SYSTEM

Our recommendations for improving the academic performance of CTE students draw heavily on the Math-in-CTE study (Stone et al., 2006), the authentic literacy study (Park et al., in press), and the Science in CTE study (NRCCTE Curriculum Integration Workgroup, 2010) discussed in Chapter 4. These studies are to our knowledge the only randomized control trials that have demonstrated the effectiveness of enhanced academic instruction in regular CTE courses. To recap, in the math study the students who received the enhanced instruction (the experimental students) scored significantly better on standardized tests of mathematics than the control students. And the differences were of a meaningful magnitude with effect sizes on TerraNova of .55 and on Accuplacer of .42. Follow-up of the teachers who participated in the study found almost three fourths (73%) of the experimental CTE teachers and two thirds (66%) of the math teachers who had worked with them continued to use methods and materials from the study in the school year that followed the experimental intervention. In light of the literature on the difficulties of achieving and sustaining change in education, these findings provide a strong base for our recommendations.

In the literacy study, the teachers assigned to the experimental groups were trained to use a variety of strategies to improve the ability of their students to read and comprehend difficult text. The students of the teachers who received this training scored significantly better, with effect sizes in the mid-20s, on the Gates-MacGinitie Reading Test than the students of the control group teachers. Some of the teachers in the experimental groups had also participated in the pilot study, and the students of these teachers scored significantly higher than the students of the teachers who participated only in the full-year study, with effect sizes of .48 on the raw scores and .45 on the extended scale scores. The intervention improved reading scores and additional training and experience in the reading strategies improved the scores even more.

In the science study, we found similar but not as pronounced effects as we did in the math and literacy studies. The positive effects occurred among students whose pretest scores were in the upper three quartiles but not among those who scored in the lowest quartile. The more students knew about science coming into the CTE classes, the more they got out of the integrated curriculum.

It bears repeating that these outcomes were achieved with self-selected teachers who were more motivated to improve their teaching ability than teachers who did not volunteer. During the experiments they had the support of the project staff and their fellow volunteers, but they did not have what is repeatedly reported as a key to successful educational change: supportive principals (e.g., Hargreaves & Fink, 2006). Their principals were aware of their participation in the studies, but they were not active members of the communities of practice. If our experimental teachers had been in schools with other teachers who had received the same professional development and were actively supported by their principals, the impact of the interventions may have been even larger.

Given that the experiments yielded meaningful differences in learning, and that most of the teachers who participated continued to use the method and materials, what would districts that may want to try our approach have to do? Rather than a set of disconnected recommendations, we offer a scenario of a possible future and then discuss if the future we portray could become a reality.

IS THIS FUTURE POSSIBLE?[1]

Superintendent Helen Smith's school district includes 11 high schools that range from small rural schools to larger schools in an urban setting. In the past 5 years, she has been able to cut her dropout rate in half. More of her graduates are leaving high school with a "credentialed" diploma. The credentials include college credits and industry certifications.

Smith attributes much of the decline in dropout to efforts to increase both the relevance and rigor of the CTE programs her district offers. In 2006 the reauthorization of the Perkins CTE legislation required the district to offer at least one program of study to be eligible for federal funds. In discussion with her CTE director, John Hughes, Superintendent Smith reviewed the performance of the Tech Programs that the district had in place and asked what would be needed to make them programs of study. Hughes identified three major challenges: increasing the academic rigor of the Tech Prep courses, improving the alignment of secondary and postsecondary programs (as part of this, more clearly identifying appropriate industry credentials), and enhancing career development. Smith asked for suggestions for addressing these challenges, and Hughes outlined the initiatives described below.

Increasing Academic Rigor

At the 2006 annual convention of the Association for Career and Technical Education, Hughes had attended a 1-day workshop presented by the NRCCTE. This workshop provided an overview of a method to enhance mathematics instruction in CTE classes and assisted Hughes to develop a tentative plan for implementing the method. He knew that he would have to recruit teams of CTE and mathematics teachers and provide them with 10 days of professional development (PD) and that this would require funding beyond his regular budget.

Ten days were a lot of PD, but since his district enrollment included a high percentage of students eligible for free and reduced lunches, the district qualified for considerable funding from both Perkins and NCLB. Hughes also knew that his state's plan for the use of its Perkins grant promised to "promote the integration of coherent and rigorous academic content standards with CTE curricula, including opportunities for appropriate academic and CTE teachers to jointly develop and implement curricula and pedagogical strategies" (Perkins IV, Sec. 122(c)(2)(A)).

Hughes outlined for Superintendent Smith his ideas for implementing the integration model. Demonstrating adequate yearly progress was the superintendent's top priority and she liked what she heard. She also was well aware of the difficulties of implementing large-scale change in her district. She asked Hughes to put together a proposal for a pilot test of the methods he was proposing. She promised that if Hughes obtained funds from the state's Perkins grant, she would find dollars to match it.

Encouraged by this response, Hughes decided to focus on the two occupational areas that had the highest number of teachers in the district: business and health. He developed a proposal to request funds for the NRCCTE to provide PD to these teachers. In addition to the fee paid to the NRCCTE, the budget included funds to cover the cost of bringing the teachers together for a summer workshop, a $100 per day stipend for the teachers when the PD occurred on nonschool days, and pay for substitute teachers when the workshops occurred on school days. The proposal also asked the state department to assign from its staff a CTE supervisor and a mathematics supervisor to assist in the PD.

The state department funded the proposal in March 2007, and Hughes began recruiting CTE teachers to participate. He sent out an announcement about the new initiative to all the teachers in the two selected CTE areas and invited them to apply to participate. The announcement described what would be asked of those who volunteered: 10 days of PD, beginning with 1 week during the summer of 2007; writing of lesson plans; and teaching all the lessons developed for their occupational areas. His initial announcement drew applications from about half of the desired 10 teachers per area. He knew he needed at least 10 because the NRCCTE research pointed to the need for a critical mass of teachers to establish a functional community of practice. Hughes met individually with those who applied and asked them to encourage colleagues who might be interested to apply. He also asked if they could recruit math teachers to work with them. Only about one third knew math teachers who were interested, so Hughes worked with the math supervisor for the district to recruit the number needed.

In July 2007 the 40 teachers, 20 CTE and 20 math, came together for PD. They met as a full group to receive an overview of the pedagogic model they would be using. After their initial briefing, the CTE teachers and their math partners separated into their two occupational areas. The first thing they did was map the CTE curricula to identify math that naturally occurs, i.e., that which is essential to the occupational skills being taught. Each group identified 10 math concepts that met this definition. Each of the CTE and math teacher teams selected one of the concepts and worked together to develop a lesson plan to teach that concept within its occupational context. Within each occupational area, each team presented a draft of its lesson to their colleagues for their critique and used the critique to revise the lesson. The CTE teachers then individually decided when they would teach the lessons that had been developed during the coming 2007–08 school year. While working with their CTE partners, the math teachers identified many examples of applications of mathematics that they could use in their classes.

During that school year, the CTE teachers taught the lessons. They met with their math partners before teaching to review concepts and obtain suggestions for presenting the material. All the teachers came together during the fall and spring semesters for 2-day "refresher" workshops to report on the lessons they had taught and the students' responses. The CTE-math teams that had developed each of the lessons used this feedback to revise their lessons.

The students who received these lessons took pretests and posttests to assess their effect. Posttest scores were 7% to 10% higher than the pretests. Armed with this evidence, Hughes received approval and funding to expand this approach to other occupational areas. Hughes recruited additional teachers in each of his occupational areas. He used the CTE and math teachers who had taken part in the pilot to provide leadership to these new groups. He continued the 5-day workshops during the summer and the 2-day "refreshers" during the school year, and he continued to draw upon the NRCCTE to provide technical assistance as needed.

One of the unexpected outcomes of these partnerships between the CTE and academic teachers was the impact on the math teacher partners. When Hughes was visiting with the teachers after the 2nd year of implementation, he found many of the math teacher partners were using the lessons they helped develop for the CTE classes in their own math classes. The math teachers told him they thought this was a richer and more useful way to help their students understand key math concepts.

After 5 years all of the teachers who were receptive to the new approach had taken part in the PD, and the effects of explicit math instruction were being seen in the statewide tests. Working together to develop the lessons had given both the CTE and math teachers increased respect for what their colleagues were teaching. The CTE teachers reported that explicit math instruction was helping their students to learn the technical skills better. The students understood the concepts rather than just rules to apply. The math teachers had more "real-world" applications to answer the perennial question, "How am I ever going to use this?"

The success of the math initiative provided support for efforts to improve the literacy skills of CTE students. The methods used in these efforts had also been tested in an experiment conducted by the NRCCTE. These methods were adapted from the MAX (Motivation, Acquisition, eXtension) model developed by Forget (2004). Implementation of this model began prior to the 2011–12 school year and used essentially the same procedures as the math initiative, but teachers were recruited from all occupational areas. The same $100 stipend for professional development conducted on nonschool days was offered to encourage participation. Many CTE teachers who had participated in math enhancement also volunteered for the literacy initiative.

The teachers who chose to take part came together for a 5-day workshop during the summer of 2011. They began the workshop by discussing the types of reading their students must do and the problems they encounter with these materials. The workshop facilitators provided an overview of the various strategies that are part of the MAX model (see Table 4.5 in Chapter

4). The facilitators explained the theory and techniques that each strategy involved and modeled its application. The teachers practiced each strategy as both teachers and learners, and worked with others to identify opportunities to apply the strategy in their own classes. A special emphasis was placed on the motivational component because many students choose CTE programs because they do not like to read.

During the 2011–12 school year the teachers applied those strategies that they found appropriate for their own occupational areas. Some of the teachers had more success than others, but most found at least some of the strategies to be effective. Twice during the school year, 2-day workshops were held at which the teachers shared their successes and challenges in applying the strategies. The facilitators who had led the summer workshop also conducted these workshops and helped the group identify ways to respond to the challenges.

Those teachers who had participated in both the math and literacy initiative saw the results of their efforts to enhance the academic content of their courses. Their students demonstrated a deeper understanding of their occupational areas and engaged in more self-directed learning. Their performance on standardized tests also improved. Many of the students had not passed the state-mandated graduation test administered near the end of the 10th grade, and had to retake it during the 11th and 12th grades until they received passing scores. As the teachers became more comfortable with teaching enhanced academics, the number of students passing the test began to increase.

Teachers who initially had been indifferent or skeptical of the enhancement efforts began to show more interest. Hughes responded to their interest by creating professional learning communities and appointing the teachers with the most experience with enhanced academics as resources for these communities. The communities identified the major learning difficulties their students were experiencing and developed and tested ways of responding to these difficulties. When they encountered particularly difficult and pervasive problems, Hughes arranged for consultants to meet with the communities to explore possible approaches. Gradually, almost all of the CTE teachers were including explicit academic instruction as an integral component of their courses.

Improving Secondary-Postsecondary Alignment Leading to Industry Credentials

During the years that the district increased the academic rigor of its CTE courses, it also converted its Tech Prep offerings into programs of study. The conversion began with a review of existing Tech Prep programs to determine if they should be continued, modified, or replaced. To conduct this review, Superintendent Smith and the president of the community college that was a partner in the articulation agreements jointly appointed a committee made up of employers, union officials, and secondary and postsecondary instructors. This POS Steering Committee drew together projections of future job openings developed by the state and the best evidence it could assemble on the employment and postsecondary educational experiences of CTE graduates. A review of this evidence led to the selection of six career areas in which programs of study would be developed: Architecture and Construction; Business, Management, and Administration; Health Sciences; Hospitality and Tourism; Information Technology; and Transportation, Distribution, and Logistics. These clusters were selected because the job projections indicated they met the Perkins criteria of high-wage/high-demand occupations and were linked to economic projections for their region.

The district had Tech Prep programs in each of these clusters and work began to convert them into programs of study. The first step was to establish a joint technical advisory committee for each of the six areas. This committee included secondary and postsecondary instructors, counselors from both education systems, employees of the industry or union representatives, and was led by one of the industry representatives. They began with a review of the articulation agreements that had been originally developed in the 1990s and updated periodically. Both the secondary and postsecondary representatives conceded that these agreements had limited impact on what happened in the classroom. To strengthen the agreements so that they influenced both curriculum and instruction, the decision was made that programs of study would be based on standards that were developed by the major stakeholders in each occupational area and that led to industry-recognized credentials. The joint technical committees acknowledged that these standards had meaning in the labor market only if they, the employers, saw value in them in the hiring process. A second decision was to move from articulated credit to dual credit. Students who obtained a B or better in a dually credited class received immediate college credit and started a college transcript.

The six joint committees used resource materials from the Career Clusters Initiative and industry standards for their occupational areas to determine the foundation knowledge and skills that all students within a given cluster should acquire as well as the knowledge and skills for the pathways that were to be offered within each of the clusters. When a consensus was reached on the learning outcomes to be achieved and what industry credentials would be included, the committees decided what instruction should occur during each year of a 4-year program of study. The committees then compared these outcomes to the content of existing courses at the secondary and postsecondary levels to determine if they were adequately aligned to deliver the necessary instruction. Areas of duplication were identified and recommended sequences of courses and the outcomes they should achieve were prepared.

Planning for the programs of study took over 2 years, and implementation began during the 2009–10 school year. Some new courses were developed to fill gaps that had been identified, a few courses were eliminated, and all the courses that were continued required some modifications. Developing and modifying courses were ongoing processes at all the cooperating institutions, but increasing secondary-postsecondary alignment required much more cooperation than had been the case prior to programs of study. The industry partners stepped forward and offered to subsidize the cost of credentialing tests. The process was prolonged, but those involved felt that the continuing interaction increased each side's understanding of the other and resulted in much higher levels of alignment than had existed previously.

Gradually, the increased alignment and enhanced academics of the programs of study began to impact student performance. To enroll in these programs students had to decide which of the six career clusters was of most interest to them. This caused many who had not seriously thought about their career goals to consider various options. The foundation courses increased their knowledge of the variety of occupations within the clusters they chose. For many, their program of study was the first time they saw a connection between what they did in school and their future lives. They became more interested in their courses and began to apply themselves more seriously. The increased engagement in their education led to higher grades and fewer withdrawals from school. Many who had never considered postsecondary education decided to give it a try, and they found a high level of alignment between what they had studied in high school with what they studied at the community college. The community college found that the students who continued the programs of study they had started in high school needed to take fewer developmental courses than other entering students.

Enhancing Career Development

As the partners continued to review the implementation progress, they began to realize that most students do not come into high school with sufficient background on career possibilities to make wise choices. Beginning in 2012, the middle schools serving the 11 high schools required all students to develop an individualized graduation plan (IGP). This plan had several requirements:

- All students would take a career assessment in 7th grade. The purpose of this assessment would be to give students and their parents a basis for their conversation with the guidance counselors about possible career trajectories and what kind of curricular and extra-curricular activities would be useful.

- The IGP would have a 5-year, rolling planning window. At the end of 7th grade, students and their parents would plan for the 5 years concluding with high school graduation. When the counselors, students, and parents met the next year, they would plan for the next 5 years—that would include 1 year past high school. By the time the student completed high school, their IGP would include the next 5 years after high school—college, the military, industry training, or work.
- All academic teachers would use the students' IGPs as the basis for at least one assignment in each semester beginning in 8th grade and continuing throughout the students' academic career.
- To ensure smoother transition for students in specific career path-ways, each community college would identify a staff member who would coordinate with the high school counselors.

Finally, the POS Steering Committee recognized that if the high school teachers and counselors were to be effective partners in this effort, they needed to spend time with the different POS partners. Because of its im-portance, the members of the various joint technical committees provided support for school personnel to spend time in their businesses working with industry experts identifying learning opportunities, developing lesson plans based on industry activities, and learning more about career possibilities.

This scenario is optimistic but not utopian. Everything described here is happening somewhere today. The professional development described parallels closely that which the teachers in the Math-in-CTE study received and that which is part of the technical assistance offered by the NRCCTE. By the end of the 2010–11 school year, the NRCCTE had provided tech-nical assistance on the Math-in-CTE model to 27 states, regional consor-tia, and large school districts. A total of 187 administrators, 649 CTE teachers, and 602 math teachers have participated, and it is estimated that more than 17,000 students have been directly impacted by this technical assistance.[2] The description of the planning and implementation of pro-grams of study is drawn from the ongoing studies of these programs being conducted by the NRCCTE (Programs of Study Joint Technical Working Group, 2010, 2011).

The outcomes we attribute to programs of study are those we think the changes that we propose can produce. At the time this is written, however, we have little evidence that such outcomes are actually being produced. In the following section, we discuss the conditions necessary for a school dis-trict to move in the direction presented in this scenario.

DELIVERING A CAREER AND COLLEGE CURRICULUM

In Chapter 4 we presented the five core principles that emerged from the Math-in-CTE study. The first and most important of these was "Develop and sustain a community of practice among the teachers." Since the report of that study was released, the National Staff Development Council[3] published *Professional Learning in the Learning Profession* (Wei et al., 2009). The subtitle of this document is *A Status Report on Teacher Development in the United States and Abroad*, and it represents the consensus on the policies and practices most likely to produce effective teachers. At the core of these practices is the development of communities of teachers whose primary goal is to improve the learning of their students. Here is how Stephanie Hirsch, the Executive Director of the National Staff Development Council (now Learning Forward), summarized how learning communities operate in the Preface to the report:

> Teachers meet on a regular schedule in learning teams organized by grade level or content-area assignments and share responsibility for their students' success. Learning teams follow a cycle of continuous improvement that begins with examining student data to determine the areas of greatest student need, pinpointing areas where additional educator learning is necessary, identifying and creating learning experiences to address these adult needs, developing powerful lessons and assessments, applying new strategies in the classroom, refining new learning into more powerful lessons and assessments, reflecting on the impact on student learning, and repeating the cycle with new goals as necessary. (quoted in Wei et al., 2009, pp. ii–iii)

The communities that emerged in the Math-in-CTE study did so without any specific attempt on the part of those of us who directed the study to foster them. We realized from the focus groups we conducted after the intervention had ended that the groups, established purely for the purpose of developing math-enriched lessons, had taken on dimensions beyond those we had anticipated. These groups had become communities of practice with the goal of improving the math skills of their students. For this to occur, the CTE teachers had to improve their own understanding of the math they were to teach. Working with the math teachers to develop lessons and critiquing lessons developed by their peers provided the learning experiences in math that the CTE teachers needed.

The nonthreatening nature of this approach was essential to its success. Many of the CTE teachers in the Math-in-CTE study had not completed a 4-year teacher preparation program. These teachers had worked for several years in the occupations they taught before entering teaching. They had limited training in pedagogy and were not comfortable attempting to teach academics. Many of the teachers who had completed traditional programs also expressed concerns about their ability to teach math. Working with math teachers to develop lessons increased their understanding and built their confidence. Throughout the school year, the CTE teachers met with their math partners prior to teaching the lessons to review concepts and obtain suggestions for explaining the most difficult aspects. If instead of creating teams to develop lessons, we had asked the math teachers to explicitly teach math to the CTE teachers, it is highly unlikely that communities of practice would have emerged.

Time for teachers to meet and work together is critical for learning communities, and it may well be the resource most difficult to provide. As currently structured, American schools have little time for teachers to meet. Classes must be "covered," that is, a teacher must be in the classroom. Schools do not have enough teachers to cover all classes and also provide time during the school day for meetings to improve instruction. If learning communities were to become standard practice, either more teachers would have to be hired or the workday of teachers lengthened, and both alternatives have major financial implications. These implications raise questions about the pace and extent to which learning communities will become integral to American schools, but without them the collaboration needed to improve the academic rigor of the CTE curriculum will not occur.

Learning communities are essential, but creating a career and college curriculum also requires career pathways based on the realities of the labor market and opportunities for students to experience those realities. Programs that lead to industry-recognized certification and active advisory committees can provide the labor market linkage. Career guidance, work-based learning (WBL), and career-technical student organizations (CTSO) can provide opportunities for testing one's interests and abilities outside the classroom. In Chapter 2, we discussed the growth and exploratory stages of the career development process and the need for a distributed approach to guidance/counseling that involves all significant adults in students' lives. A stronger emphasis on careers is needed. The counseling function should do more than assist students to prepare for the next level of education. The benefits of WBL and CTSOs were discussed in Chapter 4. Both provide experiences that develop the problem-solving and interpersonal skills highly desired by employers. Students value the opportunities to apply what they study in the classroom to tasks with real-world consequences. Past attempts to expand WBL have demonstrated that employers need to see tangible benefits from the students they hire. The small number who offer internships, apprenticeships, and cooperative placements report high levels of satisfaction with the students they employ, but most employers remain reluctant to offer training of any depth to young people in their teens and early twenties.

SUMMING UP

The argument may be raised that if the approach to enhanced academics that we propose were to be followed, students would learn only content related to the occupations they study. Students in auto technology, for example, would learn about the physics of motors, brakes, and electrical systems, but no biology or physiology. Students in health occupations, in contrast, would learn biology and physiology, but little physics. Emphasizing occupational applications of academics does restrict coverage, but it can produce more in-depth understanding of the topics covered. Most occupationally specific CTE courses are taught in the last 2 years of high school. Students are likely to have had previous exposure to the academics inherent in these courses, but many will not have developed a full understanding of the concepts. Explicitly teaching the concepts that underlie the application of the academics can contribute to more complete learning.

Some educators may object, but we consider much of the pedagogy of CTE as consistent with the principles of the Coalition of Essential Schools (2010). These principles place "Learning to use one's mind well" as the central purpose of education. Fundamental to using one's mind is a strong foundation in basic academics. One must have a level of language, mathematical, and scientific knowledge and understanding sufficient to identify and apply the information needed to deal with the challenges life presents. Developing such a base, however, does not require that students study superficially a wide variety of unrelated subjects.

The first Coalition principle is "Less is more, depth over coverage." While this may appear to exclude the teaching of occupational skills, we think studying occupations can provide the "more." Occupational relevance can provide the context and motivation to learn academics that were not acquired in traditional classrooms. Many high school reform efforts, such as those discussed by Oakes and Saunders (2008), are built around an occupational focus. In the approach we propose, however, teaching academics is not the primary goal. The goal is to teach those academics that contribute to the learning of occupational skills. In this way, the integrity of both the academic and occupational content is preserved. Students choose CTE in the expectation that they will learn skills that will be of value in the labor market, and these expectations should be honored. If secondary CTE were to become just a "disguise" by which to teach academics, we doubt that it would retain its appeal to students.

Secondary CTE should emphasize improving academic skills because deficiencies in these skills are the primary barriers to the success of its students in postsecondary education (Bailey, Jeong, & Cho, 2008; Bragg et al., 2002; Castellano et al., 2007). Typically half or more of the CTE graduates who start postsecondary education must take developmental courses, and many never progress beyond these into the technical programs they want to study.

Another reason for enhancing academics is the developmental nature of career choice (Osipow & Fitzgerald, 1996). When high school students choose a program to study, most are engaging in career exploration. Many do not find employment in the occupations they study in high school or continue to study them at the postsecondary level. This is not a failure of either the programs or the students. It is part of the normal developmental process. Learning more about one's self and the demands of occupations represents positive growth. An explicit effort to teach academics in an occupational context will promote learning that will be useful regardless of the occupations that graduates eventually enter.

The need for rigor in both the academic and technical content of CTE programs has been accepted by the leadership of the field. The Association for Career and Technical Education (2006) has published *Reinventing the American High School for the 21st Century*. This is a position paper endorsed by the leadership of the field that proposes three purposes for secondary CTE programs. The first purpose is "Support students in the acquisition of rigorous core knowledge, skills, habits, and attitudes needed for success in postsecondary education and the high-skilled workplace" (p. 1). The National Association of State Directors of Career Technical Education Consortium (NASDCTEc) has as its members the officials responsible for state leadership of CTE. NASDCTEc (2010b) has published *Reflect, Transform, Lead: A New Vision for Career Technical Education*. In this paper, the state directors commit themselves to develop programs of study (as described in Perkins IV) that prepare students for further education and careers. These programs will follow the career clusters/career pathways model, discussed briefly in Chapter 1, which has been adopted by most states as the method of organizing their programs (NASDCTEc, 2010a).

As part of their vision, the state directors foresee the blurring of the lines that separate CTE and academic education: "The dichotomous silos of academics versus CTE must be eliminated and their supporting infrastructures must be re-imagined to meet the needs of the economy" (NASDCTEc, 2010b, p. 8). While we would like to see this occur, we think it unlikely that it will. The grammar/core of schooling is too strong. The college preparatory curriculum is doing what its students, and more importantly, the parents of its students want it to do. We hope, however, that the endorsement of rigorous academics as integral to CTE will result in increased efforts to strengthen such instruction. Even this modest goal will be hard to achieve, but it is far more feasible than attempting to change the full high school curriculum.

Finally, we think the mantra of "college for all" does more harm than good. It demeans those students, at least half of all who enter high school, who will never complete a college program. Workers with high levels of mathematical, scientific, and innovative skills are needed to keep the United States competitive in the global economy, but the evidence indicates that our colleges and universities are producing more graduates with these skills than the labor market can absorb. There is little need to encourage young people to aspire to occupations they have little chance of entering when there is widespread demand for workers with skills. Our society needs technicians of all kinds as well as plumbers, mechanics, truck drivers, manufacturing workers, grocery clerks, bank tellers, secretaries, file clerks, waiters, fire fighters, and millions of other workers who take pride in what they do. Even assuming that those performing these jobs may have aspired to something different, surveys of the general population, such as the General Social Survey (National Opinion Research Center, 2010), consistently find the majority of workers to be completely or very satisfied with their jobs and less than 10% to be dissatisfied. Everyone dreams of what might have been, but most of us come to terms with the reality of what actually is. Stressing the goal of college for all implies that those who do not go on to college are failures. We would like to see our schools instill a respect for the value of all work. John Gardner (1961) expressed our position far better than we can in the following frequently quoted passage:

> An excellent plumber is infinitely more admirable than an incompetent philosopher. The society which scorns excellence in plumbing because plumbing is a humble activity and tolerates shoddiness in philosophy because it is an exalted activity will have neither good plumbing nor good philosophy. Neither its pipes nor its theories will hold water. (p. 102)

So we conclude where we began, high school must matter. It must matter in more ways than simply focusing on college for all. Schools play a major role in preparing students for future occupational roles. As a society, we should attempt to make this process as independent of circumstances of birth as possible, but school performance will continue to have a strong influence on occupational aspirations and expectations. For the already engaged student, CTE can provide a career focus and help them become more career ready. CTE provides for many students a reason to stay in school, and a setting that is more engaging than the academic classroom. The challenge for CTE is to use its appeal to the many disengaged students to improve their academic skills so they will be prepared to adapt and respond to the technological and economic changes they are sure to experience. And thus, to help them prepare to be truly career and college ready.

Notes

Chapter 1

1. The statistics in the following paragraphs are from *Career and Technical Education in the United States: 1990 to 2005* (Levesque et al., 2008). This is the most recent report of CTE data in a series that is published once every 5 years by the National Center for Education Statistics (NCES). The 2008 report draws together information from 11 different NCES surveys that collect data on CTE.

2. The 1984 act was the first to carry the name of Carl D. Perkins, a long-time advocate for vocational education who died while still serving in Congress. The three reauthorizations of this act in 1990, 1998, and 2006 are typically referred to as Perkins II, III, and IV.

Chapter 2

1. This discussion is based on what ACT describes as an executive summary. Repeated requests to ACT for the original report from which the summary is derived have been unsuccessful. It appears that the original report is not available for scholarly review.

2. For more information about career clusters and career pathways, the reader is referred to the webpage of the States' Career Cluster Initiative: http://www.career-clusters.org.

3. Full disclosure requires that we note *Pathways to Prosperity* acknowledges Jim Stone as a contributor to the work of the project and cites unpublished analyses conducted by him that indicate requiring high school students to earn additional credits in mathematics and science may lower, not increase, graduation rates.

4. This section originally appeared as Chapter 4 in an NRCCTE report by Lewis and Kosine (2008). It has been edited for inclusion in this book.

5. The Levesque et al. (2008) and Bishop (1989) findings are based on national longitudinal studies in the United States. Similar results have been obtained in Australia (Smith & Green, 2005).

Chapter 3

1. While the origins of this phrase have not been clearly attributed, it is closely associated with former president George W. Bush's advocacy for NCLB.

2. Agodini and Deke refer to these as "vocational," but we use the newer label for the field.

3. Ad hoc analyses that compared AHS students to their full-grade cohorts at C-AHS (including students who had not attended Academy Middle School) yielded larger differences favoring AHS.

Chapter 4

1. Information on the AOIT during the 2009–10 school year was provided by the academy director, Julie Oster, on April 7, 2010. Mrs. Oster is also the CTE director for Apex High School.

2. Roberta Floyd, Instructional Coordinator, provided information on integration efforts at the East San Gabriel Valley ROP on April 13, 2010.

3. Harvey Burniston, Jr., head of the Agricultural Education Department, provided information about his program on April 30, 2010.

4. Jeffrey Dole, Career Preparation Specialist with Ingham Intermediate School District, provided information on LAMP, on April 15, 2010.

5. The full report of the pilot study is presented in Stone, Alfeld, Pearson, Lewis, and Jensen (2005).

6. These percentage differences reflect effect sizes on TerraNova of .55 and on Accuplacer of .42. An *effect size* is a measure of the difference between the means of two groups in comparison to the overall variation of the scores in the groups.

7. The CTSOs recognized by the U.S. Department of Education as eligible to receive funding under Perkins IV are as follow: Business Professionals of America; DECA (formerly Distributive Education Clubs of America); Future Business Leaders of America (FBLA); Family, Career and Community Leaders of America; FFA; Health Occupation Students of America (HOSA); SkillsUSA; and Technology Student Association.

Chapter 5

1. This section is an edited version of material from Chapter 2 of an NRCCTE report by Lewis and Kosine (2008).

2. The exploratory stage of career development is discussed at length in the section on Career Guidance in Chapter 2.

3. We estimated this percentage by dividing the 1,200,000 enrolled in dual credit courses reported by Waits et al. (2005) by the 14,067,000 enrollment in Grades 9 through 12 in the fall of 2002 reported in Table 2 of the *Digest of Educational Statistics: 2007* (retrieved from http://nces.ed.gov/programs/digest/d07/tables/dt07_002. asp?referrer=list). The percentages taking dual credit courses may be slightly inflated because of duplicate counting of students taking more than one such course.

4. "Participants" were students who had selected a CTE major or taken one CTE course. "Concentrators" had completed one third of the credits required by their programs. "Completers" had received certificates, diplomas, or AA or AAS degrees.

5. This section is taken from the NRCCTE report by the Programs of Study Joint Technical Working Group (2011).

6. In addition to the four legislative components, the Office of Vocational and Adult Education collaborated with major stakeholders in CTE to develop a POS Design Framework. This framework sets forth 10 components and subcomponents

that support the planning and implementation of effective POS. The Design Framework can be accessed at http://cte.ed.gov/nationalinitiatives/rposdesignframework.cfm

Chapter 6

1. For a more complete discussion of the differences between the BLS and Carnevale et al. (2010) methods, see Appendix 4 to the Carnevale et al. report that can be retrieved from http://www9.georgetown.edu/grad/gppi/hpi/cew/pdfs/Appendices.pdf

2. For the logistic regressions, these percentages are the Nagelkerke (1991) coefficient of determination, or pseudo R^2.

3. The findings on postgraduate reverse transfers presented here represent a synthesis based on the following studies of state or institutional samples: California Postsecondary Education Commission (2006) statewide data; Pope, Turner, and Barker (2001); Oklahoma City Community College data; Quinley and Quinley (1999) data from an unidentified community college serving a large urban area in North Carolina; Reusch (2000) statewide Illinois data; Winter, Harris, and Ziegler (2001) statewide Kentucky data.

4. Agricultural education, especially in rural areas, has been the exception to this generalization. Agricultural education is often taught at a college preparatory level.

5. The term "Linked Learning," which was discussed in Chapter 2, has replaced multiple pathways in the initiative being directed by ConnectEd.

Chapter 7

1. The following is a modification of a scenario originally published in Lewis and Pearson (2007).

2. Unpublished data compiled by the NRCCTE. The estimate of students impacted is based on students of the CTE teachers who participated in the professional development. It does not include students of math teachers many of whom reported they used examples of math applications they had developed with the CTE teachers in their own classes.

3. After this report was published, the National Staff Development Council changed its name to Learning Forward.

References

Achieve. (2004). *Ready or not: Creating a high school diploma that counts.* Washington, DC: Author. Retrieved from http://www.achieve.org/files/ADPreport_7.pdf

Achieve. (2008). *The building blocks of success: Higher level math for all students.* Washington, DC: Author. Retrieved from http://www.achieve.org/files/BuildingBlocksofSuccess.pdf

Achieve. (2010). *Closing the expectations gap: Fifth annual 50-state progress report on the alignment of high school policies with the demands of college and career.* Washington, DC: Author. Retrieved from http://www.achieve.org/files/AchieveClosingtheExpectationsGap2010.pdf

ACT. (2006). *Ready for college and ready for work: Same or different.* Iowa City, IA: Author. Retrieved from http://www.act.org/research/policymakers/pdf/ReadinessBrief.pdf

Adelman, C. (2006). *The toolbox revisited: Paths to degree completion from high school through college.* Washington, DC: U.S. Department of Education. Retrieved from http://www.ed.gov/rschstat/research/pubs/toolboxrevisit/toolbox.pdf

Agodini, R., & Deke, J. (2004). *The relationship between high school vocational education and dropping out.* Princeton, NJ: Mathematica Policy Research. Retrieved from http://www.mathematica-mpr.com/publications/PDFs/voc-ed%20dropping%20out.pdf

Alfeld, C., Stone, J. R., Aragon, S. R., Hansen, D. M., Zirkle, C., Connors, J., . . . Woo, H.-J. (2007). *Looking inside the black box: The value added by career and technical student organizations to students' high school experience.* St. Paul: National Research Center for Career and Technical Education, University of Minnesota.

Aliaga, O. A., Stone, J. R., III, Kotamraju, P., & Dickinson, E. R. (2011, September 28). *Career and technical education as a strategy to prevent dropping out of high school.* Paper presented at the Indiana Dropout Prevention Leadership Summit, Indianapolis, IN.

Allen, D., Nichols, P., Tocci, C., Hochman, D., & Gross, K. (2006). *Supporting student success through distributed counseling: A core principle for small schools.* New York: National Center for Restructuring Education, Institute for Student Achievement, Teachers College, Columbia University. Retrieved from http://www.tc.columbia.edu/ncrest/onlinepub/ISA%20DC.SP.FINAL.pdf

American Association of Family and Consumer Sciences. (2011). *AAFCS: American Association of Family and Consumer Sciences.* http://www.aafcs.org/

American Institutes for Research (AIR). (2011). *Evaluation of the early college high school initiative: Impact study overview.* Retrieved from http://www.earlycolleges.org/publications.html#evaluations

American Institutes for Research (AIR) & SRI International. (2004). *Early College High School Initiative evaluation intermediate summary report: 2003–2004.* Washington,

DC: American Institutes for Research. Retrieved from http://www.earlycolleges.org/Downloads/ECHSIntermediaryReport04.pdf

American Institutes for Research (AIR) & SRI International. (2005). *Early College High School Initiative evaluation year end report: 2003–2004.* Washington, DC: American Institutes for Research. Retrieved from http://www.earlycolleges.org/Downloads/ECHSI2005Synthesis.pdf

American Institutes for Research (AIR) & SRI International. (2006). *Early College High School Initiative: 2003–2005 Evaluation report.* Washington, DC: American Institutes for Research. Retrieved from http://www.earlycolleges.org/Downloads/ECHS_Eva_2003-2005.pdf

American Institutes for Research (AIR) & SRI International. (2007). *Evaluation of the Early College High School Initiative: Select topics on implementation.* Washington, DC: American Institutes for Research. Retrieved from http://www.earlycolleges.org/Downloads/ECHSI_ Synth%20Report2007.pdf

American Institutes for Research (AIR) & SRI International. (2009*). Six years and counting: The ECHSI matures.* Washington, DC: American Institutes for Research. Retrieved from http://www.earlycolleges.org/Downloads/Fifth%20Annual%20Early%20College%20High%20School%20Initiative%20Evaluation%20Synthesis%20Report.pdf

Andrew, E. N. (Ed.). (1996). *As teachers tell it: Implementing all aspects of the industry: The case studies.* Berkeley, CA: University of California, Berkeley, National Center for Research in Vocational Education. Retrieved from http://www.eric.ed.gov/PDFS/ED401465.pdf

Apple, M. W. (2004). *Ideology and curriculum* (3rd ed.). New York: RoutledgeFalmer.

Arthur, M. B., Hall, D. T., & Lawrence, B. S. (1989). Generating new directions in career theory: The case for a transdisciplinary approach. In M. B. Arthur, D. T. Hall, & B. S. Lawrence (Eds.), *Handbook of career theory* (pp. 7–25). New York: Cambridge University Press.

Association for Career and Technical Education. (2006). *Reinventing the American high school for the 21st century: A position paper.* Alexandria, VA: Author.

Association for Career and Technical Education. (2007). *Expanding opportunities: Postsecondary career and technical education and preparing tomorrow's workforce: A position paper.* Alexandria, VA: Author.

Association for Career and Technical Education, National Association of State Directors of Career Technical Education Consortium, & Partnership for 21st Century Skills. (2010). *Up to the challenge: The role of career and technical education and 21st century skills in college and career readiness.* Washington, DC: Authors. Retrieved from http://www.p21.org/documents/CTE_Oct2010.pdf

Au, W. (2009). *Unequal by design: High-stakes testing and the standardization of inequality.* New York: Routledge.

Auger, R. W., Blackhurst, A. E., & Wahl, K. H. (2005). The development of elementary-aged children's career aspirations and expectations. *Professional School Counseling, 8*(4), 322–329.

Autor, D. (2010). *The polarization of job opportunities in the U.S. labor market: Implications for employment and earnings.* Washington, DC: Center for American Progress and The Hamilton Project. Retrieved from http://www.americanprogress.org/issues/2010/04/pdf/job_polarization.pdf

Autor, D. H., Katz, L. F., & Kearney, M. S. (2006). The polarization of the U.S. labor market. *American Economics Association Papers and Proceedings, (96)*2, 189–194.

Auty, W. P., Goodman, J., & Foss, G. (1987). The relationship between interpersonal competence and work adjustment. *Vocational Evaluation & Work Adjustment Bulletin, 20*(2), 49–52.

Bailey, T. (1993a). Can youth apprenticeship thrive in the United States? *Educational Researcher, 22*(3), pp. 4–10.

Bailey, T. (1993b). Youth apprenticeship in the context of broad education reform. *Educational Researcher, 22*(3), 16–17.

Bailey, T., Jeong, D. W., & Cho, S. W. (2008). *Referral, enrollment, and completion in developmental education sequences in community colleges.* New York: Columbia University, Teachers College, Community College Research Center. Retrieved from http://ccrc.tc.columbia,edu/ContentByType.asp?t=1

Bartlett, K. R. (2004). *The signaling power of occupational certification in the automobile service and information technology industries.* St. Paul, MN: National Research Center for Career and Technical Education.

Barton, P. (2005). *One-third of a nation: Rising dropout rates and declining opportunities.* Princeton, NJ: Educational Testing Service. Retrieved from http://www.ets.org/Media/Education_Topics/pdf/onethird.pdf

Barton, P. (2006). *High school reform and work: Facing labor market realities.* Princeton, NJ: Educational Testing Service. Retrieved from http://www.ets.org/Media/Research/pdf/PICHSWORK.pdf

Beatty, A., Neisser, U., Trent, W. T., & Heubert, J. P. (Eds.). (2001). *Understanding dropouts: Statistics, strategies, and high-stakes testing.* Washington, DC: National Academies Press.

Becker, G. S. (1964). *Human capital: A theoretical and empirical analysis, with special reference to education.* New York: National Bureau of Economic Research.

Berlin, G. L. (2007). Rewarding the work of individuals: A counterintuitive approach to reducing poverty and strengthening families. *The Future of Children 17*(2), 17–42. Retrieved from http://www.eric.ed.gov/ERICDocs/data/ericdocs2sql/content_storage_01/0000019b/80/3d/d6/17.pdf

Berliner, D. C., & Biddle, B. J. (1995). *The manufactured crisis: Myths, fraud, and the attack on the American public school.* Reading, MA: Addison-Wesley.

Berliner, J. S. (1957). *Factory and manager in the U.S.S.R.* Cambridge, MA: Harvard University Press.

Bishop, J. (1989). Occupational training in high school: When does it pay off? *Economics of Education Review, 8*(1), 1–15.

Bishop, J., & Mane, F. (2004). The impacts of career-technical education on high school labor market success. *Economics of Education Review, 23*, 381–402.

Bloch, D. P. (1996). Career development and workforce preparation: Educational policy versus school practice. *The Career Development Quarterly, 45*, 20–39.

Blustein, D. L. (1988). The relationship between motivational processes and career exploration. *Journal of Vocational Behavior, 32*, 345–357.

Blustein, D. L. (1997). A context-rich perspective of career exploration across the life roles. *The Career Development Quarterly, 45*, 260–274.

Blustein, D. L. (1999). A match made in heaven? Career development theories and the school-to-work transition. *The Career Development Quarterly, 47*, 348–352.

Blustein, D. L., Devenis, L. E., & Kidney, B. A. (1989). Relationship between the identity formation process and career development. *Journal of Counseling Psychology, 36*(2), 196–202.

Borek, J. (2008, April). "A nation at risk" at 25. *Phi Delta Kappan, 89*(8), 572–574.

Bottoms, G., Han. L. L., & Murray, R. (2008). *High school experiences that influence reading proficiency: What states and schools can do.* Atlanta, GA: Southern Regional Education Board. Retrieved from http://publications.sreb.org/2008/08V21_Improving_Reading_Proficiency.pdf

Bowles, S., & Gintis, H. (1976). *Schooling in capitalistic America: Education reform and the contradictions of economic life.* New York: Basic Books.

Bragg, D. D., Loeb, J. W., Gong, Y., Deng, C.-P., Yoo, J., & Hill, J. L. (2002). *Transition from high school to college and work for Tech Prep participants in eight selected consortia.* St. Paul: National Research Center for Career and Technical Education, University of Minnesota. Retrieved from http://www.nccte.org/publications/infosynthesis/r%26dreport/Transition-Bragg%20ALL.pdf

Briggs, T. W. (2000, October 12). Farm nurtures economy of scales Tennessee teacher hooks young minds on hydroponics, fish instead of tobacco crop. *USA Today.* Retrieved from http://pqasb.pqarchiver.com/USAToday/access/62456534.html?FMT=ABS&FMTS=ABS:FT&date=Oct+12%2C+2000&author=Tracey+Wong+Briggs&pub=USA+TODAY&edition=&startpage=11.D&desc=Farm+nurtures+economy+of+scales+Tennessee+teacher+hooks+young+minds+on+hydroponics%2C+fish+instead+of+tobacco+crop

Brynjolfsson, E., &McAfee, A. (2011). *Race against the machine: How the digital revolution is accelerating innovation, driving productivity, and irreversibly transforming employment and the economy.* Lexington, MA: Digital Frontier Press.

Bush, G. W. (2004, September 2). President Bush's acceptance speech to the Republican national convention. *Washington Post.* Retrieved from http://www.washingtonpost.com/wp-dyn/articles/A57466-2004Sep2.html

California Postsecondary Education Commission. (2006). *Back to college: Are university graduates returning to community colleges?* (Working Paper 06/01). Sacramento, CA: Author. Retrieved from http://www.eric.ed.gov/PDFS/ED493535.pdf

Campbell, D. T. (1975). Assessing the impact of planned social change. In G. Lyons (Ed.), *Social research and public policies: The Dartmouth/OECD conference* (pp. 3–45). Hanover, NH: Public Affairs Center, Dartmouth College.

Cappelli, P. (2008, Summer). Schools of dreams: More education is not an economic elixir. *Issues in Science and Technology, 24*(4), 60–64. Retrieved from http://www.issues.org/24.4/cappelli.html

Carnevale, A. P., & Desrochers, D. M. (2003). The democratization of mathematics. In B. L Madison & L. A. Steen, (Eds.), *Quantitative literacy: Why numeracy matters for schools and colleges* (pp. 21–31). Proceedings of the National Forum on Quantitative Literacy held at the National Academy of Sciences in Washington, D.C., December 1–2, 2001. Princeton, NJ: National Council on Education and the Disciplines. Retrieved from http://www.maa.org/ql/qltoc.html

Carnevale, A. P., Smith, N., & Strohl, J. (2010). *Help wanted: Projections of jobs and educational requirements through 2018.* Washington, DC: Center on Education and the Workforce, Georgetown University. Retrieved from http://www9.georgetown.edu/grad/gppi/hpi/cew/pdfs/FullReport.pdf

Carnevale, A. P., Strohl, J., & Melton. M. (2011). *What's it worth? The economic value of college majors.* Washington, DC: Center on Education and the Workforce, Georgetown University. Retrieved from http://www9.georgetown.edu/grad/gppi/hpi/cew/pdfs/whatsitworth-complete.pdf

Carpenter, T. P., Blanton, M. L., Cobb, P., Franke, M. L., Kaput, J., & McClain, K.

(2004). *Scaling up innovative practices in mathematics and science.* Madison: University of Wisconsin, National Center for Improving Student Learning and Achievement in Mathematics and Science.

Cassidy, R. A. (2007). The benefits of a comprehensive K–12 career development system. *Techniques: Connecting Education & Careers, 82*(4), 44–46.

Castellano, M., Stone, J. R., III, Stringfield, S., Farley, E. N., Overman, L. T., & Hussain, R. (2007). *Career-based comprehensive school reform: Serving disadvantaged youth in minority communities.* St. Paul: National Research Center for Career and Technical Education, University of Minnesota.

Castellano, M., Stone, J. R., III, Stringfield, S., Farley, E. N., & Wayman, J. C. (2004). *The effect of CTE-enhanced whole-school reform on student coursetaking and performance in English and science.* St. Paul: National Research Center for Career and Technical Education, University of Minnesota.

Castellano, M., Stringfield, S., & Stone, J. R., III. (2001). *Career and technical education reforms and comprehensive school reforms in high schools and community colleges: Their impact on educational outcomes for at-risk youth.* St. Paul: National Research Center for Career and Technical Education, University of Minnesota.

Castellano, M., Stringfield, S., & Stone, J. R., III. (2002). *Helping disadvantaged youth succeed in school: Second-year findings from a longitudinal study of CTE-based whole-school reforms.* St. Paul: National Research Center for Career and Technical Education, University of Minnesota.

Castellano, M., Stringfield, S. C., Stone, J. R., III, & Wayman, J. C. (2003). *Early measures of student progress in schools with CTE-enhanced whole-school reform: Math course-taking patterns and student progress to graduation.* St. Paul: National Research Center for Career and Technical Education, University of Minnesota.

Cataldi, E. F., Green, C., Henke, R., Lew, T., Woo, J., Shepherd, B., & Siegel, P. (2011). *2008–09 Baccalaureate and Beyond Longitudinal Study (BB:08/09): First look* (NCES 2011-236). Washington, DC: U.S. Department of Education, Institute of Education Sciences, National Center for Education Statistics. Retrieved from http://nces.ed.gov/pubs2011/2011236.pdf

Center on Education Policy. (2008). *State high school exit exams: A move toward end-of-course exams.* Washington, DC: Author. Retrieved from http://www.eric.ed.gov/PDFS/ED504468.pdf

Chronicle of Higher Education. (2011, January 23). *Adults with college degree in the United States by counties.* Retrieved from http://chronicle.com/article/Adults-With-College-Degrees-in/125995

Clinton, B. (1991). Apprenticeship American style: Why the governor of Arkansas believes apprenticeship is a cure for what ails education. *Vocational Education Journal, 66*(7), 22–23.

Coalition of Essential Schools. (2010). *The CES common principles.* Providence, RI: Author. Retrieved from http://www.essentialschools.org/items/4

Coburn, M., Dooling, L., McGinnis, R., & Nelson, B. (2010, December). *Academic integration in action.* Presentation to the Annual Convention of the Association for Career and Technical Education, Las Vegas, NV.

Commission on National Aid to Vocational Education. (1974). Report. In M. Lazerson & W. N. Grubb (Eds.), *American education and vocationalism: A documentary history, 1870–1970* (pp. 116–132). New York: Teachers College Press. (Original work published 1914)

Common Core State Standards Initiative. (2011). *In the states.* Retrieved from http://www.corestandards.org/in-the-states

Council on Competitiveness. (2005). *Innovate America: National innovation initiative summary and report.* Washington, DC: Author. Retrieved from http://www.compete.org/images/uploads/File/PDF%20Files/NII_Innovate_America.pdf

Covey, S. (1998). *The seven habits of highly effective teens: The ultimate teenage success guide.* New York: Simon & Schuster.

Crain, R. L., Allen, A., Thaler, R., Sullivan, D., Zellman, G. L., Little, J. W., & Quigley, D. D. (1999). *The effects of career magnet education on high schools and their graduates.* Berkeley: National Center for Research in Vocational Education, University of California. Retrieved from http://www.eric.ed.gov/PDFS/ED428295.pdf

Crawford, F. (2007). High skilled jobs in finance and medical research going to India, study shows. *ChronicleOnline.* Retrieved from http://www.news.cornell.edu/stories/July07/ILRKuruvilla.html

Crawford, M. B. (2009). *Shop class as soulcraft: An inquiry into the value of work.* New York: The Penguin Press.

Csikszentmihalyi, M., & LeFevre, J. (1989). Optimal experience in work and leisure. *Journal of Personality and Social Psychology, 56,* 815–822.

Damon, W. (2008). *The path to purpose: Helping our children find their calling in life.* New York: Free Press.

Dewey, J. (1974). An undemocratic proposal. In M. Lazerson & W. N. Grubb (Eds.), *American education and vocationalism: A documentary history, 1970–1970.* (pp. 143–147). New York: Teachers College Press. (Original work published 1913)

Dougan, C. P. (2005). The pitfalls of college courses for high school students. *Chronicle of Higher Education, 52*(10), B20.

Dykeman, C., Wood, C., Ingram, M., Gitelman, A., Mandsager, N., Chen, M. Y., & Herr, E. L. (2003). *Career development interventions and academic self-efficacy and motivation: A pilot study.* St. Paul: National Research Center for Career and Technical Education, University of Minnesota.

Dykeman, C., Wood, C., Ingram, M. A., Pehrsson, D., Mandsager, N., & Herr, E. L. (2003). The structure of school career development interventions: Implications for school counselors. *Professional School Counseling, 6*(4), 272–278.

Dynarski, M., Gleason, P., Rangarajan, A., & Wood, R. (1998). *Impacts of dropout prevention programs: Final report.* Princeton, NJ: Mathematica Policy Research.

Eck, A. (1993). Job-related education and training: Their impact on earnings. *Monthly Labor Review, 116*(10), 21–38. Retrieved from http://www.bls.gov/opub/mlr/1993/10/art2full.pdf

Edmunds, J. A., Bernstein, L., Unlu, F., Glennie, E. J., Arschavsky, N., & Smith, A. (2011, April). *Keeping students in school: Impact of a high school reform model on students' enrollment and progression in school.* Paper presented at the annual meeting of the American Educational Research Association (AERA), New Orleans, LA.

Education Alliance at Brown University. (2011). *Adolescent literacy in the content areas.* Providence, RI: Brown University. Retrieved from http://knowledgeloom.org/adlit/index.jsp

Elmore, R. F. (1980). Backward mapping: Implementation research and policy decisions. *Political Science Quarterly, 94,* 601–616.

Elmore, R. F. (1996). Getting to scale with successful educational practice. In S. H. Furhman & J. A. O'Day (Eds.), *Rewards and reform: Creating educational incentives that work* (pp. 294–329). San Francisco: Jossey-Bass.

Erikson, E. H. (1959). Identity and the life cycle: Selected papers. *Psychological Issues, 1*, 1–171.

Erikson, E. H. (1963). *Childhood and society.* New York: Norton.

Farr, M., & Shatkin, L. (2009). *300 best jobs without a four-year degree* (3rd ed.). Indianapolis, IN: JIST Works.

Farrell, D., Laboissière, M., Rosenfeld, J., Stürze, S., & Umezawa, F. (2005). *The emerging global labor market: Part II—the supply of offshore talent.* San Francisco: McKinsey Global Institute. Retrieved February 9, 2009 from http://www.mckinsey.com/mgi/reports/pdfs/emerginggloballabormarket/Part2/MGI_supply_executivesummary.pdf

Fletcher, E. C., Jr., & Zirkle, C. (2009). The relationship of high school career track to degree attainment and occupational earnings. *Career and Technical Education Research, 34*(2), 81–102. Retrieved from http://acter.metapress.com/content/b1431031708124t7/fulltext.pdf

Forget, M. (2004). *MAX teaching with reading and writing: Classroom activities for helping students learn new subject matter while acquiring literacy skills.* Victoria, British Columbia, Canada: Trafford.

Fredricks, J. A., Blumenfeld, P. C., & Paris, A. H. (2004). School engagement: Potential of the concept, state of the evidence. *Review of Educational Research 74*(1), 59–109.

Fried, R. L. (2005). *The game of school: Why we play it, how it hurts kids, and what it take to change it.* San Francisco, CA: Jossey-Bass.

Fullan, M. (2007). *The NEW meaning of educational change* (4th ed.). New York: Teachers College Press.

Gardner, J. W. (1961). *Excellence: Can we be equal and excellent too?* New York: Perennial Library, Harper & Row.

Giannantonio, C. M., & Hurley-Hanson, A. E. (2006). Applying image norms across Super's career development stages. *The Career Development Quarterly, 54*(4), 318–330.

Giles, C., & Hargreaves, A. (2006). The sustainability of innovative schools as learning organizations and professional learning communities during standardized reform. *Educational Administration Quarterly, 42,* 124–156.

Ginzberg, E., Ginsburg, S. W., Axelrad, S., & Herma, J. L. (1951). *Occupational choice.* New York: Columbia University Press.

Giroux, H. A. (1983). *Theory and resistance in education: A pedagogy for the opposition.* South Hadley, MA: Bergin & Garvey.

Grabinger, R. S. (1996). Rich environments for active learning. In D. H. Jonassen (Ed.), *Handbook of Research for Educational Communications and Technology* (pp. 665–692). New York: Macmillan.

Gray, K. C., & Herr, E. L. (2006). *Other ways to win: Creating alternatives for high school graduates* (3rd ed.). Thousand Oaks, CA: Corwin Press.

Greene, J. P. (2005). *Education myths: What special interest groups want you to believe about our schools—and why it isn't so.* Lanham, MD: Rowland & Littlefield Publishers.

Greene, J. P., & Winters, M. A. (2006, April). Leaving boys behind: Public high school graduation rates. *Civic Report* (No. 48). New York: Manhattan Institute for Policy Research. Retrieved from http://www.manhattan-institute.org/html/cr_48.htm

Gushue, G. V., Clarke, C. P., Pantzer, K. M., & Scanlan, K. R. L. (2006). Self-efficacy, perceptions of barriers, vocational identity, and the career exploration behavior of Latino/a high school students. *The Career Development Quarterly, 54*, 307–317.

Gushue, G. V., Scanlan, K. R. L., Pantzer, K. M., & Clarke, C. P. (2006). The relationship of career decision-making self-efficacy, vocational identity, and career exploration behavior in African American high school students. *Journal of Career Development, 33*(1), 19–28.

Halperin, S. (Ed.). (1998). *The forgotten half revisited: American youth and young families, 1988–2008.* New York: W. T. Grant Foundation. Retrieved from http://www.wtgrantfoundation.org/usr_doc/TheForgottenHalfRevisited.pdf

Hamilton, M. A., & Hamilton, S. F. (1993). *Toward a youth apprenticeship system: A progress report from the youth apprenticeship demonstration project in Broome County New York.* Ithaca, NY: Cornell Youth and Work Program, Cornell University. Retrieved from http://www.eric.ed.gov/PDFS/ED393970.pdf

Hamilton, S. F. (1990). *Apprenticeship for adulthood: Preparing youth for the future.* New York: Free Press.

Hamilton, S. F. (1993). Prospects for an American-style youth apprenticeship system. *Educational Researcher, 22*(3), 11–16.

Hamilton, S. F., & Hamilton, M. A (1999). Creating new pathways to adulthood by adapting German apprenticeship in the United States. In W. R. Heinz (Ed.), *From education to work: Cross-national perspectives* (pp. 194–213). Cambridge, UK: Cambridge University Press.

Handel, M. J. (2007). *A new survey of workplace skills, technology, and management practices (STAMP): Background and descriptive statistics.* Boston: Northeastern University. Retrieved from http://www7.nationalacademies.org/CFE/Future_Skill_Demands_Michael_Handel_Paper.pdf

Hansen, L. S. (1999). Beyond school to work: Continuing contributions of theory and practice to career development of youth. *The Career Development Quarterly, 47*(4), 353–358.

Hargreaves, A., & Fink, D. (2006, September). Redistributed leadership for sustained professional learning communities. *Journal of School Leadership. 16*(5), 550–565.

Hargreaves, A., & Goodson, I. (2006). Educational change over time? The sustainability and nonsustainability of three decades of secondary school change and continuity. *Educational Administration Quarterly, 42*(1), 3–41.

Haworth, J. T., & Hill, S. (1992). Work, leisure and psychological well-being in a sample of young adults. *Journal of Community & Applied Social Psychology, 2*, 147–160.

Heckman, J. J., & LaFontaine, P. A. (2006). Bias-corrected estimates of GED returns. *Journal of Labor Economics, 24*(3), 661–700. Retrieved from http://www.jstor.org/pss/10.1086/504278

Heckman, J. J., & LaFontaine, P.A. (2007). *The American high school graduation rate: Trends and levels* (Discussion Paper No. 3216). Bonn, Germany: Institute for the Study of Labor. Retrieved from ftp://repec.iza.org/RePEc/Discussionpaper/dp3216.pdf

Heilig, J. V., & Darling-Hammond, L. (2008). Accountability Texas style: The progress and learning of urban minority students in a high stakes testing environment. *Education Evaluation and Policy Analysis, 30*(2), 75–110.

Helwig, A. A. (2004). A ten-year longitudinal study of the career development of students: Findings. *Journal of Counseling & Development, 82*(1), 49–57.

Henderson, S. J. (2000). "Follow your bliss": A process for career happiness. *Journal of Counseling & Development, 78*(3), 305.

Herr, E. L. (1977). *Research in career education: The state of the art* (Information Series No. 106). Columbus, OH: ERIC Clearinghouse on Career Education, Ohio State University. Retrieved from http://www.eric.ed.gov /PDFS/ED149177.pdf

Herr, E. L. (1997). Super's life-span, life-space approach and its outlook for refinement. *The Career Development Quarterly, 45*, 238–246.

Herrnstein, R. A., & Murray, C. A. (1994). *The bell curve: Intelligence and class structure in American life.* New York: Free Press.

Hershey, A. M., Silverberg, M. K., Owens, T., & Hulsey, L. K. (1998). *Focus for the future: The final report of the national Tech-Prep evaluation.* Princeton, NJ: Mathematica Policy Research. Retrieved from http://www.eric.ed.gov/ERICDocs/data/ericdocs2sql /content_storage_01/0000019b/80/15/cb/7c.pdf

Hoachlander, G. (1999, September). Integrating academic and vocational curriculum. Why is theory so hard to practice? *Centergram 7*, National Center for Research in Vocational Education. University of California Berkeley. Retrieved from http://www.eric.ed.gov/PDFS/ED433454.pdf

Hollenbeck, K., & DebBurman, N. (2000). *Use and effectiveness of formal course and career planning forms in secondary schools in the Ottawa area intermediate school district: Final report.* Kalamazoo, MI: Upjohn Institute for Employment Research.

Holzer, H. J. (2010). *Is the middle of the U.S. job market really disappearing? A comment on the "polarization" hypothesis.* Washington, DC: Center for American Progress and The Hamilton Project. Retrieved from http://www.americanprogress.org/issues/2010/05/pdf/Holzer_memo.pdf

Holzer, H. J., & Lerman, R. I. (2009). *The future of middle-skill jobs* (CCF Brief #41). Washington, DC: Center for Children and Families, Brookings Institution. Retrieved from http://www.brookings.edu/~/media/Files/rc/papers/2009/02_middle_skill_jobs _holzer/02_middle_skill_jobs_holzer.pdf

Hord, S. M. (2004). Professional learning communities: An overview. In S. M. Hord (Ed.), *Learning together, leading together: Changing schools through professional learning communities* (pp. 5–14). New York: Columbia University, Teachers College Press; Oxford, OH: National Staff Development Council.

Hughes, K. L., Bailey, T. R., & Mechur, M. J. (2001). *School-to-work: Making a difference in education.* New York: Institute on Education and the Economy, Columbia University. Retrieved from http://www.eric.ed.gov/PDFS/ED449364.pdf

Hughes, K. L., & Karp, M. M. (2004). *School-based career development: A synthesis of the literature.* New York: Institute on Education and the Economy, Columbia University.

Hull, D. (2004). *Career pathways: The next generation of Tech Prep.* Wasco, TX: CORD. Retrieved from http://www.cord.org/uploadedfiles/Career%20PathwaysNext%20Generation%20of%20Tech%20Prep%20(Nov%2004).pdf

Hursh, D. (2008). *High-stakes testing and the decline of teaching and learning: The real crisis in education.* New York: Rowman & Littlefield.

Hurst, D., Kelley, D., & Princlotta, D. (2004). *Educational attainment of high school dropouts 8 years later. Issue brief* (NCES 2005-026).Washington, DC: U.S. Department of Education, Institute of Education Sciences, National Center for Education Statistics. Retrieved from http://nces.ed.gov/pubs2005/2005026.pdf

International Center for Leadership in Education. (2009). *Lexile analysis of occupational reading materials* (Rev. ed.). Rexford, NY: Author.

ISEEK Careers (2011). *Science, technology, engineering, and math (STEM) careers.* Retrieved from http://www.iseek.org/careers/stemcareers.html.

Jacobson, L., & Mokher, C. (2009). *Pathways to boosting the earnings of low income students by increasing their educational attainment.* Washington, DC: Hudson Institute and CNA. Retrieved from http://www.hudson.org/files/publications/Pathways%20to%20 Boosting.pdf

Johnson, A. B., Charner, I., & White, R. (2003). *Curriculum integration in context: An exploration of how structures and circumstances affect design and implementation.* St. Paul, MN: National Research Center for Career and Technical Education, University of Minnesota.

Jones, M. G., Jones, B. D., & Hargrove, T. Y. (2003) *The unintended consequences of high-stakes testing.* Lanham, MD: Rowland & Littlefield Publishers.

Jordaan, J. P. (1963). Exploratory behavior: The formation of self and occupational concepts. In D. E. Super, R. Stariskevsky, N. Matlin, & J. P. Jordaan (Eds.), *Career development: Self-concept theory* (pp. 42–78). New York: College Entrance Examination Board.

Kali, Y., Linn, M. C., & Roseman, J. (2008). *Designing coherent science education: Implications for curriculum, instruction, and policy.* New York: Teachers College Press.

Karp, M. M., Calcagno, J. C., Hughes, K. L., Jeong, D. W., & Bailey, T. R. (2007). *The postsecondary achievement of participants in dual enrollment: An analysis of student outcomes in two states.* St. Paul: National Research Center for Career and Technical Education, University of Minnesota. Retrieved from http://www.nccte.org/publications/Dual_Enrollment.pdf

Kemple. J. J., & Scott-Clayton, J. (2004). *Career academies: Impacts on labor market outcomes and educational attainment.* New York: MDRC.

Kemple, J. J., & Snipes, J. C. (2000). *Career academies: Impacts on students' engagement and performance in high school.* New York: MDRC. Retrieved from http://www.eric.ed.gov/PDFS/ED441075.pdf

Kemple, J. J., & Willner, J. (2008). *Career academies: Long-term impacts on labor market outcomes, educational attainment, and transitions to adulthood.* New York: MDRC.

Kempner, K., & Warford, L. (2009). The promise of the College and Career Transition Initiative. *Techniques, 84*(7), 40–43. Retrieved from http://www.eric.ed.gov/PDFS/EJ858237.pdf

Kotamraju, P. (2005, April). *The Minnesota Post-Secondary Enrollment Options Program: Does participation in dual enrollment programs help high school students attain career and technical education majors and degrees in college?* Paper presented at the 47th annual conference of the Council for the Study of Community Colleges, Boston, Massachusetts.

Krueger, C. (2006). Dual enrollment: Policy issues confronting state policymakers. *Policy Brief Dual/Concurrent Enrollment.* Denver, CO: Education Commission of the States. Retrieved from http://www.eric.ed.gov/ERICDocs/data/ericdocs2sql/content_storage_ 01/0000019b/80/1 b/ef/aa.pdf.

Kulik, J. (1998, June). Curricular tracks and high school vocational education. *The Quality of Vocational Education.*

Lacey, T. A., & Wright, B. (2009). Occupational projections to 2018. *Monthly Labor*

Review, 132(11), 82–123. Retrieved from http://www.bls.gov/opub/mlr/2009/11/art5full.pdf

Lapan, R. T., Aoyagi, M., & Kayson, M. (2007). Helping rural adolescents make successful postsecondary transitions: A longitudinal study. *Professional School Counseling, 10*(3), 266–272.

Leithwood, K., Louis, K. S., Anderson, S., & Wahlstrom, K. (2004). *How leadership influences student learning.* Minneapolis: Center for Applied Research and Educational Improvement, University of Minnesota and Toronto, ON: Ontario Institute for Studies in Education, University of Toronto.

Lekes, N., Bragg, D. D., Loeb, J. W., Oleksiw, C. A., Marszalek, J., LaRaviere, M. B., . . . Hood, L. K. (2007). *Career and technical education pathway programs, academic performance, and the transition to college and career.* St. Paul: National Research Center for Career and Technical Education, University of Minnesota. Retrieved from http://www.nccte.org/publications/infosynthesis/r&dreport/CTE_Pathway_Programs.pdf

Lent, R. W., & Worthington, R. L. (1999). Applying career development theories to the school-to-work transition process. *The Career Development Quarterly, 47,* 291–296.

Levesque, K., Laird, J., Hensley, E., Choy, S. P., Cataldi, E. F., & Hudson, L. (2008). *Career and technical education in the United States: 1990 to 2005* (NCES 2008-035). Washington, DC: U.S. Department of Education, Institute of Education Sciences, National Center for Education Statistics. Retrieved from http://nces.ed.gov/pubsearch/pubsinfo.asp?pubid=2008035

Levy, R., & Murnane, R. J. (2004). *The new division of labor: How computers are creating the next job market.* New York: Russell Sage Foundation.

Lewis, M. V. (1997). *Characteristics of successful school-to-work initiatives: What the research says* (Information Series No. 370). Columbus, OH: ERIC Clearinghouse on Adult, Career and Vocational Education, Ohio State University. Retrieved from http://www.eric.ed.gov/PDFS/ED410433.pdf

Lewis, M. V., & Kosine, N. R. (2008). *What will be the impact of programs of study? A preliminary assessment based on similar previous initiatives, state plans for implementation, and career development theory.* Louisville, KY: National Research Center for Career and Technical Eduation, University of Louisville.

Lewis, M. V., & Pearson, D. (2007). *Sustaining the impact: A follow-up of the teachers who participated in the Math-in-CTE study.* St. Paul: National Research Center for Career and Technical Education, University of Minnesota. Retrieved from http://www.nrccte.org/PDFS/ED508974.pdf

Lieber, J., Butera, G., Hanson, M., Palmer, S., Horn, E., & Czaja, C. (2010). Sustainability of a preschool curriculum: What encourages continued use among teachers? *NHSA Dialog: A Research-to-Practice Journal for the Early Intervention Field, 13*(4), 225–242.

Lieberman, J. E. (1986). *Middle college: A ten-year study.* New York: LaGuardia Community College. Abstract for document ED271153. Retrieved from http://www.eric.ed.gov

Lieberman, J. E. (2004). *The early college high school concept: Requisites for success.* Retrieved from http://www.earlycolleges.org/Downloads/ECHSConcept.pdf

Lowell, B. L., & Salzman, H. (2007). *Into the eye of the storm: Assessing the evidence on science and engineering education, quality and workforce demand.* Washington, DC: Urban Institute. Retrieved from http://www.urban.org/UploadedPDF/411562_Salzman_Science.pdf

Lowell, B. L., Salzman, H., Bernstein, H., & Henderson, E. (2009, November). *Steady as she goes? Three generations of students through the science and engineering pipeline.* Paper presented at the annual meetings of the Association for Public Policy Analysis and Management, Washington, DC. Retrieved from http://policy.rutgers. edu/faculty/salzman/SteadyAsSheGoes.pdf?utm_source=Solutions+at+Work&utm_ campaign=8550936f7c-Heldrich%2BNovember_Newsletter&utm_medium=emai

Madaus, G. F., Russell, M., & Higgins, J. (2009). *The paradoxes of high-stakes testing: How they affect students, their parents, teachers, principals, schools, and society.* Charlotte, NC: Information Age.

Mathematica Policy Research, Inc. (2002). *Job Corps: An education and training program for disadvantaged youth that works.* Princeton, NJ: Author.

Mathews, J. (1988). *Escalante: The best teacher in America.* New York: Holt.

McCharen, B. (2008). The success of implementing programs of study in health careers through career clusters and pathways. *Career and Technical Education Research, 33*(3), 203–216.

McGinley, S. (2002). *High-stakes testing isn't the answer.* Agricultural Experiment Station Research Report. Tucson: University of Arizona, College of Agriculture and Life Sciences. Retrieved from http://ag.arizona.edu/pubs/general/resrpt2002/13. pdf

McNeil, L., & Valenzuela, A. (2001). The harmful impact of the TAAS system of testing in Texas: Beneath the accountability rhetoric. In G. Orfield & M. L. Kornhaber (Eds.), *Raising standards or raising barriers? Inequality and high-stakes testing in public education* (pp. 127–150). New York: Century Foundation Press.

Meer, J. (2007). Evidence on the returns to secondary vocational education. *Economics of Education Review, 26,* 559–573. Retrieved from http://www.stanford.edu/~jmeer/ Meer_Evidence_on_the_Returns_to_Vocational_Education.pdf

Morgan, R., Forget, M., & Antinarella, J. (1996). *Reading for success: A school-to-work approach.* Cincinnati, OH: South-Western.

Morris, S. B., & DeShon, R. P. (2002). Combining effect size estimates in meta-analysis with repeated measures and independent-groups designs. *Psychological Methods, 7,* 105–125. doi: 10.1037/1082-989X.7.1.105

Mueller, M. K. (2003). Take this job and love it: Factors related to job satisfaction and career commitment among physical therapists. (Doctoral dissertation, Union Institution and University, 2002). *Dissertation Abstracts International: Section B. Sciences and Engineering, 63,* 11B.

Murray, C. A. (2008). *Real education: Four simple truths for bringing American schools back to reality.* New York: Crown Forum.

Nagelkerke, N. (1991). A note on a general definition of the coefficient of determination. *Biometrika, 78*(3), 691–692.

National Academy Foundation. (n.d.). *National Academy Foundation* [Brochure]. New York: Author. Retrieved from http://naf.org/files/NAF_brochure.pdf

National Assessment of Educational Progress. (2011). *The nation's report card: Science, Grade 12 national results.* Retrieved from http://nationsreportcard.gov/science_2009/g12_ nat.asp?tab_id=tab2&subtab_id=Tab_1#tabsContainer

National Association of Secondary School Principals. (2004). *Breaking ranks II.* Reston, VA: Author.

National Association of State Directors of Career Technical Education Consortium. (2010a). *A look inside: A synopsis of CTE trends. Focus: Teacher and faculty shortages.* Silver Spring, MD: Author. Retrieved from http://www.careertech. org/uploaded_files/Synthesis_-_CTE_Teacher_Shortage_FINAL.pdf

National Association of State Directors of Career Technical Education Consortium. (2010b). *Reflect, transform, lead: A new vision for career technical education.* Silver Spring, MD: Author. Retrieved from http://www.careertech.org/uploaded_files/2010_Vision_Paper.pdf

National Center for Education Statistics (2010). Common Core of Data. Retrieved from http://nces.ed.gov/ccd/schoolsearch/school_detail.asp?Search=1&City=Phoenix&State=04&DistrictName=Glendale+Union+High+School&SchoolType=1&SchoolType=2&SchoolType=3&SchoolType=4&SpecificSchlTypes=all&IncGrade=-1&LoGrade=-1&HiGrade=-1&ID=040345000283National

National Center for Higher Education Management Systems (NCHEMS). (2011). *College-going rates of high school graduates—directly from high school.* Retrieved from http://www.higheredinfo.org/dbrowser/index.php?submeasure=63&year=2008&level=nation&mode=data&state=0

National Center for Public Policy and Higher Education. (2004). *Measuring up 2004: The national report card on higher education.* San Jose, CA: Author. Retrieved from http://www.eric.ed.gov/PDFS/ED508096.pdf

National Center on Education and the Economy. (2007). *Tough choices or tough times: The report of the New Commission on the Skills of the American Workforce.* San Francisco: Wiley.

National Commission on Excellence in Education. (1983). *A nation at risk: The imperative for educational reform.* Washington, DC: Government Printing Office.

National Commission on Secondary Vocational Education. (1984). *The unfinished agenda: The role of vocational education in the high school.* Columbus: National Center for Research in Vocational Education, Ohio State University.

National FFA Organization. (2009). *The FFA mission.* Retrieved from http://www.ffa.org/index.cfm?method=c_about.mission

National Governors Association Center for Best Practices (NGA Center). (2007). *Retooling career technical education.* Washington, DC: Author. Retrieved from http://www.nga.org/files/live/sites/NGA/files/pdf/0706TECHED.PDF

National Governors Association Center for Best Practices (NGA Center) & Council of Chief State School Officers (CCSSO). (2011). *States that have formally adopted the common core state standards.* Retrieved from http://www.corestandards.org/in-the-states

National Opinion Research Center. (2010). *Online trend chart for years 1989, 1998, and 2006 for question: "How satisfied is respondent with his/her job?"* Retrieved from http://www.norc.org/GSS+Website/Browse+GSS+Variables/Subject+Index/

National Research Center for Career and Technical Education (NRCCTE), Curriculum Integration Workgroup. (2010). *Capitalizing on context: Curriculum integration in career and technical education.* Louisville, KY: National Research Center for Career and Technical Education, University of Louisville. Retrieved from http://www.nrccte.org/

National Research Council (NRC) & the Institute of Medicine. (2004). *Engaging schools: Fostering high school students' motivation to learn.* Washington, DC: National Academies Press.

National Summit on Competitiveness. (2005). *Investing in U.S. innovation.* Washington, DC: Author. Retrieved from http://www.nist.gov/mep/upload/competitiveness-innovation-2.pdf

Nelson, D. (2004). *Design-based learning delivers required standards in all subjects, K–12.* Retrieved from http://www.csupomona.edu/~dnelson/library.html

Newmann, F. M. (1996). *Authentic achievement: Restructuring schools for intellectual quality.* San Francisco: Jossey-Bass.

Nichols, S. L., & Berliner, D. C. (2007). *Collateral damage: How high-stakes testing corrupts America's schools.* Cambridge, MA: Harvard Education Press.

Oakes, J. (1985). *Keeping track: How schools structure inequality.* New Haven, CT: Yale University Press.

Oakes, J. (2005). *Keeping track: How schools structure inequality* (2nd ed.). New Haven: Yale University Press.

Oakes, J., & Saunders, M. (Eds). (2008). *Beyond tracking: Multiple pathways to college, career, and civic participation.* Cambridge, MA: Harvard Education Press.

Orfield, G., & Kornhaber, M. L. (2001). *Raising standards or raising barriers? Inequality and high-stakes testing in public education.* New York: The Century Foundation Press.

Organisation for Economic Cooperation and Development (OECD). (2008). *Education at a glance: OECD indicators.* Paris: Author. Retrieved from http://www.oecd.org/dataoecd/23/46/41284038.pdf

Organisation for Economic Cooperation and Development (OECD). (2010). *Learning for jobs: Synthesis report of the OECD reviews of vocational education and training.* Paris: Author.

Osipow, S. H., & Fitzgerald, L. F. (1996). *Theories of career development.* Boston: Allyn & Bacon.

Oswald, K. (2002). *Career and technology education: Program evaluation report, 2000–2001.* Austin, TX: Office of Program Evaluation, Austin Independent School District. Retrieved from http://www.eric.ed.gov/ERICDocs/data/ericdocs2sql/content_storage_ 01/0000019b/80/1a/22/49.pdf

Park, T. D., Santamaria, L. A., van der Mandele, L., Keene, B. L., & Taylor, M. K. (in press). *Authentic literacy in career and technical education.* Louisville, KY: National Research Center for Career and Technical Education, University of Louisville.

Parnell, D. (1985). *The neglected majority.* Washington, DC: Community College Press.

Parsons, F. (1909). *Choosing a vocation.* Boston: Houghton Mifflin.

Partnership for 21st Century Skills. (2009). *Framework for 21st century learning.* Tucson, AZ: Author. Retrieved from http://www.21stcenturyskills.org/documents/P21_Framework.pdf

Patton, W., & McMahon, M. (2006). *Career development and systems theory: Connecting theory and practice* (2nd ed.). Rotterdam, The Netherlands: Sense Publishers.

Pearson, D., Sawyer, J., & Park, T., Sanatamaria, L., van der Mandele, E., Keene, B., & Taylor, M. (2010). *Capitalizing on context: Curriculum integration in career and technical education.* Louisville, KY: National Research Center for Career and Technical Education, University of Louisville.

Phelps, R. P. (Ed.). (2005a). *Defending standardized testing.* Mahwah, NJ: Erlbaum.

Phelps, R. P. (2005b). Persistently positive. In R. P. Phelps (Ed.), *Defending standardized testing* (pp. 1–22). Mahwah, NJ: Erlbaum.

Phelps, R. P. (Ed.). (2009a). *Correcting fallacies about educational and standardized testing.* Washington, DC: American Psychological Association.

Phelps, R. P. (2009b). Educational achievement testing: Critiques and rebuttals. In R. P. Phelps (Ed.), *Correcting fallacies about educational and standardized testing* (pp. 89–146). Washington, DC: American Psychological Association.

Plank, S. (2001). *Career and technical education in the balance: An analysis of high school persistence, academic achievement, and postsecondary destinations.* St. Paul: National Research Center for Career and Technical Education, University of Minnesota.

Plank, S., DeLuca, S., & Estacion, A. (2005). *Dropping out of high school and the place of career and technical education: A survival analysis of surviving high school.* St. Paul: National Research Center for Career and Technical Education, University of Minnesota.

Plant, M., & Provasnik, S. (2007). *High school coursetaking: Findings from the the condition of education* 2007. Washington, DC: U.S. Department of Education Institute of Education Sciences, National Center for Education Statistics

Pope, M., Turner, M., & Barker, J. (2001, July). *Post-baccalaureate reverse transfer: Implications for community college student services.* Paper presented at the conference, Transfer: The Forgotten Function of the Community College, at the annual meeting of Johnson County Community College and Oakton Community College, Overland Park, KS. Retrieved from http://www.eric.ed.gov./PDFS/ED469895.pdf

Powell, A. G., Farrar, E., & Cohen, D. K. (1985). *The shopping mall high school: Winners and losers in the education marketplace.* Boston: Houghton Mifflin.

Programs of Study Joint Technical Working Group. (2010). *Programs of study: Year 2 joint technical report.* Louisville, KY: National Research Center for Career and Technical Education, University of Louisville.

Programs of Study Joint Technical Working Group. (2011). *Programs of study: Year 3 joint technical report.* Louisville, KY: National Research Center for Career and Technical Education, University of Louisville.

Quinley, J. W., & Quinley, M. P. (1999). The urban postbaccalaureate reverse transfer student: Giving new meaning to the term second chance. *New Directions for Community Colleges, 106,* 35–45.

Rampey, B. D., Dion, G. S., & Donahue, P. L. (2009). *NAEP 2008 trends in academic progress* (NCES 2009-479). Washington, D.C: National Center for Education Statistics, Institute of Education Sciences, U.S. Department of Education. Retrieved from http://nces.ed.gov/nationsreportcard/pdf/main2008/2009479.pdf

Ravitch, D. (2010). *The death and life of the great American school system.* New York: Basic Books.

Reindl, T. (2006). *Postcards from the margin: A national dialog on accelerated learning.* Bolder, CO: Western Interstate Commission for Higher Educations; Boston, MA: Jobs for the Future. Retrieved from http://www.eric.ed.gov/PDFS/ED494186.pdf

Reusch, D. L. (2000). *The nature and characteristics of post-baccalaureate reverse transfer students and their utilization of career guidance.* Carbondale. IL: Southern Illinois University. Retrieved from http://www.eric.ed.gov/PDFS/ED458930.pdf

Rojewski, J. W., & Kim, H. (2003). Career choice patters and behavior of work-bound youth during early adolescence. *Journal of Career Development, 30*(2), 89–108.

Rosenbaum, J. E. (2001). *Beyond college for all: Career paths for the forgotten half.* New York: Russell Sage Foundation.

Rosenbaum, J. E., Deil-Amen, R., & Person, A. E. (2006). *After admission: From college access to college success.* New York: Russell Sage Foundation.

Rosenbaum, J. E., Stephan, J. L., & Rosenbaum, J. E. (2010). Beyond one-size-fits-all college dreams: Alternative pathways to desirable careers. *American Educator 34*(3), 2–13. Retrieved from http://www.aft.org/pdfs/americaneducator/fall2010/Rosenbaum.pdf

Rosenbaum, J. E., Stern, D., Hamilton, S. F., Hamilton, M. A., Berryman, S. E., & Kazis, R. (1992). *Youth apprenticeship in America: Guidelines for building an effective system.* Washington, DC: W. T. Grant Foundation Commission on Youth and America's Future. Retrieved from http://www.eric.ed.gov/PDFS/ED355340.pdf

Rubin, M. (June, 2011). *Meaningful connections—The Wisconsin opportunity*. Paper presented at the Wisconsin Career Pathways Summit, Madison, WI.

Rudy, D. W., & Rudy, E. L. (2001). *Report on career pathways: A success story in Berrien County, Michigan*. Berrien Springs, MI: Berrien County Intermediate School District. Retrieved from http://eric.ed.gov/PDFS/ED457408.pdf

Ruffing, K. (2006). *History of career clusters*. Retrieved from http://www.careertech.org/ uploaded_files/The_History_of_Career_Clusters_by_Katherin

Saunders, M., & Chrisman, C. (2011). *Linking learning to the 21st century: Preparing all students for college, career, and civic participation*. Boulder, CO: National Education Policy Center. Retrieved from http://nepc.colorado.edu/publication/ linking-learning

Savickas, M. L., & Super, D. E. (1993). Can life stages and substages be identified in students? *Man and Work, 4*(1), 71–78.

Schlafly, P. (1997). School-to-work and Goals 2000. *The Phyllis Schlafly Report, 30*(9). Retrieved from http://www.eagleforum.org/psr/1997/apr97/psrapr97.html

Schrag, P. (1970, March 21). Growing up on Mechanic Street. *Saturday Review, 53*(12) 57–61, 78–79.

Schug, M. C., & Western, R. D. (1999). *School to work in Wisconsin: Inflated claims, meager results*. Milwaukee: Wisconsin Policy Research Institute, University of Wisconsin–Milwaukee.

Schultheiss, D. E. P., Palma, T. V., & Manzi, A. J. (2002, August). *Career development in childhood: A qualitative inquiry*. Paper presented at the annual meeting of the American Psychological Association, Chicago, IL.

Schultheiss, D. E. P., & Stead, G. B. (2004). Childhood career development scale: Scale style construction and psychometric properties. *Journal of Career Assessment, 12*(2), 113–134.

Schumer, R., & Digby, C. (in press). Programs of study: Development efforts in six states. *International Journal of Educational Research*.

Scribner, J., & Wakelyn, D. (1998). Youth apprenticeship experiences in Wisconsin: A stakeholder-based evaluation. *High School Journal, 82*(1), 24. Retrieved from http:// wf2dnvr9.webfeat.org/PFRIK153/url=http://wf2dnvr9.webfeat.org:80/PFRIK153/ url=http://search.ebscohost.com/login.aspx?direct=true&db=aph&AN=1572209& site=ehost-live&scope=site.

Secretary's Commission on Achieveing Necessary Skills. (1991). *What work requires of schools*. Washington, DC: U.S. Department of Labor. Retrieved from http://www. eric.ed.gov/PDFS/ED332054.pdf

Senge, P. (1990). *The fifth discipline: The art and practice of the learning organization*. New York: Doubleday.

SERVE Center. (2010). *A better 9th grade: Early results from an experimental study of the Early College High School Model*. Greensboro, NC: Author. Retrieved from http://www.serve.org/FileLibraryDetails.aspx?id=179

Shoffner, M. F., & Newsome, D. W. (2001). Identity development of gifted female adolescents: The influence of career development, age, and life-role salience. *Journal of Secondary Gifted Education, 12*(4), 201.

Silverberg, M., Bergeron, J., Haimson, J., & Nagatashi, C. (1996). *Facing the challenge of change: Experiences and lessons of the school-to-work/youth apprenticeship demonstration: Final report*. Princeton, NJ: Mathematica Policy Research. Retrieved from http://www.eric.ed.gov/ERICDocs/data/ericdocs2sql/content_ storage_01/0000019b/80/1 5/0a/d1.pdf

Silverberg, M., Warner, E., Fong, M., & Goodwin, D. (2004). *National assessment of vocational education: Final report to Congress.* Washington, DC: U.S. Department of Education, Office of the Under Secretary, Policy and Program Studies Service. Retrieved from http://www2.ed.gov/rschstat/eval/sectech/nave/navefinal.pdf

Skomsvold, P., Radford, A. W., & Berkner, L. (2011). *Web tables: Six-year attainment, persistence, transfer, retention, and withdrawal rates of students who began postsecondary education in 2003–04* (NCES 2011-152). Washington, DC: National Center for Education Statistics, U.S. Department of Education. Retrieved from http://nces.ed.gov/pubs2011/2011152.pdf

Smith E., & Green, A. (2005). *How workplace experiences while at school affect career pathways.* Adelaide, SA, Australia: National Centre for Vocational Education Research. Retrieved from http://www.eric.ed.gov/PDFS/ED494040.pdf

Snyder, T. D., Dillow, S. A., & Hoffman, C. M. (2009). Table 147: Average number of Carnegie units earned by public high school graduates in various subject fields, by selected student characteristics: Selected years, 1982 through 2005. In *Digest of education statistics 2008* (pp. 214–216; NCES 2009-020). Washington, DC: National Center for Education Statistics, Institute of Education Sciences, U.S. Department of Education. Retrieved from http://nces.ed.gov/programs/digest/d08/tables/dt08_147.asp

Southwest Educational Development Laboratory. (2003). *Follow-up study of schools implementing comprehensive school reform in the southwest.* Retrieved from http://www.sedl.org/pubs/change93/csr-followup-report.pdf

Sparks, S. D. (2011, June 18). Panel finds few learning benefits in high stakes testing. *Education Week, 30*(33), 1. Retrieved from http://www.edweek.org/ew/articles/2011/06/08/33academy-2.h30.html

Stead, G. B., & Schultheiss, D. E. P. (2003). Construction and psychometric properties of the Childhood Career Development Scale. *South African Journal of Psychology, 33*(4), 227–235.

STEM Education Coalition. (2011). Retrieved from http://www.stemedcoalition.org

Stern, D., Stone, J. R., III, Hopkins, C., McMillion, M., & Crain, R. (1994). *School-based enterprise: Productive learning in American high schools.* San Francisco: Jossey-Bass.

Stipanovic, N., & Stringfield, S. (in press). A qualitative inquiry of career exploration in highly implemented CTE programs of study. *International Journal of Educational Research.*

Stone, J. R., III. (2009, February). A Perkins challenge: Assessing technical skills in CTE. *Techniques, 84*(7), 21–22.

Stone, J. R., III. (2011). Adolescent employment. In B. B. Brown & M. J. Prinstein (Eds.), *Encyclopedia of adolescence* (Vol. 2, pp. 59–67). San Diego: Academic Press.

Stone, J. R., III, & Alfeld, C. (2006). The neglected majority—revisited. *Journal of Career and Technical Education, 21,* 61–74.

Stone, J. R., III, Alfeld, C., & Pearson, D. (2008). Rigor and relevance: Enhancing high school students' math skills through career and technical education. *American Educational Research Journal, 45,* 767–795.

Stone, J. R., III, Alfeld, C., Pearson, D., Lewis, M. V., & Jensen, S. (2005). *Building academic skills in context: Testing the value of enhanced math learning in CTE. Pilot study.* St. Paul: National Research Center for Career and Technical Education, University of Minnesota.

Stone, J. R., III, Alfeld, C., Pearson, D., Lewis, M. V., & Jensen, S. (2006). *Building academic skills in context: Testing the value of enhanced math learning in CTE.* St. Paul: National Research Center for Career and Technical Education, University of Minnesota.

Stone, J. R., III, & Aliaga, O. A. (2003). *Career and technical education, career pathways, and work-based learning: Changes in participation 1997–1999.* St. Paul: National Research Center for Career and Technical Education, University of Minnesota.

Stott, M. B. (1970). What is occupational success? *Occupational Psychology, 44,* 205–212.

Super, D. E. (1957). *The psychology of careers.* New York: Harper & Row.

Super, D. E. (1963). Self-concepts in vocational development. In D. E. Super, R. Stariskevsky, N. Matlin, & J. P. Jordaan (Eds.), *Career development: Self-concept theory* (pp. 1–26). New York: College Entrance Examination Board.

Super, D. E. (1984). Career and life development. In D. Brown & L. Brooks (Eds.), *Career choice and development* (pp. 192–234). San Francisco: Jossey-Bass.

Super, D. E. (1990). A life-span, life-space approach to career development. In D. Brown, L. Brooks, et al. (Eds.), *Career choice and development: Applying contemporary theories to practice* (2nd ed., pp. 197–261). San Francisco: Jossey-Bass.

Super, D. E., Savickas, M. L., & Super, C. M. (1996). The life-span, life-space approach to careers. In D. Brown & L. Brooks (Eds.), *Career choice and development* (3rd ed., pp. 121–178). San Francisco: Jossey-Bass.

Swail, W. S., & Kampits, E. (2004). *Work-based learning and higher education: A research perspective.* Washington, DC: Educational Policy Institute. Retrieved from http://inpathways.net/work-based.pdf

Swarthout, L. (2006). *Paying back, not giving back: Student debt's negative impact on public service career opportunities.* Sacramento, CA: CALPIRG. Retrieved from http://cdn.publicinterestnetwork.org/assets/_41DxuH1iAd4_OaMGzE4cg/Paying_Back_Giving.pdf

Symonds, W. C., Schwartz, R. B., & Ferguson, R. (2011). *Pathways to prosperity: Meeting the challenge of preparing young Americans for the 21st century.* Cambridge, MA: Harvard Graduate School of Education. Retrieved from http://www.gse.harvard.edu/news_events/features/2011/Pathways_to_Prosperity_Feb2011.pdf

Tews, N. M. (2011). Integrated curricula: Implementing English and math credits into CTE. *Techniques, 86*(1), 44–47.

Tews, N. W., Spencer, J., & Sharp, J. (2010, December). *Integrated curriculum: Implementing English and math credit into career and technical curriculums.* Presentation to the Annual Convention of the Association for Career and Technical Education, Las Vegas, NV.

Tinto, V. (1996). Persistence and the first-year experience at community college: Teaching new students to survive, stay, and thrive. In J. Harkin (Ed.), *The community college: Opportunity and access for America's first-year students* (pp. 97–104). Columbia: National Resource Center for the Freshman Year Experience and Students in Transition, University of South Carolina.

Tough, P. (2008). *Whatever it takes: Geoffrey Canada's quest to change Harlem and America.* Boston: Houghton Mifflin.

Trice, A. D. (1991a). A retrospective study of career development: I. Relationship among first aspirations, parental occupations, and current occupations. *Psychological Reports, 68*(1), 287–290.

Trice, A. D. (1991b). Stability of children's career aspirations. *Journal of Genetic Psychology, 152*(1), 137.

Trice, A. D., Hughes, M. A., Odom, C., & Woods, K. (1995). The origins of children's career aspirations: IV. Testing hypotheses from four theories. *The Career Development Quarterly, 43*(4), 307–322.

Trice, A. D., & King, R. (1991). Stability of kindergarten children's career aspirations. *Psychological Reports, 68*(3), 1378.

Trice, A. D., & Knapp, L. (1992). Relationship of children's career aspirations to parents' occupations. *Journal of Genetic Psychology, 153*(3), 355.

Trice, A. D., & McClellan, N. (1993). Do children's career aspirations predict adult occupations? An answer from a secondary analysis. *Psychological Reports, 72*(2), 368.

Tripp, R. L. (1993). *The game of school: Observations of a long-haul teacher.* Seven Fountains, VA: Loft Press.

Tyack, D. B., & Tobin, W. (1994). The grammar of schooling: Why has it been so hard to change? *American Educational Research Journal, 31*, 453–479.

U.S. Census Bureau. (2011a, April 26). More working women than men have college degrees, Census Bureau reports. *Newsroom.* Retrieved from http://www.census.gov/newsroom/releases/archives/education/cb11-72.html

U.S. Census Bureau. (2011b). Table 225. Educational attainment by race and Hispanic origin: 1970–2009. *The 2011 Statistical Abstract.* Retrieved from http://www.census.gov/compendia/statab/2011/tables/11s0225.pdf

U.S. Census Bureau. (2011c). *Apex, NC: 2005–2009 American Community Survey 5-Year Estimates.* Retrieved from http://factfinder.census.gov/servlet/ACSSAFFFacts?_event=Search&geo_id=&_geoContext=&_street=&_county=Apex&_cityTown=Apex&_state=04000US37&_zip=&_lang=en&_sse=on&pctxt=fph&pgsl=010

U.S. Census Bureau. (2011d). *Johnson County, TN: 2005-2009 American Community Survey 5-Year Estimates.* Retrieved from http://www.factfinder.census.gov/servlet/ACSSAFFFacts?_event=Search&geo_id=&_geoContext=&_street=&_county=Johnson+County&_cityTown=Johnson+County&_state=04000US47&_zip=&_lang=en&_sse=on&pctxt=fph&pgsl=010

U.S. Census Bureau. (2011e). *Glendale, AZ: 2005–2009 American Community Survey 5-Year Estimates.* Retrieved from http://www.factfinder.census.gov/servlet/ACSSAFFFacts?_event=Search&geo_id=&_geoContext=&_street=&_county=Glendale&_cityTown=Glendale&_state=04000US04&_zip=&_lang=en&_sse=on&pctxt=fph&pgsl=010

U.S. Department of Education, Institute of Education Sciences, National Center for Education Statistics (NCES). (2010a). *Education Longitudinal Study of 2002 (ELS:2002). Overview: Purpose.* Retrieved from http://nces.ed.gov/surveys/els2002/

U.S. Department of Education, Institute of Education Sciences, National Center for Education Statistics (NCES). (2010b). *Search for public schools, Glendale Union High School District.* Retrieved from http://nces.ed.gov/ccd/schoolsearch/school_detail.asp?Search=1&City=Phoenix&State=04&DistrictName=Glendale+Union+High+School&SchoolType=1&SchoolType=2&SchoolType=3&SchoolType=4&SpecificSchlTypes=all&IncGrade=-1&LoGrade=-1&HiGrade=-1&ID=040345000283

U.S. Department of Labor. (2008). *Office of Apprenticeship, statistics for FY 2003–2007.* Retrieved from http://www.doleta.gov/oa/statistics.cfm

Vondracek, F. W., Schulenberg, J., Skorikov, V., Gillespie, L. K., & Wahlheim, C. (1995). The relationship of identity status to career indecision during adolescence. *Journal of Adolescence, 18*, 17–29.

Wadhwa, V., Gereffi, G., Rissing, B., & Ong, R. (2007). Seeing through preconceptions:

A deeper look at China and India. *Issues in Science and Technology, Online.* Retrieved from http://www.issues.org/23.3/wadhwa.html

Waits, T., Setzer, J. C., & Lewis, L. (2005). *Dual credit and exam-based courses in U.S. public high schools: 2002–03* (NCES 2005–009). Washington, DC: U.S. Department of Education, Institute of Education Sciences, National Center for Education Statistics. Retrieved from http://nces.ed.gov/pubs2005/2005009.pdf

Wallace-Broscious, A., Serafica, F. C., & Osipow, S. H. (1994). Adolescent career development: Relationships to self-concept and identity status. *Journal of Research on Adolescence, 4*(1), 127–149.

Wang, J. L., Lesage, A., Schmitz, N., & Drapeau, A. (2008). The relationship between work stress and mental disorders in men and women: Findings from a population-based study. *Journal of Epidemiology & Community Health, 62*(1), 42–47.

Warr, P. (2007). *Work, happiness, and unhappiness.* Mahwah, NJ: Erlbaum.

Wei, R. C., Darling-Hammond, L., Andree, A., Richardson, N., & Orphanos, S. (2009). *Professional learning in the learning profession: A status report on teacher development in the United States and abroad.* Dallas, TX: National Staff Development Council. Retrieved from http://www.srnleads.org/resources/publications/pdf/nsdc_profdev_tech_report.pdf

Wenger, E. (1998). *Communities of practice: Leaning, meaning, and identity.* Cambridge, UK: Cambridge University Press.

Wenger, E. (2010). *Communities of practice: A brief introduction.* Retrieved from http://www.ewenger.com/theory/index.htm

Weyhing, R. S., Bartlett, W. S., & Howard, G. S. (1984). Career indecision and identity development. *Journal of Psychology and Christianity, 3*(1), 74–78.

Wichowski, C. P. (n.d.). *Selected student gains related to teacher participation in the Temple center reading project.* Philadelphia: Center for Professional Development in Career and Technical Education, College of Education, Temple University.

Wichowski, C. P., & Garnes, D. C. (2004). *Facilitator guidebooks for reading strategy workshops in: reciprocal teaching, scaffolding, journaling.* Philadelphia: Center for Professional Development in Career and Technical Education, College of Education, Temple University.

Wichowski, C. P., & Heberley, G. (2009). *An examination of the impact of the Temple University reading project on the delivery of instruction and its influence on CTE students.* Philadelphia: Center for Professional Development in Career and Technical Education, College of Education, Temple University.

Willett, J. B., & Singer, J. D. (1991). From whether to when: New methods for studying student dropout and teacher attrition. *Review of Educational Research, 61*(4), 407–450.

Wimberly, G. L., & Noeth, R. J. (2005). *College readiness begins in middle school. ACT policy report.* Ames, IA: American College Testing (ACT).

Winter, P. A., Harris, M. R., & Ziegler, C. H. (2001). *Community college reverse transfer students: A discriminate analysis of completers and noncompleters.* Paper presented to the annual meeting of the American Education Research Association, Seattle, WA. Retrieved from http://www.eric.ed.gov/PDFS/ED452895.pdf

Wood, C., & Kaszubowski, Y. (2008). The career development needs of rural elementary students. *The Elementary School Journal, 108*(5), 431–444.

Woodward, C. M. (1974). The fruits of manual training. In M. Lazerson & W. N. Grubb (Eds.), *American education and vocationalism: A documentary history, 1870–1970* (pp. 60–66). New York: Teachers College Press. (Original chapter published 1883)

Worthington, R. L., & Juntunen, C. L. (1997). The vocational development of non-college bound youth: Counseling psychology and the school-to-work transition movement. *The Counseling Psychologist, 25*, 323–363.

W. T. Grant Foundation Commission on Work, Family, and Citizenship. (1988). *The forgotten half: Pathways to success for America's youth and young families*. New York: W. T. Grant Foundation. Retrieved from http://www.wtgrantfoundation.org/ usr _doc/TheForgottenHalf.pdf

Yang, P. (2006). Reverse transfers and the multiple missions of community colleges. *Community College Review, 33*(3–4), 55–70.

Zhang, Y. (2009). *State high school exit exams: Trends in test programs, alternate pathways, and pass rates*. Washington, DC: Center on Education Policy. Retrieved from http://www.cep-dc.org/document/docWindow.cfm?fuseaction=document.viewDocument&documentid=297&documentFormatId=4558

Zinth, K., & Dounay, J. (2007). *Aligned to the research: Science and mathematics graduation requirements*. Denver, CO: Education Commission of the States. Retrieved from http://www.ecs.org/clearinghouse/74/52/7452.pdf

Zirkle, C., & Connors, J. (2003). The contribution of career and technical student organizations (CTSO) to the development and assessment of workplace skills and knowledge: A literature review. *Workforce Education Forum, 30*(2), 15–26.

Index

AAI (all aspects of the industry), 17, 32
Academy High School (AHS), 64, 65, 182 n. 3
Academy Middle School (AMS), 64, 182 n. 3
Accountability, 2–3, 53. *See also* No Child Left
    Behind Act (NCLB) of 2001
Accuplacer, 90, 167
Achieve, Inc., 14, 21, 114
Achievement. *See* Employability skills
ACT, 9, 22–24, 46, 86, 181 n. 1
ACTE (Association for Career and Technical
    Education), 9, 11, 17, 77, 84, 114, 117,
    127, 169, 179
Adelman, C., 21
Adolescent Literacy Support Framework, 98–99
Advanced Placement (AP) courses, 33, 132–
    133, 144
Age
    high school graduation rates and, 59–60
    role in exploration and career decisions, 45
Agodini, R., 60–61, 181 n. 2
Agricultural educational programmatic model,
    80–82
Alfeld, C., 18, 19, 22, 72, 73, 75, 90, 111–112,
    167, 182 n. 5
Aliaga, O. A., 60, 61, 119, 123
All aspects of the industry (AAI), 17, 32
Allen, A., 66
Allen, D., 49
American Association of Family and Consumer
    Sciences, 8
American Diploma Project (Achieve), 14, 21
American Educational Research Association
    (AERA), 128
American Educator, 26
American Federation of Teachers (AFT), 26
American Institutes for Research (AIR), 138,
    139, 141
American Vocational Association, 9, 127
Anderson, C. J., 93
Anderson, S., 73
Andree, A., 76, 167, 176
Andrew, E. N., 17
Aoyagi, M., 45
AP (Advanced Placement) courses, 33, 132–

133, 144
Apex High School, Academy of Information
    Technology (AOIT; North Carolina),
    77–79, 182 n. 1
Appalachian Regional Commission, 80–81
Apple, M. W., 161
Apprenticeships, 110, 115, 117, 126–131
Aragon, S. R., 18, 111–112
Archway Model (Super), 40
Arizona, academic integration at Washington
    High School (Glendale), 84–85, 89
Arschavsky, N., 141
Arthur, M. B., 38
ASE, 20
Ash Framework, 98–99, 101–104
Association for Career and Technical Education
    (ACTE), 9, 11, 17, 77, 84, 114, 117, 127,
    169, 179
Au, W., 54, 56
Auger, R. W., 42
Austin (Texas) Independent School District, 125
Authentic Literacy study (Park et al.), 88–89,
    90, 97–104, 106, 107, 113, 167, 168
Automotive technology, 20, 82–84, 107
Autor, D. H., 147–149
Auty, W. P., 37
Axelrad, S., 43

Baby Boomers, 1
Bailey, Thomas R., 7, 128, 129, 131–134,
    136–137, 179
Barker, J., 183 n. 3
Bartlett, K. R., 20
Bartlett, W. S., 44
Barton, Paul, viii, 6, 14, 16, 19
Basic academic, 60, 61
Beatty, A., 7
Becker, G. S., 1
Bell, Terrel, 1
Bell Curve, The (Herrnstein & Murray), 25
Bergeron, J., 110, 117, 130
Berkner, L., 27–28, 28n.
Berlin, G. L., 115, 116
Berliner, David C., 53, 55

About the Authors

James R. Stone, III is a Distinguished University Scholar at the University of Louisville. A professor of Work and Human Resource Education, he is also the Director of the National Research Center for Career and Technical Education, a position he has held since 2002. Previously, Stone held professorial rank at the University of Minnesota and before that, the University of Wisconsin–Madison. His scholarly work focuses on connecting education for youth and adults to the workplace. He has published more than 100 journal articles, books and book chapters, and reports of research, more than a dozen of which have received national awards. Because of his expertise in this field, Stone is asked to provide advice to such organizations as the National Science Foundation, the National Center for Education Statistics, the ERIC system, the National Academies of Science, many states' education departments, and large urban school districts' agencies.

Frequently called upon to keynote state and national conferences and participate in international conferences and meetings, Stone has delivered more than 200 speeches and presentations of research in the past decade.

Morgan V. Lewis is a consultant to the National Research Center for Career and Technical Education at the University of Louisville. Lewis has over 40 years of experience in research, policy analysis, and evaluation of education and training programs. His focus has been primarily on school-based programs designed to prepare young people for employment, but he has also studied programs in correctional institutions, parole offices, day care centers, and public welfare agencies. He is the author or coauthor of more than 150 publications.

Lewis received his doctorate in Industrial/Organizational Psychology from Pennsylvania State University. While in his doctoral program, he worked on a multistate evaluation of vocational education and that experience set the direction for his future career. After receiving his degree, he remained at Penn State for 13 years conducting research and evaluation studies for state and federal agencies. In 1978 Ohio State University was awarded the contract for the first National Center for Research in Vocational Education and Lewis joined its staff. When the national center moved to the University of California–Berkeley, Lewis continued at Ohio State as a staff member of the Center on Education and Training for Employment until his retirement in 2006. During his years at Ohio State, he served as a consultant to vocational education and workforce agencies in China, Turkey, Kyrgyzstan, and the Philippines.